Compendium of Those Who Count

THE
RIGHT
PEOPLE

Books by STEPHEN BIRMINGHAM

YOUNG MR. KEEFE

BARBARA GREER

THE TOWERS OF LOVE

THOSE HARPER WOMEN

FAST START, FAST FINISH

"OUR CROWD"

THE RIGHT PEOPLE

THE
RIGHT
PEOPLE

A Portrait of the American Social
Establishment

Stephen Birmingham

Little, Brown and Company · Boston · Toronto

Published simultaneously in Canada
by Little, Brown & Company (Canada) Limited

PRINTED IN THE UNITED STATES OF AMERICA

*For
Harry Sions*

Preface

A little more than ten years ago, I first met the man to whom this book is dedicated in the office of the late and justly celebrated literary agent, Carl Brandt. I was a young writer who had published a few short stories, a bit of verse (a secret vice), and was at the time working on my first novel, or First Novel. I had been led, by the best of Eastern-college creative-writing courses, and by the newest of the New Critics, to believe that fiction was somehow holier than nonfiction (though most modern fiction wasn't very good), and that factual reportage was a somewhat spurious endeavor. There was a world of difference, I had been taught, between an author (of novels) and a mere "journalist." The purpose of the meeting in Carl Brandt's office was to discuss whether I might also "turn my hand" — my phrase — to nonfiction.

The first article I wrote for Harry Sions was returned to me rather promptly for repairs. Let us say they were extensive. Indeed, they were total. Grimly, I attacked the piece again, and once more it was returned for repairs only slightly less extensive than before. I don't remember how many times this sequence of events repeated itself after this, but I do know that by the time the article was finally accepted I hated Harry Sions. It was several days before my equanimity returned and I realized that I was grateful.

For a number of years Harry Sions edited, scolded, stimulated, badgered, inspired, charmed, and browbeat *Holiday* writers. He is not a hand-holding sort of editor. Great is his glee when he can find a reason for requiring this or that Great Name in American literature to revise, repair, rewrite, or when he can reject altogether a piece of writing that does not meet his stiff and spiky standards. Harry Sions taught me two things. He taught me how to write nonfiction. And he taught me that the American upper-class surroundings and training (including The Right School) and institutions (including the "junior dances") which I had grown up with, and had merely endured, were both interesting and exceptionally worth writing about.

Over the years, I wrote a number of pieces for Harry Sions which dealt with Society and the institutions it supports (and which, in turn, support it and help keep High Society aloft), and these pieces, along with quite a bit of new material, the result of further researches and reflections, are at the heart — if that is not too strong a word — of this book.

S. B.

Contents

Illustrations

Post-debutantes Patsy Pulitzer and Fern Tailer at the April in Paris Ball

Most of the photographs in this book were taken by Slim Aarons. The exceptions are the portrait of Mrs. Adolph B. Spreckels as a young woman, which is from Mrs. Spreckels's collection, and the photograph of the Auchincloss family reunion, which appears through the courtesy of Louis Auchincloss.

S.B.

Part One

THE SOCIAL
ESTABLISHMENT:

Growing Up "Upper"

1

Who Are Who?

IN America, there is Society. Then there is Real Society. Real Society is a part of Society — the upper part. Everybody who is in Society knows who the people in Real Society are. But the people in Real Society do not necessarily know who the other Society people are. The two groups seldom mix. Real Society is composed of older people. It is composed of older families. Older families are better people. Better people are nicer people. Newer people may be richer people than older people. That doesn't matter. Ordinary Society people may get to be Real Society people one day only if they work at it. It sounds confusing, but it is really very simple. Cream rises to the top.

Once, in my extreme youth, I had the difference between Society and Real Society demonstrated to me rather vividly. I was perhaps fifteen, and I was at a dinner party in New York in a very grand — or so it seemed to me — town house in the East Sixties. (The house seemed grand because it had one room, called "the music room," which contained no furniture whatever except a huge golden cello in a glass case.) The party was a children's party before one of the "junior dances," I forget which, and we were offered our choice (it seemed a grand choice, too) of sauterne or tomato juice. It was the first party to which I had worn a black tie. My clothes were new, my shave was new and I, too, was very new. I was so new that I made the mistake of offering to carry the plate of the young lady I was escorting, along with

my own plate, back to the buffet table for seconds of creamed chicken
in timbales and petits pois. And, in the process of carrying the two
laden plates back to our seats, my cummerbund, newly acquired and
only dimly understood, became undone. I was in the center of the
room when I felt it begin to slip, and I clapped my elbows tight against
my sides to stop it. But it continued to slide down about my hips.
Lowering myself to a half-crouch, and jabbing my right elbow into my
upper thigh, I became aware that the plate I held in my left hand had
emptied itself of peas and chicken, and I felt this warm, moist mass
flowing along my arm, inside the sleeve of my dinner jacket.

This was not a Real Society dinner party. I know because, a few
days later, when I told this story in all its detail to a lady who *was* a
member of Real Society, she said, "Do you mean they served *Sauterne*
and not Dubonnet? How dreadful!" She might have added, too, that
no young gentleman of Real Society would have found himself in such
a predicament. He would not have carried a young lady's plate to the
serving table. He would have let her take care of herself.

Real Society people, I once thought, do not listen to what other
people are saying. But I was wrong. They listen, but their ears are
attuned to different sounds; they respond to different cues. It is not
that they miss ordinary conversations, but they pick up different drifts.
It is as though most people were on AM and they were on FM. Once,
at a Saltonstall wedding in the 1940's, one guest was overheard whis-
pering to another, "Did you know that she was for Wallace?" There
was a pause, and then the other guest said thoughtfully, "Really?
Wallace *Who?*"

In Philadelphia recently, a matron was exclaiming to a visitor over
the great supply of books and plays that have been written about the
Philadelphia social scene — *Kitty Foyle, The Philadelphia Story,* and
more recently, Richard Powell's *The Philadelphian.* The visitor commented that he, personally — as an outsider — had found parts of Mr.
Powell's novel hard to credit. "Oh, really?" said the lady eagerly. "So
did *I.* Tell me what it was that bothered you." The visitor cited the
opening section of the book, which centers about a Philadelphia
Society wedding. As readers of the novel will remember, when the
fictional bride and groom have settled in their wedding-night rooms
at the Bellevue-Stratford, the bride makes the belated discovery that
her husband is impotent. In her distress, she runs out of the hotel into

Broad Street where, walking in the opposite direction, she encounters a burly construction worker whom she has eyed admiringly in the past. He is drunk, and walking arm in arm with a prostitute. In the convenient darkness, the young bride pays off the prostitute and takes the arm of the construction worker, who does not notice the artful substitution. The bride and her new beau now proceed to a handy shed where their union is consummated. (And, in the best tradition of modern fiction, where one encounter guarantees a pregnancy, the young woman nine months later gives birth to the child who becomes the novel's hero.) Meanwhile, back at the Bellevue-Stratford, the young bridegroom is so distraught at his wife's discovery that he, too, races off into the night in a fast sports car and is killed in a hideous accident, thereby easing things considerably for his wife's future. All this, said the visitor, "I simply found impossible to believe." "I completely agree," said the Philadelphia lady quickly. "It's absurd. *Nobody* would ever spend their wedding night at the Bellevue-Stratford."

An Englishman, who has made a hobby of studying American Society, feels that Real Society people are indeed different from you and me. "You can spot them immediately," he says. "They have a special way of talking, a special way of thinking, and a special look. They even smell a special way. I love the way they smell."

Though I am still unable to identify Real Society people by their odor, his other points of difference seem perfectly valid. And these differences provide the most formidable obstacles to the social climber. Such is the nature of Society that a person can live his whole life, quite happily and quite successfully, without being aware of Society, or feeling its effect in any way. Only when he attempts to move into it does he discover that it was there all along, like a wall, stern and unscalable, a wall with a small grilled door in it — locked.

Perhaps a better image than a wall with a door in it would be a series of walls, arranged in a crazy-quilt pattern like a bit of New Hampshire farm country seen from the air. Social climbing is like a game. You play it by climbing the walls and crossing the little squares between, one after another. Progress is slow and arduous, and often you must rely on guesswork. Through it all, your goal is *Real* Society, and as you approach its fringes, the going becomes harder. You must learn to recognize, even though you may have not yet seen one, a Real Society person. And one way to do this is to remember a few things a Real Society person is not.

People who go regularly to charity balls, who have been photographed dancing with the Duke of Windsor, who have played poker on the yacht of a Greek shipping magnate, are not necessarily all members of Real Society. Some may be, but most are the other kind. There are Real Society people who have never set foot on a yacht of any sort and who, if the Duke of Windsor walked into the room, would fail to identify him. Sheer splash has nothing to do with Real Society. There were few Real Society people in attendance, for instance, at the wedding of Luci Johnson. ("An August wedding in *Washington?*" people murmured.) Nor were there Real Society people at the wedding of Grace Kelly and Prince Rainier of Monaco. ("I hear that they met," said a Philadelphia Society woman at the time, "at the home of a mutual friend in Ocean City, New Jersey. But how can that be? No one has gone to Ocean City for years.") To this day, the best Philadelphia people make a point of explaining that they did not attend these nuptials; there are a number of princesses in Real Society, but Grace is not one of them. When a splash does occur at a Real Society function, it occurs by coincidence or by accident more often than by design. The wedding of Janet Jennings Auchincloss, a Real Society occasion, generated a good deal of inadvertent splash — and upset the bride so much that she burst into tears.

The *Social Register* is no longer — if it ever was — a reliable guide to who is Real Society and who is not. The little black and red "stud book" has always been published for profit, and has depended on its listees' willingness to be listed, as well as on their subscriptions. The *Social Register* grows thicker in times of economic boom, and shrinks when the economic pendulum falls the other way. The number of *Social Register* families may wax and wane, but the size of *Real Society* remains constant. Many Real Society families ridicule the *Register* now, and make the familiar comment, "It's just a telephone book." In New York, for instance, it is still smaller and more wieldy than the Manhattan directory. As often as not, however, when an entrant is "dropped" from the *Register,* he has simply neglected to — or chosen not to — fill out the necessary annual forms. Still, many Society people feel as the writer Louis Auchincloss does. "The *Social Register* has gotten so enormous," he says, "that it looks rather peculiar if you're *not* in it."

One can frequently recognize a woman of Real Society by the way she dresses. Real Society women's clothes have a way of staying in style longer than other peoples' because Real Society fashions do not change markedly from year to year. Neither the junior-cut mink coat nor the beaver jacket has gone through many transitions since the introduction of the designs, nor has the cut of the classic camel's hair topper. The short-sleeved, round-collared McMullen blouse is ageless, and the hemline of the Bermuda short has hardly been known to fluctuate. What is more classic than a double strand of good pearls? The poplin raincoat is as suited to suburban shopping today as it was to the Smith campus in 1953. It has been said that were it not for the tastes of the young Society woman, the great firm of Peck & Peck would soon go out of business, and all the knitwear on the second floor of Abercrombie & Fitch would quickly fall prey to the moth.

The look is easy, tweedy. Hair is a blond mixture, streaked from the sun, of middle length, and is often caught at the back of the neck in a little net bag. This style is as much at home on the back of a horse as it is with a full-length dinner dress; it has also been with us since the 1920's. Real Society women are often tanned the year round — from riding and playing golf and tennis wherever the sun shines — and a perpetual tan may lead to a leathery look, with crinkled squint lines about the eyes. It is a look exemplified in both the Mrs. Nelson Rockefellers, who had identically impeccable Real Society origins. It is a look that is instantly recognizable but, because of its particular composition, quite difficult for the outsider to simulate.

Then there is the Society voice. Trying to duplicate the American Society accent has provided the greatest stumbling block for the parvenu. Some say you must be born with it to speak it properly and convincingly, but it is safe to say that graduates of such private schools as St. Paul's, Foxcroft, and Madeira, who may not have had the accent to begin with, can emerge with a reasonably close facsimile of it. It is a social accent that is virtually the same in all American cities, and it is actually a blend of several accents. There is much more to it than the well-known broad A. Its components are a certain New England flatness, a trace of a Southern drawl, and a surprising touch of the New York City accent that many people consider Brooklynese. Therefore, in the social voice, the word "shirt" comes out halfway between "shirt" and "shoit." Another key word is "pretty," which, in the social voice, emerges sounding something like "prutty." There is also the word "circle," the first syllable of which is almost whistled through pursed lips, whereas the greeting, "Hi," is nearly always heavily diphthonged as "Haoy." This speech has been nicknamed "the Massachusetts malocclusion," since much of it is accomplished with the lower jaw thrust forward and rigid, and in a number of upper-class private schools, children are taught to speak correctly by practicing with pencils clenched between their teeth.

Accent and appearance help Real Society people to recognize one another quickly, but other factors also weld them into a recognizable unit. The school, college, and clubs are just as important considerations as how much money one has to spend, or where one lives. Addresses have become of minor importance to members of Real Society. They may own estates on Long Island which they call places, palaces in Newport which they call cottages, duplexes on Fifth Avenue which they call houses. A number simply own houses which they call houses. Though, for the most part, Real Society lives on the better streets of America's larger cities, and in the more affluent of these cities' suburbs, Real Society can still be encountered on beachheads along the Carolina coast, in tiny hamlets in Vermont, or in the Mojave Desert.

Society has always had a matriarchal cast — particularly in the United States. But in Real Society the male reigns over his own preserve. Real Society wives have no need to be pushy. The male has his club, even though a number of the most exclusive clubs have been forced to admit ladies at the dinner hour. And, if the men's club has become less important than it used to be, this is not blamed upon women but on urban economics and, of course, newcomers. New money has been inexorably pushing the old money out of the leather club chair, and the result is that men of Real Society have retreated to their homes again. Here, their position is secure. Their wives would never think of accepting an invitation or planning a party without consulting them. And the man may even, provided he is able to afford it, be permitted to keep a mistress.

In Real Society it is less a matter of which club, which school, which street, and what clothes, than it is a matter of *who*. *Who* will always count more than how, or how much. One does *not* ask, "Where

are you from?" or "Where did you go to school?" or "What do you do?"
Such questions are considered as tactless as "How much did it cost?" If
you have to ask such questions, you have no right to the answers. On
the other hand, you may ask without fear of rebuke, "Who . . . ?"
"Who is she?" as a question may mean, "What was her maiden
name?" It may also mean what was her mother's maiden name, and
what was her grandmother's maiden name, and so on. The members of
the family are the family's most precious family jewels. Grandfather
may have been Ambassador to The Hague or an alcoholic suicide; it
doesn't matter, if he belongs. Family talk is a favorite cocktail-hour
diversion wherever Real Society gathers. Each genealogical fact is
brought out lovingly and tenderly, examined meticulously, then carefully put away. To talk family properly, you never need a reference
book or printed family tree, or any other aid; the facts are at your
fingertips with dates, with snippets of incidental history, with little
anecdotes. Done well, family talk is a beautiful and bewildering thing
to listen to — a concerto of whos. Done poorly — by the poseur or dis-
sembler — it can be disastrous. A social climber can sometimes fake an
ancestor, but he had better examine his company carefully before he
tries it. "All we Van Rensselaers," says a Van Rensselaer significantly,
"*know* our Van Rensselaers." And the parvenu had better be prepared
to let family values dominate all other values. Not long ago in Phila-
dephia the talk turned to art and, parochially enough, to Philadelphia's two most prominent woman painters, Mary Cassatt and Cecilia
Beaux — both of whom were members of distinguished families. In
the middle of a debate on their relative artistic merits, with Miss Cassatt seemingly favored, someone commented sharply, "But the Cassatts
weren't anybody!"

People named Vanderbilt are not necessarily in Real Society, but
people named Vanderlip are. In Real Society, the name Morris means
somewhat more than Belmont. Rockefellers now are safely in Real Society, though they didn't use to be, and Astors, who used to be, are
pretty much out. Roosevelts always were and always will be of Real
Society, despite the political affiliations of one of the family's branches.
Other impeccable Society names are, in New York: Aldrich, Auchincloss, Blagden, Burden, French, Stillman, Wickes, and Woodward; in
Boston you are safe with Sedgwicks and Gardners and Fiskes, as

well as with Adamses, Cabots, Lowells, and Saltonstalls. In Philadelphia, there are Drinkers and Ingersolls and Chews and Robertses.
There are Biddles, but there are also other Biddles. There are Cadwaladers. It is said that a true Philadelphian can distinguish between
single-*l* Cadwaladers, who are Real Society, and double-*l* Cadwal-
laders, who are not, simply by the way the name is pronounced.

There are, furthermore, in every American city, families who might
be called *local* Real Society. Thus the Fords, who are Real Society in
Detroit, lose a bit of their Reality in Philadelphia or Boston. The Uih-
lein family and their beer may have made Milwaukee famous, but
their name does not carry imposing social weight in New York. The
phenomenon also works in reverse. The Kennedys, who are *from* Boston, are closer to Real Society elsewhere than they were — or ever will
be — on their native soil.

Certain social critics have claimed that Society has been "killed" by
publicity. This is rather like saying that Dacron has killed the fashion
industry. There has always been a small but colorful segment of Real
Society that has labored to see that its name and picture got in the
papers, just as there has always been an element more fond of going to
clubs and bars and bistros than of staying home. Café Society,
whether by that label or any other, is no new phenomenon, and
the spiritual descendants of C. K. G. Billings's famous dinner-on-
horseback at Sherry's dance today at the Electric Circus. Publicity
filled out the "image" of American Society in the eighteenth and nineteenth centuries, just as it does today, providing it with gaudy accents.
The only difference is that the outlets for publicity, thanks to modern
mass communications, have escalated. It should never be assumed that
publicity and Society are alien concepts, and that one can flourish only
at the expense of the other. On the contrary, Society enjoys — and is
grateful for — its publicity-seeking members. They, the few, in many
ways protect and support the many. Far from killing Society, these
busy few provide a facade and a showcase — a deceptively glossy showcase, to be sure — for what has become an enduring structure in America, the Social Establishment. Behind the facade and the showcase, the
others of the Establishment like to feel they are being given a little
peace. It is not *they* who will be asked to give the interviews.

Publicity, by making Society appear glamorous and celebrated, also provides the greatest lure for social climbers. And Society could not exist without its climbers.

When a person says, with a little sigh, that Real Society is dead and gone, it is reasonably safe to assume that that person is not a member. People in Real Society know that their world is very much alive. But they don't think it is quite polite to say so.

2

Was It Ever What It Used to Be?

OF course there are very few women in Society today who lead the sort of life that was led, just a couple of dozen years ago, by Mrs. Edward T. Stotesbury. She received, as wedding presents from her husband, the senior Morgan partner in Philadelphia, a simple $100,000 diamond-and-sapphire necklace and $4,000,000 in cash to make up for it. She enjoyed such luxuries as a flotilla of maids who were in charge of nothing but her clothes. Every afternoon Mrs. Stotesbury would summon her wardrobe staff — who arrived carrying massive costume books and catalogues of jewelry — to help her decide what to wear for dinner. Even such a seemingly small task as deciding which diamond bracelet to wear, can, when one has sixty-five, take time.

Mrs. Stotesbury's way of life, people in Society often point out, is one that has gone the way of all 1040 forms. But it was fairly uncommon even in her own day. Her parties were criticized as being a touch garish. A generation or so earlier, the famous Bradley-Martin ball — where the hostess appeared in a twenty-foot-long train, a crown, and $100,000 worth of diamonds on her stomacher alone and Mrs. Astor managed to support $200,000 worth on her head — drew so much criticism in the international press that the Bradley-Martins exiled themselves to England forever. Mrs. Stotesbury's guests did not overlook the fact that her husband had been nothing but a six-dollar-a-week clerk before becoming one of the country's richest men. And, even at the peak of her career as America's most spectacular hostess, Mrs. Stotesbury was not considered a bona fide member of Society. Even so she has become, today, a more or less permanent constellation in the social firmament. Some people insist that it takes at least three generations for a family, starting with nothing but money, to elevate itself to the highest Society. (Given another three generations' time, it is also said, the same family will fritter its way back to the ash heap.) Mrs. Stotesbury proves that an individual can be elected to Society posthumously.

Mrs. Stotesbury's children — one is the former wife of the late General Douglas MacArthur, and the other a former husband of Doris Duke — lead lives of comparative quiet and obscurity, as do other members of other families whose wealth once glittered in the public eye. The descendants of Belmonts and Goulds and Goelets, of Biddles and Bakers and John Wanamakers have, as real estate taxes have gone up, moved from brownstone and marble palaces on Fifth Avenue and Rittenhouse Square, into apartments; here they achieve a certain anonymity. The offspring of Astors, Gardners, Vanderbilts, Fishes, Harrimans and Iselins can be found in made-over gardeners' cottages on country estates. A number of Society people are, very quietly, doing something that formerly would have been thought very odd indeed: they live in places like Newport and Tuxedo Park, *year round*. ("The season here," says one Tuxedo butler discreetly, "is now from January first to December thirty-first.")

But are our great Society families languishing for lack of funds? Let us not weep too bitterly for them. Taxes may have scaled down some families' living habits. Quite a number of Society families are, comparatively speaking, poor. But a number of others are just as rich as their grandfathers were, or even richer. The late Vincent Astor, for instance, who inherited $87,200,000 in 1912, increased his fortune — right through the Great Depression — to the point where it amounted to $200,000,000 by the time he died in early 1959.

Money may be spent in less conspicuous ways than in making a woman topheavy with precious stones, but it is still spent. Mrs. J. Denniston Lyon of New York, for instance, who only recently was gathered to her ancestors, spent it on her tiny Pekingese, Peaches. Peaches had been trained to relieve himself in Mrs. Lyon's garden in her country place on the North Shore of Long Island. In winter, lest

Peaches be confused or disturbed by the move back to Fifth Avenue, Mrs. Lyon directed her butler to make weekly trips out to Long Island. There he spaded up a square of Long Island lawn and returned with it to New York for Peaches. Peaches indeed was so particular that though he loved to eat caramel candies, he would only eat the imported Italian ones sold at the expensive food shop Maison Glass. Mrs. Lyon, among other expenses, maintained a yacht anchored off Palm Beach. A year-round staff of five was required for its maintenance. When its owner died she had not sailed the boat, or set foot upon it, for fully fifteen years. Her house in Aiken, South Carolina, stood similarly unvisited, though the house was ritually opened at the beginning, and closed at the end, of each Aiken "season." "And it was not," says one member of the family, "an easy house to open and close. The silver and the paintings had to be taken out of the vault and then put back again — that sort of thing."

Nearby, a neighbor of Mrs. Lyon's, Mrs. Dorothy Killiam, had an extraordinary swimming pool constructed. Of average width, it was of surprising length — appearing like a long, blue canal through the garden. This was because, though its owner liked to swim, she disliked having to turn around. Taking her architect to Palm Beach one winter, she waded into the sea and began to swim along the shore. When she tired, she emerged, and said, "Measure it off. That's how long I want my swimming pool to be." For parties, a hundred and fifty guests for a sit-down dinner was not uncommon, and in summer — since North Shore weather could not be relied upon — she had tables set for a hundred and fifty in the house as well as out of doors. At the last minute, then, she could decide where to sit her party. To place the centerpiece over the largest table, her houseboy used to swing from a large, thick rope, slung from an overhanging eave above her terrace. Cleaning Mrs. Killiam's massive plunge was a chore tantamount to mowing John Nicholas Brown's lawn at Newport. Because the lawn slopes at a forty-five-degree angle into the water, gardeners and their mowers must be lashed with heavy ropes from the crest of the rise lest men and machines be plunged into Narragansett Bay.

The servant problem is, of course, a problem. It is certainly no longer possible to acquire a "good, honest, healthy and well-trained chambermaid" for twenty dollars a month, as a 1914 advertisement in the New York *Times* put it. It sometimes seems as though there are no well-trained chambermaids at any price. "It isn't the upper class that's dying out, it's the servant class," says a New York lady, anxiously eyeing her courtly, but creaky, majordomo. Mrs. George Roberts of Philadelphia has said, with a good deal of accuracy, "The only good servant is a person who thinks it's *nice* to be a servant. Nowadays people simply don't think that being a servant is a nice way to earn a living." As a result of this, there are Society people who still live in houses with rooms for twenty servants and yet have to pick up and deliver their maids each day. Many live in houses with private switchboards, and answer their own telephones. Some who maintain boxes at the Opera must hire sitters in order to attend.

On the rolling acres of Penllyn, Pennsylvania, there are a number of imposing houses which, as a matter of family pride, the present generation of Philadelphia's distinguished Ingersoll family is determined to keep up. The late Charles E. Ingersoll managed to run his house with three men for outside work, a chauffeur, a cook, two maids, a butler, and a pageboy called, in the English manner, the buttons. (Once, in the 1920's, after a slight misadventure in the stock market, Mr. Ingersoll advised his family that some stringent belt-tightening was in order, and in a drastic economy measure he dismissed the buttons. But it so distressed him to see his family thus deprived that he sent them all off to White Sulphur Springs for an extended rest and holiday while he hired another buttons.) In the old days, the Ingersoll staff at Penllyn was such that the meandering gravel drives of the estate could be freshly raked after each vehicle passed. But on the Ingersoll place the other day, Mr. Ingersoll's son John and his wife sat down for cocktails feeling tuckered. The two (she is a Cadwalader) had spent the afternoon replacing a hundred feet of iron fencing. Far from entering a decline, Real Society is often working very hard.

And yet here again we are faced with a contradiction. For all the talk of the servant problem, there are a number of Society families who seem not to have been affected by it at all. On the North Shore of Long Island, throughout the Great Servant Shortage of the Second World War, one hostess managed to muddle through with fourteen maids who did nothing but arrange flowers. (How do fourteen young women busy themselves with nothing but flowers? Among other things, they implanted large Styro-Foam balls with broom straws and, at the end of each straw, secured a rose; the huge floral globes were used as table centerpieces. In the conservatory, an organ-pipe cactus grew nearly two stories high. Each day, the girls decorated it by placing a camellia bloom on each needle. Striking color effects were sometimes worked out with, say, red blossoms on the base of the cactus, fading to pink, and to white at the top. "That sort of thing," commented an awed guest when he saw one of the floral fountains, "ought to be government-subsidized.")

At "Viking's Cove," her summer place at Oyster Bay, as well as at her houses in New York and Palm Beach, Mrs. George F. Baker appears to have successfully overcome the servant problem. A year or so ago her English butler of many years' service expressed a desire to return to England for a visit. Mrs. Baker agreed to let him go and, moreover, made him a gift of his passage on a boat. But he had no sooner sailed out of New York Harbor than Mrs. Baker remembered a party she was having for Senator Barry Goldwater two weeks later. She cabled the butler on shipboard, and when he reached Southampton, he took one brief look at his native land — his first in nearly twenty years — and boarded a boat to take him home again. "I could never have given the party without him," said Mrs. Baker.

Even in Spartan, unshowy old Boston, the servant problem seems to be more a matter of how you look at it. Here, when a young debutante asked a friend if she would enjoy helping her pick out a gown for a coming party, the friend said that she would be delighted. The friend was startled, however, when the debutante sat her down on a sofa and spread open a Sears, Roebuck catalogue between them. When the friend murmured something about the uncertainty of getting a proper fit, the young lady said, "Oh, I can always have Anna take it in." Anna, needless to say, was her governess.

Anthropologists will journey to remote corners of the earth to find those rare spots where a species, or form of life, is still in the process of evolution. Any aboriginal society is a rewarding study, best observed before the missionaries have arrived and instructed all the natives to wear Mother Hubbards, and so it is with the American concept of a social elite. There are only a few places left where the Real Society notion can still be glimpsed evolving, where one can see how it started, and why. In such Eastern cities as Philadelphia, Charleston, and Boston, the evolutionary process was completed in the early 1900's, when

Society began to congeal into a more or less consistent pattern, and to begin its continuous and stately celebration of genealogy. San Francisco, on the other hand, a newer city, was just beginning to emerge from the primordial ooze when it suffered its historic fire and had to start all over again. Since then, it has had to work extra hard and fast to establish for itself an Old Guard. If Society ever *was* what it used to be, San Francisco should be a good place to observe it.

"But how can there *be* a Real Society out there?" perplexed Bostonians are likely to ask. "After all, nobody's been there for longer than three generations — and who were they originally? Gold prospectors and prostitutes, from what I'm told — the worst sort of ragtag and bobtail." But Thomas Carr Howe, director of San Francisco's California Palace of the Legion of Honor, has said, "The fascinating thing about Society here is that the leaders of the city today are the grandchildren of the people who *made* the place." It has been a long time since any Easterner could make such a statement. "I gather they just copy what we do here," says a Philadelphia lady somewhat sniffily. To this, few San Franciscans would seriously demur. But they would certainly add that, in San Francisco, they have, in the copying process, learned how to do it better. A cold war has raged for years between the social capitals of the East and West Coasts, and nothing pleases an Easterner more than an opportunity to put a San Franciscan in his place. In Boston not long ago, a San Francisco woman was being entertained at a party on Beacon Hill, and, before dinner, was offered a cocktail — that curious Bostonian concoction, the Sweet Martini. When, in due time, no second drink was offered, the San Francisco lady turned to her hostess and, holding out her empty glass, said brightly, "In San Francisco, we have a saying — 'You can't fly on one wing!' " Her hostess smiled coolly and replied, "In Boston, we fly on one wing."

Though the pick and shovel did indeed come first to San Francisco, and though several mining fortunes were quickly made, most of them were quickly spent. The most substantial money in the city today represents fortunes made in places where the miners spent theirs. San Francisco's famous Big Four, for instance — Charles Crocker, Collis P. Huntington, Leland Stanford, and Mark Hopkins — were Sacramento merchants who collected the little sacks of gold that the miners brought down from the hills, and parlayed them into fortunes large enough to build the Central Pacific and Southern Pacific Railroads.

Then there was another quartet of families — the Floods, the Fairs, the Mackays, and the O'Briens — the great Irish "Silver Kings" of the Comstock Lode, who quickly put their Comstock fortunes to work in other areas. (From the Fairs, San Francisco acquired its Fairmont Hotel; Clarence H. Mackay made millions in telephones, telegraphs, and cables.)

These eight names are still liberally sprinkled throughout the pages of the San Francisco telephone book. They might be called the core of the San Francisco *Social Register.* To them have been added names from more recent — but only slightly more recent — banking, mercantile, and shipping fortunes, names such as Sutro, Blyth, and Monteagle (finance), Spreckels (sugar), Folger (coffee), Ghirardelli (chocolate), and Lapham (shipping). Other now impeccable San Francisco families include the Newhalls (married to Spreckelses and O'Briens), the Metcalfs (married to Huntingtons), the Hendersons (married to Crockers), the Redingtons (John Redington is married to Diana Crocker; William W. Crocker lives on Redington Road), the Nickels (married to Morses, of the Code family), the Meins (married to Nickels), the Olivers (married to Fays), the Tobins (married to Fays and de Youngs), the Thieriots (married to Tobins and de Youngs), the Millers (married to Folgers), and the Fays (married to Millers, Meins, Tobins, and practically everybody else).

Also important to San Francisco Society are a number of wealthy Jewish families — the Haases, the de Youngs, the Hellmans, the Zellerbachs, the Dinkelspiels, the Schwabachers, and the Fleishhackers, to mention a few — and, because members of these families have intermarried with non-Jewish Society families, a number have found their way into the *Social Register,* despite that publication's customary "policy." "We are fortunate," says a San Francisco woman, "in having a perfectly lovely group of Jewish people here." This sentiment is echoed almost as often as those extolling San Francisco's hilltop views of the Bay. With it, of course, goes the implication that the Jewish families should feel fortunate, too, to be so favorably regarded.

Local retailing money is represented socially by the Prentis Cobb Hales (Hale Brothers' department store), the Carl Livingstons (Livingstons' specialty store), the Magnins (I. Magnin & Company, another specialty store), the Hector Escobosas (he is president of I. Magnin), the James Ludwigs (head of the local Saks Fifth Avenue), and

the Baldocchis. (Podesta Baldocchi is a chic flower shop but, as one matron puts it, "All the Baldocchis aren't in flowers, just as all the Aliotos
aren't in fish." Alioto's is an eating establishment on Fisherman's
Wharf.)

One factor that has helped the rapid growth of a Social Establishment in San Francisco has certainly been the burgeoning growth of the
city itself. San Franciscans bewail the presence of so many "new
people," but the new people have certainly done their share to make
things pleasanter for those who have been there somewhat longer.
Since many of the makers of early fortunes bought land, the present generation is not only rich by inheritance but growing richer. For example,
when Mrs. George T. Cameron's father, the late Meichel H. de
Young, told her he was making her a gift of "some sand dunes," Mrs.
Cameron thought little of it. It did not occur to her that, after a few
years, those dunes would form a considerable piece of metropolitan
real estate, now being divided into building lots selling for thousands
of dollars apiece.

In San Francisco it is possible to see that being a member of an
emerging elite can be a complicated experience — giddy, and yet
baffling; full of unexpected pleasures, and yet at the same time full of
unforeseen headaches. With plentiful money, which everyone in San
Francisco Society has begun to take for granted, and with the idea of
"Society" still a fresh, bright, important-seeming notion, it is certainly
fun to pamper oneself. A kind of careless self-indulgence that was
characteristic of Eastern Society a generation ago, in the 1920's, now
pervades the San Francisco air. A generation from now, frivolity may
have gone out of fashion, but at the moment it is still fun in San
Francisco to dash off to Scandinavia in search of a pair of "really good
house servants," as one couple recently did. It is still fun to buy up
whole rooms from French châteaux, have them dismembered, shipped
home, and reassembled in suburban Burlingame, a practice which
palled in other sections of the country three decades ago, at least. No
one in San Francisco is bored with his gold-plated bathroom fixtures.
Many houses are still putting them in, and the old line, first attributed
to Mrs. Stotesbury, about gold being easy to care for "because it
doesn't need polishing" is being trotted out all over the town. Dorothy
Spreckels Munn's chinchilla bedspread is not considered in the least
outré. It is fun.

It is fun to dress up in white tie and tails or a long gown twice a week, and sit in a golden box at the Opera — though Opera-going in Eastern cities has become a pastime for older folks. In San Francisco it is fun to dress up for *all* occasions — and here, of course, is where the city's climate has been such a boon to fashion-minded women. It is "dress-up weather" for suits, hats, furs, gloves, and jewelry all year round. San Francisco is known as one of the world's dressiest cities, and San Franciscans would not have it otherwise. While Boston women "have a hat," and are said never to need to buy one, San Francisco ladies buy hats by the dozens of dozens; they may even wear bits of veiling and fluff in their hair for luncheon in their own houses, and carry silk reticules from room to room. In San Francisco it is fun to have small, informal luncheons cooked to perfection by an imported Swiss chef, with two wines and gold utensils, served in Directoire plates at a table decked with scores of saucer-sized camellias fresh from the garden.

Lest such pleasurable splendors seem vulgar, great care is taken to make them seem effortless, even ordinary, and yet authoritative and correct. San Franciscans make it a point to know good food from bad, *véritable* French furniture from reproductions, diamonds from rhinestones, mink from muskrat. San Francisco Society works with astonishing intensity at making itself the genuine article, not an imitation. Great stress is placed on manners. "Never point," one San Francisco mother teaches her children, "except at French pastry." Do's and don'ts are rampantly important. "We'd never wear diamonds before lunch," says one woman. "Anyone who'd wear a mink stole in the daytime is automatically *out*," says another. "I think it's almost *insulting* not to serve wine with meals," says Mrs. Michael Tobin. "Even to people I didn't really want to meet, I'd serve wine — and not a California wine, either. As for food, we simply won't serve the ordinary. Steak is for butchers."

San Francisco people believe in entertaining in their homes, and this is one of the most house-proud cities in America. It matters little whether one's house is large or small, built last year or "before the fire"; what matters is how it is "done," and how it is run. San Francisco is an interior decorator's paradise. "We wouldn't dream of asking anyone to dinner in a public restaurant," says one young hostess. "I can't remember when I was last inside one." Sixteen for dinner is her favorite number; usually it is black tie. There is a strong Southern flavor, carefully cultivated, in San Francisco; many Gold Rush families came from the South, and at the time of the Civil War, it was touch and go whether California would side with the Union or the Confederacy. When you are entertained in some of the houses of San Francisco Society, it is often possible to imagine yourself on a plantation in ante-bellum Virginia.

Public interest in the doings of Society has gone somewhat stale in the East. Not so in San Francisco. While apathy and indifference have reduced Society pages to a few columns in New York, San Francisco Society receives page after page of fulsome glowing attention in the daily press, and twice as much on Sundays. And this news, further-more, is read by everyone in the state of California. The opening of the San Francisco Opera is more than a major social function; it is a public pageant and fashion show, with worshipful teenagers lining the streets beforehand. At the annual Opera Fol de Rol, an Opera Guild benefit at which the stars give free performances, the main floor of the Civic auditorium is filled by the few hundred Society sponsors who buy tables, but the vaulting gallery above is packed with some six thousand non-Society faces which gasp and crane forward as each new Society figure makes an entrance. After one of these affairs, a housewife from the gallery said, "Of course I love to hear the artists sing, but the real reason I come is to see the Society women in their beautiful dresses." Opera patronage has become the most profitable avenue for the San Francisco social climber, as it was in New York in the days of Otto Kahn.

Riding up Washington Street in a taxi recently, a visitor was sur-prised to have the driver point, with more than a touch of civic pride, to the A. B. Spreckels mansion. He then proceeded to describe some of the features of the house — the $30,000 French commodes, the wall-to-wall carpeting in the servants' rooms, the $25,000 motor-operated movable glass swimming-pool enclosure with its $2000 built-in radiant-heating mechanism, its owner's venerable custom-built wicker-sided Rolls-Royce with its mink lap robe and, of course, Dorothy Spreckels Munn's celebrated chinchilla bedspread. The taxi driver had seen none of these things (except the Rolls), but he loyally approved of all of them. (Though San Franciscans never tire of deploring the "showiness" of Los Angeles, San Franciscans nonetheless allow their houses to be photographed for use on tourist postcards.)

But for all the fun of cultivating the grand manner, there are drawbacks. A developing Society can develop growing pains, and in San Francisco, one of these has been a fierce social competitiveness which, more than anything else, is reminiscent of the New York of Edith Wharton in *The Age of Innocence*. San Francisco has an obsessive concern with class. Newcomers, who may not realize it, are carefully sized up and then ticked off according to a local shorthand system. To the question, "What's so-and-so like?" the answer may be, "N.O.C.D.," which means, "Not our class, dearie." Acceptable souls are classified O.C.D., while those with no class are labeled N.C. A fourth category is P.C., which stands, according to one young San Franciscan, for "Pittsney-Classney," and *that,* according to another, is San Francisco baby talk that means "fifth class — the kind of people who sit in the dress circle at the Opera, and who serve potato-chip dips made out of dried onion soup mix and sour cream."

San Francisco Society is divided into sets and cliques and circles and the circles intersect, and meet, and blur like rings on a college beerhall table — with an effect just about as chaotic and untidy. Everyone has his group, but each group exists at the expense of another group, and the rivalry is stern and sometimes ferocious. There is, of course, an older group and a younger group, and a quiet group and a "jetty" group, but it doesn't stop there. "We have," as one of the younger nonjetty group explains, "our A Group — the people we adore and can't see too much of. Then we have the B Group, containing people we adore *less*. Then we have the Bidet Group, our little nickname for the people connected with the European embassies and consulates in the city, and the Wetback Group — people with the Latin American consulates. Of course we put some of the Wetback Group and the Bidet Group into the A Group, and some into the B Group, and often we invite the A Group and the B Group together, but there's sort of a subsection of the B Group which we call the C Group, who are the people we see only about once a year, at Christmastime."

Then there is the Political Group — "People who get terribly interested in politics and who are always inviting the mayor for dinner," and there is a Mumsy Group — "Their daughters come out in the afternoon, at little teas," and a Dress-Up Group which buys its clothes in Rome and Paris and whose daughters come out at spectacular balls. Each of these groups is convinced the other is doing it wrong. There is an organization known as the Spinsters, a postdebutante club rather than a group but, according to a member, the Spinsters splinter into groups of their own. The Spinsters' male counterparts are called the Bachelors. The Spinsters give a flossy ball each year, and shortly after it, the Bachelors give a flossy ball "to repay the Spinsters and certain debutantes to whom the Bachelors are indebted." The Bachelors stress that only *certain* debutantes are invited. "Others will knock vainly for admission to our ball," says one Bachelor. There is also an informal men's group called the Downtown Operators' Association which strives for social acceptance but which, according to Gorham Knowles, a former president of the Bachelors, is made up of men who couldn't get into the Bachelors. The Downtown Operators, needless to say, don't give a ball of any kind.

San Francisco Society is terribly worried these days that it may be getting too big, and that too many people who don't deserve to may be managing to get themselves in. "To be accepted here, a new person simply must be *attractive*," says one woman. She suggests that new-comers seeking acceptance by Society arrive with at least two letters of introduction and recommendation. Then, she explains, "We'll give them the go-around with invitations once. If they seem attractive, we'll give them the go-around a second time. After that, we'll either drop them or take them in. If we drop them, I'm very afraid they're dropped for good." San Francisco insists that the social fatalities are numerous and that, as a result, the number of people who are in Real Society remains small. San Francisco is not at all embarrassed to admit that it is snobbish. "Frankly, I'm a snob," Mrs. Michael Tobin has said. "So many *un*attractive people have come to California that I'm determined to see to it that my children mingle only with their own kind."

San Francisco Society is now in a kind of social-arbiter stage, as the East was a couple of generations back. It is in a Ward McAllister phase, and a short while ago it lost an excellent local equivalent of that famous screener. He was, of all things, a headwaiter. Just as Mr. Mc-Allister used to maneuver guests into, and keep others out of, Mrs. Astor's gold-and-white ballroom, so Ernest, headwaiter in the St. Francis Hotel's Mural Room, conferred social status upon some and stripped it from others. One of the city's most venerable traditions is

"Monday lunch" at the St. Francis. This lunch, attended by all of San Francisco's would-be and actual socialites, as well as by columnists from the press who make avid note of who is there, includes a fashion show which is somewhat desultory since the real show is at the tables where San Francisco ladies are eating. (The forty-year-old tradition supposedly began when certain ladies decided to make it publicly clear that they were not bound to the ordinary chores of washday.) For over a generation Ernest smoothly seated the best San Francisco women at the best tables — on either side of the center aisle, the closer to the door the better. Slightly less important women were accommodated on the encircling balcony. Climbers of the garden variety were placed in the outer reaches of the room, called Siberia. As a woman either advanced socially or slid down the social scale, Ernest, with corklike dryness, saw to it that her table location changed accordingly. Like all arbiters of elegance, Ernest was incorruptible, unmoved by the most lavish bribery. One learned to dread his look of icy disapproval as he accepted the too large tip. Alas, Ernest is no more. His replacement in the Mural Room is doing his best, but according to one woman, "He has made a number of serious mistakes."

San Francisco is competitive about addresses, and which suburban area is "better" — Marin County to the north, or the Peninsula to the south — is a point of stormy controversy and hard feeling. "Burlingame is San Francisco's Long Island," says an old-time resident of Ross (in Marin County), implying that Burlingame is all rather *nouveau riche* and dreadful. "Really, I don't see why anyone would want to live there — you might as well be living in Akron." Burlingame counters such snide comments by referring to Marin County as "pure-push Marin" because, according to one woman, "Marin people are pushy — purely pushy." "Of course," says a Burlingame woman, "people do still move out to Marin, but I don't know what happens to them. They sort of disappear, and we never see them again."

Burlingame, with its elegant country club housed in an old Crocker mansion, undoubtedly outranks Marin in snob appeal and, probably, in per capita wealth as well. But even in Burlingame things are not entirely stable. Brushing Burlingame so closely that it is hard to tell where one leaves off and the other begins is the somewhat amorphous township of Hillsborough. Of the two places, everyone agrees that Hillsborough is better, but you must be careful when you use the word

Hillsborough as an address. "We always say we live in Burlingame," says Mrs. Tobin, who actually lives in Hillsborough. "If you hear people say they live in Hillsborough, you can be certain they are parvenus or climbers."

Still another social island, south of Burlingame, is the more rural and woodsy town of Woodside, and though Woodside and Burlingame people understand each other and have not formed mutually exclusive groups, there is the general feeling that Burlingame people are the more stylish, while Woodside people are horsier, and go in for dog breeding, Black Angus, and polo.

A newcomer soon finds that not only is it wise to look askance at, and speak with disfavor of, Los Angeles; it is also well to deplore Oakland and Piedmont across the Bay. "Over there," says a San Francisco woman with a Piedmontward wave of her hand, "they put on their jewels for breakfast and wear long, sweeping gowns for tea." San Franciscans are willing to admit that there may be a Society in Portland and Seattle — a greater likelihood of it in Portland — and, just possibly, in Denver. But they give the nod to hardly any other Western cities. The rolling coastal range of mountains, the rich towns of the Central Valley, the Sierras, the Rockies — they might just as well not exist. As far as Society is concerned, Society recommences at the Pennsylvania Turnpike where, in terms of which Eastern prep school or college one's son attends, the San Francisco competitiveness and rivalry starts all over again.

New York, Philadelphia, and Boston do not spend much time arguing over who, in each city, is that city's Social Leader. In San Francisco this is a matter of fierce importance and, as the arguments rise to battle pitch, a certain frontier flavor pervades the San Francisco air — an odor of saloons and gunsmoke — and, with several able-bodied contenders for top position, the fights are about as orderly as a Barbary Coast poker party. Beneath a veneer of politeness and gentility lurk the scruples and politics of the mining camp. Social claim-jumping goes on all the time and, whenever it occurs, the socially dispossessed quickly muster their forces and charge out red-eyed for revenge. "I think we must all agree," said one woman at a cocktail party recently, "that Helen Cameron is *unquestionably* the social leader of San Francisco." The woman to whom she was speaking, obviously of a different camp, replied sweetly, "Oh, I agree that Helen is a darling. I simply *adore* her. She's one of my *dearest* friends, but —" She let the sentence hang a moment, heavy with unspoken meaning, and then added, "Well . . ." And then she smiled and said, "After *all* . . ." (One of the "problems" with de Young was that he was Jewish.)

There has never been an undisputed social leader in San Francisco. There are only disputed ones. Other than Mrs. Cameron, there is her sister, Mrs. Nion Tucker, but Mrs. Tucker may be slightly behind Mrs. Charles Blyth, whose house in Burlingame, "Strawberry Hill," is one of the most beautiful estates in California. Though placed in retirement for a while after the death of her banker husband, Mrs. Blyth has since made, according to a friend, "a very strong comeback," and now considers herself "the grandest woman in San Francisco." But another lady who considers herself equally grand is Mrs. Blyth's neighbor and arch rival, Mrs. Edmunds Lyman. When Mrs. Blyth gave a party a while back for the visiting Queen of Holland, the Lymans were not invited. (To make the snub as inconspicuous as possible, the Lymans hastily scheduled a trip to Hawaii and were out of town on the day of the party.) Mrs. Lyman was overheard to murmur, "Kay Blyth seems obsessed with the idea of entertaining royalty these days. Is it true she's thinking of changing the name of 'Strawberry Hill' to 'The Orangerie'?"

Then there are Mrs. Paige Monteagle and Mrs. Kenneth Monteagle, sisters-in-law who appear together from time to time looking cordial but who, it is generally assumed, actually loathe one another. Hard feeling is said to stem from the time their mother-in-law died and one of the items left behind was a huge grid of diamonds. The daughters-in-law flipped a coin for the stones, and Mrs. Kenneth Monteagle won the toss, but her sister-in-law is said to feel that those diamonds would look far better on her own bosom. Socially, each woman has her own crops of staunch backers. "Lucile is an absolute peach," says one group. "But Louise —" And, says another group, "Louise is the most marvelous woman alive. On the other hand, Lucile —" And so it goes.

"I detest the term 'social leader,' simply detest it!" says Mrs. Robert Watt Miller. "It implies a certain amount of *striving*, don't you think?" Actually, with rather little striving, she herself might be considered a social leader. She is the dowager of the large and prosperous Miller clan, and her daughter Marian is one of San Francisco's great beauties. But the Millers may have a certain black mark against them, too. They came originally from Oakland.

For the most part, however, since San Franciscans cannot compete with the East on the old-family level, they choose to turn that shortcoming into an asset. Mrs. Miller, for example, was a Folger. "My father's family came from Nantucket," she explains — where Folgers can still be found — "and they were all pirates, but as far as I know none of them were jailbirds, quite." And as for the great Flood family, young James Flood, a banker, rancher, and yachtsman, makes no bones of the fact that his grandfather was a bartender and his grandmother a chambermaid. "Why should he?" asks a friend. "The point is that Floods today are ladies and gentlemen." Another San Franciscan says, "Isn't it better to come up in the world than down?" And everyone enjoys citing the case of the elegant and ancient Markoe family of Philadelphia. (The Markoes, originally Marcous, were a French Huguenot family who settled in St. Croix, Virgin Islands, in the seventeenth century, a few of whom migrated north to America prior to the Revolution; when Mrs. Gordon Fetterman, a family-proud descendant of the first American Markoes, journeyed to St. Croix not long ago in a search for distant cousins, she found a few but was unprepared for the fact that all the Virgin Island Markoes are now Negroes.) Today, according to one San Franciscan, "The *really* chic thing is to be able to find one honest-to-gosh prostitute in your family tree."

One of the younger set in San Francisco says, "It takes three generations of education and breeding to rub the rough edges off first-generation money. That's the state San Francisco is in today — all the roughness smoothed out." And yet, oddly enough, one San Francisco woman who, though she might not exactly qualify as a social leader, certainly belongs among the city's *grandes dames*, has, on the surface, what might appear as rough edges. She is Mrs. Adolph B. Spreckels — tall, stately and imposing, but a woman who slaps her knee loudly and roars at a good joke. Mrs. Spreckels's Washington Street house, high on a hill overlooking the Bay and most of the city, is a fantastic white-stone sculpture with so many carved garlands and furbelows on its fa-

cade that, in the San Francisco sunshine, it glitters like a confection of
spun sugar which, when you remember where the money comes from,
perhaps it is. Yet its mistress is forthright, direct, anything but delicate, and, when she encounters artificiality (or "a phony" as she calls
it), or rudeness, she responds with a total squelch. (Once, when Elsa
Maxwell asked her how old she was, Mrs. Spreckels replied, "Old
enough to remember when there was no such person as Elsa Maxwell.")

Mrs. Spreckels has met, known, and been entertained by nearly
every member of the European royalty of her time. But when her
daughter, Dorothy Munn, sent her a photograph of herself sitting next
to the Duke of Windsor, along with a note that said coyly, "Look who
I'm sitting with!" Mrs. Spreckels said, "Well, I give up. Who is it?"
She is a good friend of King Frederick and Queen Ingrid of Denmark
and points out, "I've got a signed photograph of them hanging in my
bathroom." Another friend was Queen Marie of Rumania. "The
Queen gave me a *lot* of gold furniture," she says. "I kept it out in the
hall for a while." Among the pieces was the Queen's gold throne; "very
comfortable," says Mrs. Spreckels. The precious collection now resides
in the Maryhill Museum in the state of Washington, one of several
museums for which Mrs. Spreckels is entirely or partly responsible.
(Once, referring to the royal furniture, Mrs. Spreckels said with a
wink, "Actually, pet, I bought it," meaning that the Queen parted
with it in return for a contribution to a favorite royal cause.)

With the millions left by Adolph Spreckels when he died, his
widow began an enormous and continuing program of personal and
public philanthropy. Her most impressive gift has been the California
Palace of the Legion of Honor in Lincoln Park, a replica of the Palais
de la Legion d'Honneur in Paris. This was erected not as a memorial
to herself or her husband, but to the California men who lost their
lives in World War I. The building alone cost three and a half millions when it was built, and Mrs. Spreckels added a vast art collection.
She also established the San Francisco Maritime Museum and gave *it*
a collection. More recently, she has assembled a collection devoted to
the dance and theatre which she hopes will one day become the nu-
cleus of still another museum. The cavernous garages of her house
have for many years been used as a Salvage Shop which she runs for

the benefit of at least five different causes. During World War II she entertained servicemen continually and always presented each man's wife with an electric washing machine from what was apparently an inexhaustible supply. Those around her insist that if her unpublicized gifts were ever tallied they would far exceed her public ones.

She is, however, far from one's vision of a Lady Bountiful. She likes to entertain guests in her bedroom. Coming in from a busy day, she will toss a large floppy hat over the swan's-neck post of her bed ("A king made love in it, of course") and accept a drink from her butler while she removes her stockings, talking full-steam to her visitors all the while. She may also entertain in one of her bathrooms. There are twenty-five, all capacious, and for years she kept a bridge table set up in each in case a foursome happened to gather there. She makes a game of trying to shock people, and judges people by their reactions to some of her more startling actions and pronouncements. She has been known to arrive for a quick, unscheduled visit to her Palace of the Legion of Honor with a mink blanket around her shoulders and nothing else on but a nightgown and a pair of bedroom slippers. She is fond of asking casual acquaintances over for a swim in her covered pool, and then adding, "Of course I swim in the raw — hope you don't mind, pet." She is descended from a titled French family named de Bretteville which emigrated to Denmark many generations ago, and was fairly impoverished by the time her branch of it joined the California Gold Rush and, as it turned out, found very little gold. She is proud of the fact that, as a young woman — before she met Mr. Spreckels — she used to walk two miles a day to save a five-cent streetcar fare. She is also proud of her full name, Alma Emma Charlotte Corday le Normand de Bretteville Spreckels, and claiming Marat's murderess in her family tree, usually adds, "Got anybody you want murdered, pet? I'm your girl!" At a luncheon which she gave for friends and patrons of her museums last year, she grew bored with the speeches, all of which extolled her and her good deeds and, finally, after a particularly fulsome paean, she turned to the speaker and, in her whiskey-tenor voice inquired, "Want to hear something dirty in Danish?" The speaker, nonplussed, nodded yes. Mrs. Spreckels then uttered a few Danish words. "Very interesting, dear Mrs. Spreckels, but what does it mean?" asked the speaker. "Fire up your behind!" cried Mrs. Spreckels.

One of San Francisco's great blood feuds has been conducted between the Spreckels family and the de Youngs. This is said to have resulted from old "Mike" de Young's use of his San Francisco *Chronicle* as an occasional instrument of blackmail. (There was the curious case of old Mr. Charles Crocker who, back in the 1880's, built a superlative mansion on Nob Hill, moved in, and, exactly one month later, moved out in a strange hurry, whereupon the Crocker mansion suddenly became de Young's mansion. It is widely assumed de Young "had something" on Crocker, and the house was the price of keeping it out of the newspaper.) De Young, according to the Spreckels family, also tried to frame Adolph Spreckels. In any case, one day Mr. Spreckels strode down to the *Chronicle*'s office, up to de Young's desk, and fired point-blank at the publisher — who ducked, and the bullet missed its mark. Today the feud is quiescent, and whenever Mrs. Spreckels has "Monday lunch" at the St. Francis, she greets Mr. de Young's daughters, Mrs. Cameron and Mrs. Tucker. The greeting is more polite than cordial. As she once pointed out, "Those de Young women are nice, but we just can't be very intimate since my husband shot their father."

Like many very rich people, although she has given away more millions than she can remember, Mrs. Spreckels resents being asked outright for money. When the staff of the Palace of the Legion of Honor organized a baseball team a while back, it found itself fifty dollars short of the amount needed to buy uniforms. The team, wondering whether the Palace of the Legion of Honor's wealthy benefactress might help out, approached her. The team, its manager told her, was to be called the A. B. Spreckels Memorial Baseball Team. Mrs. Spreckels nodded approvingly. The A. B. Spreckels Memorial Team needed, however, fifty dollars for uniforms, and perhaps — "*What!*" cried Mrs. Spreckels. She flung open her reticule and poured its contents — lipstick, emery boards, matches, a few coins, a handkerchief — on the table. "Where do you expect *me* to get fifty dollars?" she cried. "You people have got my skin. Now you want my guts!"

Mrs. Spreckels's less conventional antics dismay San Francisco Society; there is a feeling that someone as rich as she should be somewhat more genteel. But Mrs. Spreckels has discovered — and made the discovery long ago — that there is more to being a *grande dame* than gentility or a broad A. To be a *grande dame* one must have, among other things, the assurance to be one. Confidence of mind and clarity of purpose matter more than the Grand Manner. Grandness need have nothing to do with breeding, either, but merely with one's scale of thinking. *Grandes dames* such as Alma Spreckels are far above caring what other people think.

San Franciscans sometimes seem to harbor a mystical sense of *mission* — that they have been given the duty of introducing Good Form and the Right Thing to the wild and woolly West. San Francisco's social bellwethers are the great Eastern social cities, and San Francisco seems continually to be asking itself what the *East* might think. And yet, at the same time, one of the grandest ladies of Eastern Society is the spiritual cousin of Mrs. Spreckels. She is Mrs. Robert Homans of Boston, the former Abigail Adams, a descendant of two United States Presidents, a niece of both Henry Adams and Brooks Adams, and the present dowager of the ancient and distinguished Adams clan. Mrs. Homans possesses Mrs. Spreckel's same social audacity and verve, and ability to plunge forthrightly into situations that would surely daunt lesser folk. Once, when Beacon Street had become impassable in a blizzard, Mrs. Homans ordered her taxi to stop in front of her husband's club, the august Somerset Club, and demanded a room for the night. When the club politely explained that it had a rule against giving rooms to unescorted women, Mrs. Homans said, "Very well. In that case, I'll go out and get my taxi driver." She got her room. Now a widow in her seventies, whose hair style has not changed in forty years, she says, "When it comes to style, Boston doesn't have much. We all have what we call a hat. You know, they cover your head. My daughter makes me burn them now and then." Like Mrs. Spreckels, she is a woman above style. Though she calls herself "the last of the old Adamses," she insists that Boston still has "a regular Society, a regime under which you live and do the things you ought to do." Among the things she feels she ought to do is spend at least ten hours a day turning over her fortune to educational, cultural, and philanthropic institutions with incredibly little fanfare. And of course the existence of such a regime does not prevent Abigail Adams Homans from doing exactly what she likes. Her social position is so secure that, as she says, "If I stood in the Common on my head, people'd say, 'Oh, that's just Abigail Adams.' They wouldn't pay any attention. We're conventionally independent."

Mrs. Homans's son, Robert Homans, Jr., is married to the Winthrop Aldrich's daughter, Mary, thereby joining two of the most redoubtable families of New York and Boston. The young Homanses live quiet, successful, and conventionally independent lives in San Francisco.

3

"How Shall We Tell the Children?"

THOUGH each set of parents has its own specific formula, one of the most controversial issues in Society is the question of at what age, and how, to make the children aware of the special benefits and duties of their status. Some families, such as the Rockefellers, have traditionally made it a point to keep their children in the dark about the meaning of Rockefellerdom for as long as possible, and Rockefeller governesses were instructed to remove, from locked closets full of toys, only one toy per child daily, lest the young be overcome by the trappings of great wealth. In at least one Rockefeller nursery, a miniature kitchen was built adjoining where the children were taught to cook simple, unaffected dishes such as hamburgers, fried potatoes, and spaghetti. Once a week, furthermore, the children entertained their parents in the nursery for an evening meal the children had prepared. "I learned what it meant to be a Rockefeller long after I learned there was no Santa Claus," says one of the family. What was his reaction? "It frightened me terribly. I had nightmares for weeks. I was certain that someone would try to kidnap me." The Aldriches, who are related to Rockefellers by marriage, are similarly minded, and Lucy Aldrich Devens recalls that it was "many years before I realized that there was any money around." She was so strictly and carefully reared that she actually thought the Aldriches were poor.

Some families are more direct, and a Connecticut mother believes in

taking her small children with her on her regular rounds of personal
charity, visiting her "favorite unfortunates" and delivering Christmas
turkeys, toys, and hand-me-downs so that the children can see, without
having it painfully explained, "the difference." To some, the difference is made clear at an extremely early age. A passenger in the nursery school car pool in Westchester was awed, recently, by the size of
the home of one of his schoolmates. "Wow!" he cried. "You live in a
castle!" The young man replied crisply, "It's not a castle. It's a mansion." A youth at the Hotchkiss School was, however, sixteen years old
before he realized that everyone in the world was not precisely in his
family's circumstances. He had managed to wheedle, from the family's
cook, the promise of a bottle of whiskey to take to a party, and he had
arranged to call at her Harlem apartment to pick it up. The young man
had known the cook in terms of the coziness of the family kitchen and
the starched amplitude of her white uniform. The squalor of the Harlem apartment, and the realization that the preparer of so many delic-
ious family meals actually lived in such a place, was shock enough.
But he says, "The door to her only closet was standing open, and inside,
hanging neatly, were all my mother's old dresses. The sight of those
cast-off dresses nearly knocked me over. Nothing could have brought
home the gap — the gulf between us — with more impact. She gave
me the bottle, and I could barely bring myself to look at her, I was so
close to crying."

But most families prefer that their children make the discovery
in less dramatic fashion, that the dawning of the idea of "difference"
come gradually and painlessly by a kind of social osmosis. The theory
is that if a child is placed in the proper mixture of the right schools, the
right dancing classes, the right parties, resorts, and summer camps, the
desired result — an unsurprising marriage to someone of the same class
— will inevitably take place. Of course this formula is not foolproof
(even the most carefully brought-up young lady may fall in love with
an Italian ski instructor), but in general it can be relied upon to work.

The same osmosis principle is trusted when it comes to imparting
political values, philosophies, and eventually party affiliation. Though
one cannot guarantee it, one hopes that one's children will grow up to
be right-thinking Republicans by simply following the example of
their parents. In this endeavor, the right schools are supposed to help,
but, again and again it is a shock to parents to discover that most

schools make no attempt at all to instill political ideas. In fact, many prep school teachers take a sly delight in trying to "liberalize" Republican-oriented children. "My son has a history teacher who told him Roosevelt was okay," one father fumed recently. And Society's preference for Princeton and Yale — over Harvard — has a great deal to do with the notion that Harvard is populated largely with "Communist" and "left-wing bleeding-heart" professors. The young are nearly always rebellious, and it is distressing when they refuse to fall into line. Young Mrs. Lewis Rutherfurd, living in Hong Kong where her husband teaches, wrote home to her mother, Mrs. Hugh D. Auchincloss, with bitter things to say about the American commitment in Vietnam. "Oh, she's such a big baby!" said Mrs. Auchincloss with some exasperation.

One of the most persistent notions about growing up into Society is that the child should be subjected to rigorous discipline, that he should learn diligence and duty before shouldering the heavy responsibility of social leadership. As a result, in New York, it is possible to see on a spring Sunday, marching jauntily up Park Avenue to the strains of "St. Julien," a valiant band of two hundred little boys in white trousers, gray tunics, white belts and white caps which sport red-white-and-blue-feathered plumes; the lads, some no taller than the spring tulips which march up the center of the Avenue beside them, are armed with rifles, swords, flags, and guidons. They march with Rockette-like precision, and the effect is a bit like watching a performance on the Plain at West Point through the wrong end of a telescope. The annual occurrence of the little boys in parade confuses the majority of New Yorkers, and most passersby can seldom give a clear or cogent explanation of who the little boys are and why they are there in full battle regalia. A few, however, realize that they are witnessing nothing more startling than the annual Church Parade of the Knickerbocker Greys, "A Private Drill Class for Boys," and the New York *Social Register's* private little army.

In the ranks of the Greys, in uniformed anonymity, have marched tiny Rockefellers, Roosevelts, Vanderbilts, Van Rensselaers, and Harrimans, not to mention pint-sized Twomblys, Goulds, Fishes, Burdens, Blagdens and Schwabs, to say nothing of lilliputian Dodges, Morgans, Swopes, Sloans, Hamiltons, Reads, and Reids. Though the organization is over eighty years old, its size has been kept small. Traditionally, its membership has consisted of boys from the "best families," and, until quite recently the Knickerbocker Greys, for fear of kidnapings, permitted no publicity at all to emanate from the group. Now things have relaxed but with the exception of the Church Parade — from the Seventh Regiment Armory at Park Avenue and Sixty-sixth Street, sixteen blocks south to the steps of St. Bartholomew's Episcopal Church — the Greys make no *en masse* appearances in public.

Veterans of the Knickerbocker Greys include a number of distinguished men and, not surprisingly, the Greys do not mind assuming some of the credit. Averell Harriman, for instance, was a Grey, as was Douglas Fairbanks, Jr. Major General Pierpont Morgan Hamilton, a great-grandson of Alexander Hamilton and a wearer of the Congressional Medal of Honor, received his basic military training in the Knickerbocker Greys. There have been titled Greys from the ranks of New York's displaced royalty, among them Prince David Chavchavadze, the son of Princess Nina of Russia, and several Princes Obolensky. Former Greys in public life include journalist Robert Considine, author-lecturer Lowell Thomas, and actors John Kerr and Mel Ferrer. Young Winthrop P. Rockefeller, son of Bobo, has marched with the Greys and, since certain family disagreements have made relations somewhat strained, Winthrop had never met his first cousin, Laurance. When both young Rockefellers appeared in the ranks of the Greys, Colonel William H. Warrick, the Greys's commandant and drill master, performed the high-level introduction.

Historically, the reason for the Greys is simple enough. In 1881 a Mrs. Edward Curtis, "whose sons attended a nonmilitary school," and were, from all reports, holy terrors, felt the need of military drill for her boys. Rallying her friends, she formed the Greys. (The double meaning of the troop's name amused her; it referred to Father Knickerbocker, patron saint of New York, and also to the boys' first uniform, which included gray knickerbockers.) Appropriately, the Greys began to meet for twice-weekly drills in the ancient and elegant Seventh Regiment Armory, headquarters of the Seventh (or Society) Regiment of the New York National Guard. In addition to its drill and its Church Parade, the troop takes field trips (to nearby military installations and to West Point), and gives a Christmas tea dance. Since its formation the word "Greys" has been spelled about half the time with an *e* and half the time with an *a,* but it was with an *e* that Mrs. Curtis spelled it.

Today the *raison d'être* of the Greys is more complex — part educational, part social, part recreational, part disciplinary, part sentimental. The Knickerbocker Greys mean different things to different people. Applying for membership in the Greys is similar to applying for membership in an exclusive club. Parents fill out an application blank, answering such questions as the boy's age (eight is the minimum), height (minimum forty-eight inches), father's name, mother's maiden name, father's profession, and so forth. But in addition, each applicant must be proposed and seconded by "someone connected with the Greys" — in other words, the parent of a Grey member or ex-member. The cost of belonging is pleasantly low — under one hundred dollars a year plus another hundred-odd dollars for uniforms — but, as in all such organizations, the price of belonging is not what counts. Though the ladies who run the Greys like to play down the "snob" connotations of the group, and point out that the Greys are furiously democratic and take in "sons of advertising people, we even had Commander Whitehead's little boy, and even of theatre people, the nice ones," the emphasis is on niceness of background and, as one committee member put it bluntly, "We aren't exactly the Boy Scouts."

Because of the physical limitations of the Armory, the size of the group cannot feasibly extend beyond two-battalion strength, around two hundred, at any one time. Openings occur only as boys retire — as they must at the age of sixteen, with "honorable discharges" — or as they move out of New York private day schools and off to their prep schools in New England. Competition for admission to the Greys remains stiff and, when two equally bright, healthy, and interested boys are competing for the same opening, it is more than likely that the one with the better family and connections will be taken in.

Before he is accepted, each applicant — with his mother — is given a final screening at a tea with a few ladies of the membership committee. To an eight-year-old, it is clear that joining the Knickerbocker Greys is nothing more than the age-old boys' game of playing soldier; to his parent, it may be something else again. "Do you use *bombs?*" asked a pressed, combed, starched and Eton-collared candidate, sitting beside his mink-clad mother at an opening interview with the Greys's committee ladies. "Oh, no," murmured the committee in a chorus. "Do you use *grenades?*" "No, no." "How about swords?" "The boys do carry swords, yes," said one committeewoman.

"Boy, I'm glad of that!" replied the applicant. "Because there's one guy in the Greys I'd sure like to stick with one!"

"*Jimmy!*" cried his horrified mother, looking nervously at the committee chairman. "I'm sure Jimmy doesn't mean that," she explained.

"Oh, yes I do!" said Jimmy, standing up and giving a remarkably vivid imitation of a running-through with a bayonet.

Because of the Greys's reputation of exclusiveness, they are a sore point among non-Grey students at New York's better day schools. A perennial assertion is that the initials "K.G." on the Greys's uniforms stand for "Kitchen Grease."

Once a boy is accepted by the Greys, Colonel Warrick takes over. Trim, slim, and clear-eyed, the Colonel is a firm advocate of calisthenics, and is an excellent walking advertisement of his athletic philosophy. He claims to care not a whit for the social importance of the Greys, and to have a greater concern for what he feels is the sad physical state of New York City's youth, best families or no. Many of the boys who enter the Greys are far too flabby for the Colonel. "Some of these kids live on diets of ice cream and soda pop," he says. "I've seen boys from the wealthiest families in town who were actually undernourished!"

By drilling the Greys twice a week in the manual of arms, squad formations, company maneuvers and reviews, plus as many calisthenic periods as he can squeeze in, Colonel Warrick labors to toughen up the sons of the wealthy and well-born, and in addition to pep talks on posture and muscle tone, injects bits of advice on personal cleanliness, neatness, gentlemanly manners and morality.

Depending on his "conduct, military bearing, neatness, alertness, and cooperation," a Grey may rise from the rank of cadet private to that of cadet colonel. Needless to say, the problem of promotions is a knotty one for Colonel Warrick. Parents, who feel that cultivating the Colonel — and his pretty wife — may result in a promotion for their youngster, besiege him with invitations to cocktail parties, dinners, receptions, benefits, and theatre parties. Though he disclaims interest in Society, the Warricks lead a heady social life. They receive preferential treatment at such restaurants as "21," since the Kriendler family, which owns the place, has sent sons into the Greys. But for all this promotions are made with strict impartiality, and to insure this, the Colonel invites Army officers from nearby bases, not connected with the Greys or the Seventh Regiment, to judge the boys' performances in competition drills.

Colonel Warrick has made himself a socially attractive figure, and makes good use of his personal charm. "Working for this ladies' committee could be difficult," he admits. But it isn't. The mother of a cadet fluttered over to him at a recent party in New York, and with fluttering eyelashes said, "Tell me, Colonel, how do you *really* decide whom to promote?" Giving her a little wink and touching her hand, he replied, "Why, it's simple. I promote the boys with the most beautiful mothers." His popularity with the Greys and their parents has stood him in good stead in attracting applicants to the Adirondack Camp for Boys which Colonel Warrick operates during the summer months on the shores of Lake George. Warrick's Adirondack has become one of New York Society's favorite summer camps. On Parents' Week End in midsummer, the woods rumble with the sonorous engines of Rolls-Royces. At other times the camp, like the Greys, is run with military snap and efficiency.

A less enthusiastic observer of the Knickerbocker Greys was Mr. Harry H. Lucker of the Warnock Uniform Company which, after many years of uniforming the city's elite, finally succumbed. The Warnock firm began to make uniforms for the Greys when the organization was first established, in 1881. In his venerable emporium amid yellowing photographs and memorabilia of the great and near-great his company had outfitted and whose households he had uniformed, behind racks of military attire of every period and description, Mr. Lucker liked to brood about the past. Poring over ancient charts, catalogues, booklets, yachting manuals, warfare rule books, books on the proper assemblage of chevrons and epaulets, he would grow eloquent on the difficult problem of placing the combat ribbons and decorations on the uniform of Admiral Alan G. Kirk (Retired), a long-time customer.

For thirty-six years uniforming the Knickerbocker Greys was the personal chore of Mr. Lucker and his partner George Steinhilber, as it was of their predecessors in the company. The Greys's account grossed the company as much as $20,000 a year, and they approached the assignment with dedication and high purpose. Early in the 1950's, however, for a reason that was forever a mystery to Mr. Lucker, his company's informal franchise was suddenly taken away and the business was given to another company. This turn of events so affected Mr. Steinhilber that he was never a well man afterward, but Mr. Lucker carried on for a while alone, somewhat comforted by the fact that second- and third-generation Greys still came to him, sent by their fathers and grandfathers.

Mr. Lucker kept an enormous scrapbook bulging with clippings, all about the doings of members of the Greys. He not only outfitted each Grey, but kept track of him ever after, recording his engagement, marriage, divorce, remarriage, polo score at Meadowbrook, position in the Bermuda Cup Race, the birth of his children, and in many cases, his death. "There's so-and-so," he would say, pointing to a photograph. "Used to be fat. Thirty-eight-inch waist when he was ten. Slimmed down, though, when he was thirteen. Married a du Pont." Or, "Here's Ellery such-and-such — always losing his little service cap. Every week his nurse would come down here and order him a new cap. Too bad about him, though. Married some movie star."

Mr. Lucker felt that there had been a great decline in the quality of Society, and that this followed the same curve as the decline in the livery and uniform business. Over his scrapbooks, Mr. Lucker liked to let his thoughts wander back to the Gay Nineties, and the golden decade before the First World War, to the glittering era of the Four Hundred, to the days of carriages and uniformed coachmen, butlers, dinner parties for six hundred guests with a liveried footman behind each chair. "I used to go to their homes, all those wonderful people," he used to say, "to Newport, and Aiken, and Palm Beach, and Tuxedo Park. I'd measure their sons for uniforms for the Greys, and then I'd measure the butler, the valet, the houseman and chauffeur, and make uniforms for all the liveried help. Oh, some were nicer than others, believe me. I remember when old Mrs. John D. Rockefeller used to come here, a great lady, may she be enjoying eternal peace! She'd sit right here, in front of my desk, and place an order for little John the Third and every member of her staff. But who has that kind of money now? No, Society isn't what it used to be, believe me. I understand they sell secondhand uniforms over at the Armory now. Secondhand! Mrs. Rockefeller would turn over in her grave!"

4

The New "St. Grottlesex Set"

YOU can usually tell a Hotchkiss, Choate, Deerfield, Groton or St. Mark's man about a mile away because, for the past few years, he has been wearing a Madras plaid jacket and unpressed chino pants that ride high around his ankles. He may be sockless, but if he wears socks they will be of the white athletic variety. The shoes are loafers. The top button of his button-down shirt is usually unbuttoned (not always a sign of sloppiness so much as a sign of an outgrown shirt). His necktie may be slung over one shoulder and hanging down his back, as though a high wind blew it there or he himself put it there. Within the framework of this uniform, variations are possible, and they exist from school to school. At Hotchkiss, for example, the preference is for battered loafers, often pieced together with adhesive tape. St. Paul's shows a fondness for loafers with a hard, jewel-like polish. A curious rule operates. One concentrates either on the bottom part of one's appearance or on the top. As there are about loafers, there are two schools of thought about haircuts; they are either long and uncombed or short and slicked. Shoulder-length locks, however, hiphugging bell-bottoms and flowered Tom Jones shirts are seldom if ever seen. Carnaby Street, which has made its presence felt in public high schools across the country, has yet to have much impact on the great private boarding schools of New England where, in ways both subtle and direct, young men are reminded that they are the future leaders of America.

Since there is a fairly recognizable prep school look, it is assumed that there is also a prep school personality and a prep school frame of mind. In the outside world of his contemporaries — boys who attend public schools, and girls as well — the "preppie" is not always an object of admiration. He has long been distrusted by all but other preppies. He is brushed off as a "rich kid" going to a rich kids' school. He is called a snob. His virility is suspect. He is considered undemocratic and possibly even un-American. When he gets to college, he and his prep school friends will tend to form a group of their own. The more select fraternities and clubs will appear to favor the prep school boy. Adult critics of prep schools continue to allege that they are breeding places of the most destructive sort of social snobbery, of prejudice and bigotry, of arrogance and false values. In fact, it is ironic that today, when a prep school education is demanded or dreamed of by more parents for more children than ever before, when competition for entrance has never been stiffer, the New England prep school — as an idea — continues, among a large section of Americans, to be misunderstood if not actually resented.

This didn't matter so much a generation ago, when the schools were small, isolated, tucked away in the green New England hills, loved and understood by those who knew them and ignored by those who didn't. But now, with so much emphasis on a boy's getting into college, particularly a good college and preferably an Ivy League college, the prep schools are very much in the national consciousness. Prep schools often seem uncertain how to cope with their new importance. Prep school administrators have begun to worry about the prep school "image."

There is worry about the very phrase "prep school." Because such schools have always been considered *college preparatory* schools, their officials realize that along with the money spent on a prep school education has gone a kind of unwritten guarantee that the student will get into the college of his choice. A school can do its best, but it cannot offer or fulfill any such promise in the college-hungry world of the 1960's. It has been pointed out that the prep school education should be valued for itself, not just as a stepping-stone to Yale or Princeton but as a "total experience," and for a while, prep school headmasters discreetly suggested to parents of less-bright boys that the prep school years be made "an end in themselves," without the carrot of college held out before the donkey. But, as prep school graduates who were not heading for college began to face the prospect of military service, this argument lost much of its persuasiveness.

New phrases have been offered as substitutes for "prep school," but none has taken hold. "Private school" has that unfortunate snobbish ring. "Boarding school" is what girls go to. "Independent secondary school" is the term the academicians favor, but it has a pompous sound and is certainly a mouthful.

Meanwhile, as the popularity and importance of the prep school have grown — and as prep schools have come to fill a place in the plans of families from other than the upper class — so have the unpleasant connotations of the phrase. Not long ago, a British schoolmaster, Mr. Timothy Dymond Toswill of England's Rugby School, was completing a year as a visiting teacher at St. Paul's School, in New Hampshire, and with his homeward steamer ticket in his pocket, was in a mood to speak frankly about American prep schools as he saw them. "A bit of an anachronism, wouldn't you say?" he asked, looking across the cultivated campus of the school. "Still, if you believe in the capitalist system, which I do *not*, I suppose it's better for you Americans to spend your money sending a boy to a school like this one rather than on one of your hideous motorcars." A group of St. Paul's boys strolled by, wearing blazers of the school's two boat clubs, Halcyon and Shattuck, and school ties. Nearby, from a flagpole in the center of the school, swung an oar that had been raised shortly before, with full and solemn ceremony, by the captain of the club that won the Championship Meet. With a very British downward curl of the lips, Mr. Tosswill said, "You're awfully keen on *traditions* here, aren't you? Traditions which we at Rugby, a *somewhat* older institution, would regard as — laughable."

It is easy for an Englishman to tease America — particularly when it comes to a boys' school and its traditions. Many of the traditions, like a number of the schools themselves, were flung together in the beginning. No prep school would be having image problems today if it were not for this fact and if, in the beginning, such schools as St. Paul's, Groton, Choate, Hotchkiss — and such non-New England (but still "New England-type") schools as Lawrenceville in New Jersey, Hill in

Pennsylvania, Episcopal High School and Woodbury Forest in Virginia — had not been created to fill quite a different need from the one they are prepared to fill today. The schools are now trying to live down the specific things they started out to be.

It was natural, in the years following the Civil War, when America's great fortunes were being made, that the fortune makers and their wives should begin looking anxiously to England for cues as to what to do next. England, after all, had launched its industrial revolution more than a hundred years earlier. The results of this look across the Atlantic became quickly apparent on our shores: pompous manor houses in the English style sprawled across sooty hillsides outside Pittsburgh; rooms shipped to Tarrytown from Northumbrian castles; acres of heavy English furniture; English butlers and, for the children, English nannies. The American upper class announced itself born — in the newly acquired "social voice," a blend of the Southern accent and the Yankee but heavily powdered with inflections copied (but with an American's somewhat tin ear) from the British aristocracy. It was the period when the Anglican Episcopal faith became established as America's "fashionable" religion, and when the first loud voices of anti-Semitism were heard throughout the land.

A logical question, in the minds of the new American industrialist millionaires, was how to educate their sons. And the logical system to try to copy was that of the English "public" school. Two schools in the vicinity of Boston led the way in attempting to create the American counterparts of such ancient and aristocratic English institutions as Eton, Harrow, and Winchester. They were St. Mark's (founded in 1865) and Groton (1884). (Despite its perennial air of venerability, Groton is not the oldest but a relative latecomer among the great New England boys' schools.) St. Paul's was founded even earlier, in 1856, but it was not until the post-Civil War decades that it began to have a significant enrollment. It is not a paradox, then, but quite logical that two of the oldest and richest and largest boys' schools in New England — Andover (1778) and Exeter (1781) — are among the least fashionable and "social" today; they were successful academies long before dollars became the chief yardstick of social standing.

The great era of the birth of the New England prep school was also and by no coincidence the era of J. Pierpont Morgan who, in his day, appeared to have invented the dollar. Within ten years, either way, of

Morgan's greatest triumph, the formation of the United States Steel Company, as many as seven English-inspired private boys' schools were founded in the United States. Morgan himself (who, needless to say, had been educated in England) helped finance the Groton School. The founders of other schools represented fortunes made throughout the East — notably in New York, Philadelphia, Boston, and Pittsburgh, — and felt, as Morgan did, that the logical place to put their schools was in *New* England. The Taft School, in Watertown, Connecticut, was founded in 1890 by Horace D. Taft, a brother of President Taft. The Hotchkiss School, in Lakeville, Connecticut, was opened in 1892 by Maria Hotchkiss, the widow of the man who perfected the machine gun. St. George's School, in Newport, was built in 1896, and owes no small debt (including a million-dollar Gothic chapel) to the Providence industrialist John Nicholas Brown, of the same family that established Brown University in that city. In the same year the Choate School was established in Wallingford, Connecticut, with Andrew Mellon and Owen D. Young among its best friends (their heirs remain the school's best friends today). In 1901 a group of wealthy Bostonians, including a Lowell and a Forbes, founded the Middlesex School near Concord (and inadvertently helped give rise to the term "St. Grottlesex," the catchall used to describe all boys from Groton, Middlesex, and the "Saint" schools — Paul's, Mark's, and George's). Deerfield, which had been a local Massachusetts academy since 1797, was reorganized in 1902 as a boys' boarding school by the man who is still its headmaster, Frank L. Boyden. And, in 1906, the Kent School was founded in Kent, Connecticut, by Episcopal Father Frederick H. Sill, and has been befriended by, among others, several du Ponts.

Like Groton, which was established to educate "Christian gentlemen," and to develop "manly Christian character," St. Paul's, St. Mark's, St. George's and Kent entered the world under the firm influence of the Protestant Episcopal Church. Taft, Hotchkiss, Middlesex, and Deerfield were established as nondenominational schools, but they are hardly secular. Divine worship is part of the daily life at all of them, and as one Hotchkiss student puts it, "They call it a nondenominational service but it comes right out of the Episcopal prayer book." Andover and Exeter, though they have certain ancient Unitarian and Calvinist traditions, place the least emphasis on the religious aspect of

school life. At Exeter, for example, "morning chapel" consists of reading school announcements and, according to one Exeter boy, "to call it
chapel is a gas." For many years, wealthy Catholic families sent their
sons to Protestant schools. Then, in 1915, an important Roman Catholic boys' school, Canterbury, was established in New Milford, Connecticut. Shortly after, the Episcopal founder of St. George's had a
change of heart and became a Roman Catholic convert and, next, a
priest. In 1926 he founded the Catholic Portsmouth Priory School, six
miles north of St. George's but, according to old Newport residents, six
miles farther away from God.

The continuing belief that prep schools are snobbish has not been
helped by the fact that, in the early days, many schools maintained
subtle, unwritten quota systems by which Jews were kept in the minority. "No more than ten per cent," one headmaster used to say discreetly to parents who questioned the presence of a certain name in the
school's enrollment. When Jacob Schiff, who was J. P. Morgan's peer
and, at times, his better on Wall Street, wished to send his son Morti
to Groton, he asked that Morti, "as a conscious Jew," be excused from
the school's religious exercises. After an "amiable exchange of letters"
between Mr. Schiff and Groton's headmaster, Endicott Peabody, it
was decided that Groton was not the proper school for Morti. One
father of a former prep school boy recalls, some twenty years ago, tear-
ing up a school application that wanted to know, "Is the boy in any
part Hebraic?" "It was not only the *idea* of the question that infuriated
me," this man says. "It was the abominable semantics of the sentence.
How could I answer it? Which *part* of him was Hebraic? His left foot?
His right ear?"

As the idea of the American prep school was born, with it came the
prototype American prep school headmaster. He was supposed to be
tweedy, pipe-smoking, cuddlesome, full of homilies and wisdom, with a
strong hand but, from within, exuding warmth as mellow as his tobacco; under a tough exterior, he was supposed to possess a heart as
soft as tapioca. He was, in other words, Mr. Chips rolled into one, and,
at various schools, he was known variously as "The Head," "The
Duke," "The King," and "The Old Man." He was a kind of universal
Grand Dad. In real life his name was Endicott Peabody of Groton and,
for many years, all New England prep school headmasters were merely
pallid imitations of "The Rector," as the Reverend Mr. Peabody was

called by all who knew him. (He was the model for the hero of Louis
Auchincloss's novel, *The Rector of Justin*.) Peabody and J. P. Morgan
had much in common in addition to being good friends. Peabody's
father was a Morgan partner in London, and the younger Peabody,
after being educated at a select public school in England — Cheltenham — returned to America to work in Wall Street. His social credentials were impeccable, and he made a socially correct marriage. When,
after joining the clergy, he first dreamed of Groton and — with Morgan's help — proceeded to found it, his dream was of a school that
would, quite literally, be a spiritual extension of a well-bred boy's own
family. A Groton boy was to feel as loved and as needed at Groton as
he had been on Fifth Avenue or Beacon Hill. Endicott Peabody's biographer says, "It was the most natural thing in the world for him to
think of his school as being simply a large family. . . . At the center
of the big school family his own family grew and the beautiful home
and family life was presided over by Mrs. Peabody, the most gracious
and beautiful of wives and mothers." Like Mr. Chips, the Rector considered all Grotonians "my boys." Every night, he and Mrs. Peabody
said good night to each and every lad before he went to bed, and, on
the foreheads of the younger ones, Mrs. Peabody often bestowed a
motherly good-night kiss.

Peabody's counterpart at St. Paul's, "The Rector" Samuel S. Drury,
was almost equally lovable. His wife, it was often pointed out, was "a
Wolcott," and his mother was "a Wheeler," and for twenty-seven years
he guided St. Paul's boys *in loco parentis*. To make the transition from
home-family to school-family seem less abrupt, uniformed waitresses
waited on the boys in the school dining room, serving from the left and
removing from the right, just as the family servants would have done
at home. Faculty wives joined their husbands at the tables for meals, to
simulate a family atmosphere. In true headmasterly tradition, Drury
was stern but forgiving — the perfect parent. Once, when a group of
boys was taking an illegal swim in the nude in a pond near the campus, they heard a familiar voice bellowing through the trees: "Boys,
this is your rector speaking. I am taking a walk with Mrs. J. Lewis
Bremer of Boston. You will stay in the water until we have passed.
You will then resume your clothes and go back to the School. I have
recognized none of you." A St. Paul's tradition is the annual new-boy
picnic, called "Cricket Day," and, for each picnic, Drury and his wife

appeared to scramble eggs and butter toast for the boys. The date of
Cricket Day is always a surprise and, to announce that the jolly day
had arrived, Drury's innovation was to open morning chapel with a
special prayer which began, "O Lord, who hast promised Thy holy city
Jerusalem shall be full of children playing in the streets thereof — "
That gave it away. The chapel filled with happy shouts. What boy
could help but love and respect a man like that? This at least was the
theory.

With such heavy injections of intimacy and family feeling it was
natural that certain schools were adopted by certain families as their
very own. Sons of Groton graduates entered Groton as soon as they
were able. "It won't be like going away from home," one Groton father
told his uncertain youngster. "Groton is a *part* of home." St. Mark's
became the favorite school of Cabots, Hotchkiss of Fords, Choate of
Mellons, Taft of Tafts. Vanderbilts favored St. Paul's but, according
to a Philadelphia lady, "Those Vanderbilts were always climbers. The
main reason they sent their children to St. Paul's was to meet Philadelphia people." (This lady echoes a persistent, if totally baseless,
rumor in the highest circles of Society that the Vanderbilts — and, no
less, the Astors — are actually Jewish.)

Just as the silver cords of Groton and St. Mark's stretch toward Beacon Hill, St. Paul's for a long time was the educational outpost of
Philadelphia. It has graduated numerous Ingersolls and Biddles, but it
is Philadelphia's august Wheeler family that can say, with the greatest
degree of accuracy, "There has always been a Wheeler at St. Paul's."
Hotchkiss for years was largely a New York Society school, though it
was also popular with Middle Western families from Cleveland, Detroit, and Chicago. Polarized around certain families and certain cities,
schools became oriented toward certain colleges whether they wished
to be or not — though St. Paul's did wish it. For years, St. Paul's sent
boys to Yale, Princeton, or Pennsylvania, and spurned Harvard. This
was because Henry Augustus Coit, another longtime headmaster, considered Harvard "Godless." The school still sends the largest number
of its graduates to Yale and Princeton. (Princeton is still Philadelphia's
favorite college, and there is still a "Hotchkiss set" at Yale.) Today it
may even be that certain prep schools have become suppliers of per-
sonnel to certain corporations. Time, Inc., which has had a gaggle of
Hotchkiss alumni at its helm (including the late Henry R. Luce '16

and James A. Linen '30) has a reputation for being more than a little interested in Hotchkiss graduates.

The controversy that has always surrounded the "traditional" boys' schools in New England has prompted various individuals, from time to time, to try to alter or improve the pattern according to their private visions. Some of these experiments have been more successful than others. In the 1920's and 1930's, New York Society buzzed with talk of the super-elegant Avon Old Farm School in Avon, Connecticut, and the school's creator, an altogether curious woman called Theodate Pope Riddle. Mrs. Riddle, a wealthy bicycle heiress, was a self-styled missionary to youth, a devotee of Molyneux gowns, and a dabbler in religious cults. Theodate was not her real name, but a Greco-Roman hybrid she had manufactured for herself, meaning "gift of God." Frank N. D. Buchman, father of the Buchmanites, held Moral Re-Armament hootenannies on the lawn of her Avon "cottage." (At one of these, God Himself made one of His infrequent public utterances and announced, somewhat ambiguously through Buchman, that He "wanted" Mrs. Riddle — which apparently came as no surprise to her.)

To build her school, Mrs. Riddle spared no expense, putting up sprawling buildings in the English country style and transplanting full-grown elms to the campus so that the school, though new, immediately looked as though it had been there for centuries past. It was her notion that the blacksmith's art had been sorely neglected by young gentlemen — why she felt this has never been quite clear — and so a fully equipped forge became an integral part of the school. To tone up the place, she required the boys to dress for dinner in black tie. (Some say she would have preferred white tie and tails, but had to compromise somewhere.)

For a long time, New York parents regarded Avon as a school that was "amusing" and "different" and even "exciting." Meanwhile, excitement at the school was provided by a series of headmasters who fell into, and then quickly fell out of, Mrs. Riddle's favor. She was as arbitrary and whimsical in her choice of students, and occasionally offered a boy free tuition if she considered his parents "interesting." The school failed to prosper academically, however. Mrs. Riddle finally rejoined her admiring Maker in 1946, but even before that the school, fallen upon sorry days, had closed. During World War II it was used as a veterans' rehabilitation center, but afterward it reopened along more traditional prep school lines — for one thing, no more dressing for dinner. Recently it has been enjoying a slow renascence to academic soundness.

In 1935, another strong-minded woman, Mrs. Carmelita Hinton, founded the Putney School in Putney, Vermont. Though she, too, showed herself to be a woman of certain personal crotchets (she was opposed to tea, coffee, pepper, mustard, catsup, and several other condiments), she wisely left the administration of her school in the hands of experts and now spends most of her time in Europe where, a lady well into her seventies, she only recently gave up skiing. At Putney, an attempt was made to "break through" the traditional ideas and methods of education, and the school was established as a coeducational (boys slightly outnumbering girls) boarding school where students would call their teachers by their first names, individual talents would be encouraged, and no grades would be given. To balance the "technical and intellectual" side of education, the "emotional and sensuous" aspects would also be stressed in a program including singing, dancing, painting, carpentry, drama, and handicrafts. The school farm was also made important, and Putney students, in their afternoon work jobs, help produce a large share of the school's vegetables, including most of its potatoes, and manage the sizable herd of Holstein dairy cattle that provides all the school's milk. The youngster driving a tractor is a Putney symbol, but then so is the girl in the black leotard, moving through the slow figures of an expressive dance on the lawn. One Putney student describes the school as "an attempt to put the individual back into the community."

That may be. But Putney has been able to attract only the most intellectually enlightened of the Social Establishment to *its* community and has, in fact, become an anti-Society school. Putney boys, barefoot, in long hair and jeans, sneer at proper, preppie boys from nearby St. Paul's. "I hear they even take *baths* there," one boy says. A Putney girl says airily, "Of course most of us are Marxists here." These attitudes, plus the common assumption that coeducational boarding and freedom lead to coeducational bedding, make Society parents leary of schools like Putney and, at Putney, the students themselves do their best to shock conventional morality. "Oh, we have rules here," one boy said to a visiting parent. "No sleeping with the girls — after lights out." Another Putney joke is, "She's a terrible snob. She doesn't like her roommate because he's a Negro." ("Actually," one Putney boy said, "you get to know what girls are like here without sleeping with them." Putney encourages sexual candor, if not license.)

The school's anti-Establishment approach has had some ironic results. Lacking the support of Society, Putney has been unable to build an imposing physical plant. Nor, without generous benefactions from the titans of American finance, has Putney been able to amass an endowment the size of other schools'. It is, therefore, one of the most expensive schools around. Putney's tuition is nearly twice that of the more "fashionable" St. Paul's, whose endowment is in the tens of millions and where over $2,000,000 stands in the Scholarship Endowment Fund alone yielding income enough to send, if the school wished, seventy boys a year to school on full scholarships. At Putney, there are few scholarships available. It has become, in other words, truly a "rich kids' school," and its students in large part come from the homes of the highly paid in television, films, the theatre, and art. "Shall we name-drop some of our celebrity parents?" asks a Putney girl with a little smile.

For years, in England, schools like Eton, Harrow, Rugby, Winchester, Cheltenham, Wellington, and Epsom served a sociological as well as a social function. They managed, through the eighteenth and nineteenth centuries, to bring together the sons of the old landed gentry and the sons of the new-rich manufacturers, and to produce from this fusion an aristocracy of a special sort. It was an aristocracy which felt that, in return for the privilege of having received an expensive education, it owed a debt to the British public. Its members left school feeling that they were not only destined but obligated to lead the Empire, and lead they proceeded to do. Furthermore, the Empire not only accepted but came to rely on their leadership. Eton and Harrow became the traditional forcing-beds of Britain's military, religious, and government leaders, both Socialist and Tory. These two schools alone have turned out roughly two dozen prime ministers, plus countless cabinet ministers, members of parliament, ambassadors, Archbishops of Canterbury, marshals and generals and rulers of the Queen's Navy.

But in the days when New England's prep schools were being founded, there were no Peers of the Realm in America, and landed gentry were in short supply. As a result, the sons of the new-rich manufacturers mingled mostly with one another. Theirs was an aristocracy based on mills, mines, machines and machine guns — a Society based on the same social and economic forces that gave us the national corporation, national advertising, the brand name, and more recently, the trading stamp and the credit card. New England prep schools have been criticized for their apparent inability to match the records of Eton and Harrow in turning out national leaders and statesmen. But this has not been so much the fault of the schools as the fault of American Society people who, for so long, dominated the schools. American Society has never been much concerned with government leadership, or service.

American prep schools have, therefore, graduated many successful corporation lawyers, few Supreme Court justices; many Wall Street investment bankers, few Secretaries of the Treasury; many minstrels of Madison Avenue, but only a handful of bishops; many executives of General Foods, General Mills, and General Motors, but no Generals of the Army. The British public schools have become, so to speak, the property of the British public, through alumni who have given themselves to England. But American private schools have remained for the most part "private." And, in the tradition of American private enterprise, which believes that a share of the profits should be plowed back into the corporation, American prep school alumni have given largely to the treasuries of their alma maters.

It has been argued of course, that large numbers of Americans do not want their leaders to have fancy diplomas — that the log cabin and the school of hard knocks are more appealing than the town house and Groton. It seems to be more a case of Americans not knowing which they prefer. Franklin D. Roosevelt, a Groton alumnus, was the first American President to have graduated from a prep school. John F. Kennedy, who went to Choate, was the second. (Though the prep school influence has always been significantly Republican, our few American prep-school-educated statesmen have been Democrats. Adlai Stevenson was a Choate man, too. Perhaps these men were rebelling from the prep school influence. Political careers have always been for the rebels in American Society.)

Though Roosevelt was one of our more popular Presidents, his Groton background did little to enhance his popularity. It certainly did not with his Groton classmates, many of whom refused to attend a school

Mrs. Donald K. Clifford, granddaughter of Bronxville's founder, William Van Duzer Lawrence, in her Bronxville home

*Mrs. Winston F. C. Guest ("Cee-Zee") chats with Society
grande dame, Mrs. William Woodward*

Mrs. Thomas Schippers, wife of the conductor, the former Nonie Phipps

Mrs. Jeanne Murray Vanderbilt and escort at a New York ball

Actress Constance Carpenter dances with the Duke himself at the Duke of Windsor Ball at New York's Waldorf-Astoria. At left, the Duchess chats with Mr. Woolworth Donahue

The Princess d'Arenberg, formerly Margaret Bedford, of New York and Paris

San Francisco's Doña Francesca Ortega Brady, descendant of José Francisco Ortega, first white man to see the Golden Gate, before the Mission Dolores

*Mrs. Henry Potter Russell, a Crocker, on the terrace of her
Telegraph Hill apartment*

reunion because F.D.R. was to be there. In fact, Roosevelt's Groton-Harvard background and accent were the object of fun-poking from both sides of the political divide.

When Mrs. Robert A. Taft made her famous speech to a gathering of Ohio mine workers in 1938 — "My husband did not start from humble beginnings . . . he had a fine education at Yale" — it was widely assumed that she had dealt him a political death blow. But he went on to win the Senatorial election. During Adlai Stevenson's two Presidential campaigns, it was decided to play down his Choate-Princeton schooling. He lost both times, regardless. During William W. Scranton's gubernatorial campaign in Pennsylvania, it was deemed wise to play down Hotchkiss and Yale. He won. Senator Claiborne Pell of Rhode Island decided to play down neither his prep school (St. George's) and college (Princeton) nor his Old Family background, and won. Also in Rhode Island, William H. Vanderbilt — on the theory that, being a Vanderbilt, he would have *had* to have gone to some prep school — similarly decided neither to disown nor flaunt St. George's. He ran for a term as Governor, then lost the reelection. Most recently, New York City's Mayor, John V. Lindsay, chose the artful (and, to those who knew his school, hilarious) tactic of referring to St. Paul's as his "high school" during his campaign. (Few boys' prep schools are as unlike high school as is St. Paul's where even the match-books in the public rooms and the guest towels in the washrooms are embossed with the school's monogram, "S.P.S.," where the chapel is furnished with a vaulting, hand-carved reredos donated by a Vander-bilt, and where the school gymnasium is entered through a reception room filled with English antiques.) This Gosh-I'm-No-Better-Than-You approach may have helped Lindsay win. In short, a New England prep school education won't kill a politician's chances, but it won't do much to help them, either.

New England boys' schools themselves have, in recent years, tried to rid themselves of the St. Grottlesex tag, and to shake off the position they occupied in the public's mind fifty or sixty years ago. There has been talk of a "new look" in prep schools, and educators like to say that the schools have "changed drastically" in the years since the end of the Second World War. But they may not have changed as much as some would like to think. They have tried to lure boys from a broader geographic spectrum, and most schools today can boast enrollments from the majority of the fifty states and from a number of foreign countries. With their multi-million-dollar endowments — some of which are larger than those of many large universities — the schools have also tried to tempt boys from the other end of the economic scale with scholarships. Though it would have been something of a surprise to see a Negro boy at a prep school in the 1940's, it is now a surprise to find a school that does not have at least three or four. No prep school would dream of discriminating against Jews nowadays, though anti-Semitism among prep school students is a recurrent unpleasant theme. (When the young son of the photographer Richard Avedon, who is Jewish, was looking over prep schools in New England recently, he told his father, with a certain accuracy, "I'd probably stand a better chance of getting in if I was a Negro.") But the fact remains that prep school applications — including applications for scholarships — continue to come from the best addresses in the larger cities and the better suburbs, from families who want their sons to go to schools where they will meet "nice people" — which causes school administrators to grumble about parents who are giving their sons "the right education for the wrong reasons."

"A school," so runs a familiar prep school maxim, "is only as good as its current headmaster," and there is certainly a new look and a new wave of young and vigorous headmasters who have almost completely replaced the old, paternalistic, lovable "heads" and "Rectors" of a generation ago. These men include Mssrs. A. William Olsen of Hotchkiss, John Kemper of Andover, Seymour St. John of Choate, and Sidney Towle of Kent (where, to the astonishment of old Kent graduates, a co-ordinated school for girls was opened in 1960). The latest Old Guard headmaster to resign in favor of a younger man has been Exeter's beloved William G. Saltonstall ("Bill Salty"), who is now director of the Peace Corps mission in Nigeria, and who was replaced at the school by a forty-seven-year-old ex-paratrooper, Richard Ward Day.

Practically the last member of the Old Guard still in his post is Deerfield's Frank Boyden, who, well in his eighties, seems indestructible. It is becoming harder and harder for friends of the school to think of Deerfield without him. Still, Mr. Boyden is not at all to be regarded as behind the times. "It's that old son-of-a-gun Boyden who forced us into the public relations business," says one of the younger headmasters. "Bruce Barton got hold of his ear, and Madison Avenue came to the prep school. He made us competitive with one another. Now a headmaster has to sell his school the way an automobile dealer sells cars." Mr. Boyden is credited with having used "promotional gimmicks" to raise money for, and attract students to, Deerfield, and the success of his methods has been both admired and envied. For some of his gimmickery, however, he may owe no small debt to such "Old Dear" headmasters as Endicott Peabody; one of Mr. Boyden's devices is riding around the Deerfield campus in a horse-drawn buggy. There have been dark hints that other headmasters, to compete, have had to dream up devices or eccentricities or "trademarks" of their own. Seymour St. John at Choate, for instance, has been seen with a pet otter flopping at his heels, and the Reverend Matthew Warren, headmaster of St. Paul's, was given a red-and-white golf cart by an appreciative alumnus in which to tool around the campus.

The St. Grottlesex boy, according to prep school administrators, is no longer the snobbish, pampered Society heir or rich man's son. He is now simply "the most qualified boy." In prep school circles, he is referred to as the "M.Q.B." Prep school educators today are apt to refer to their schools as, "America in microcosm," or, as William Saltonstall once said he hoped Exeter would one day be, "a great national high school" — which is perhaps also the way Mayor Lindsay has begun to think of St. Paul's. But most prep school boys would disagree with these notions. The reason, they say, is simple. "Most of us didn't really *want* to go away to school," one boy said. "We were *told* we were going, and our parents pretty much told us which school we were going to. They wanted us to go to prep school for one of two basic reasons — because they figured it would put us in a position of superiority in later life, or because they just wanted us the heck out of the house."

He went on to say that many boys, however well-qualified, simply have no desire to go to prep school. "It just isn't an accepted American idea," he said. "It's popular only with a small minority. You take a boy who's going to a public high school in Nebraska. He's president of his class, a great athlete, and a straight-A student. He's prep school *qualified,* all right, and he'd be a great addition to any school. But you could offer him Choate or Deerfield or Exeter on a platter, *free,* and he'd turn it down. Why should he leave his home and family and friends, and all his *success* there, to come to some place in the East he's heard is a snob school? Why should he want — or even *need* — a prep school?

That kind of guy can get into any college in the country, anyway. That's the great fallacy of the M.Q.B. We want *him*. But he just doesn't think we're all that great." This boy feels that the American people do not wholeheartedly support the idea of private secondary school education; that the schools cannot be called strongholds, or even mirrors, of democracy. Instead, he says, "Most of us are upper or upper-middle class, country-club-coming-out-party, stockbroker-Tudor-French-Provincial-suburban."

Prep school boys themselves do not believe that they are America's M.Q.B.'s. They feel they are something a little different, a little special — not just a little better than other boys. At prep school, many boys begin to feel hints of the heavy weight that will one day fall on them as members of an American Establishment. A St. Mark's boy says, soberly, "For me and others it's a real problem to justify the fact that we're being given a top-grade education without deserving it more than the next fellow — except by an accident of birth. It's a heavy responsibility we're given, and often we don't feel qualified to handle it."

And prep school administrators themselves admit that, M.Q.B. or no M.Q.B., the sons of alumni are given special consideration. "It is a matter of economic necessity," says one headmaster — since alumni gifts are so important to a school's maintenance and expansion. A teenage Ford would have to be most *un*qualified indeed to be turned away from Hotchkiss, now that the splendid Ford Library reposes there. Problems like these may not keep prep school headmasters awake nights, but they are matters of continuing concern. Sons of alumni and benefactors must be served — and usually served first. When the mother of a prep school student, who had been warned that his spelling was so poor as to be far below the school's standard, confronted the headmaster, she asked, "What difference does it make whether he can spell or not? He'll always have a secretary." The headmaster admitted he had no answer to this.

And so a money and family elite are perpetuated through the medium of the prep school. As a St. Paul's sixth-former put it dryly not long ago — when a young Pillsbury from Minneapolis was applying to St. Paul's where many other Pillsburys have studied — "I kinda think he'll get in, don't you?"

5

"We're Coming Out Tonight"

HISTORY'S first debutantes were, presumably, young women of marriageable age who were presented at European Courts during the seventeenth century for the approval of Court ladies, Court gentlemen, and, sometimes, the Monarch. But there is strong evidence that the practice of introducing eligible virgins to members of the tribe began considerably before that, and that the debutante ritual dates from the Old Stone Age, if not before. The ritual has always carried strong sexual overtones — a rite of passage between the ages of puberty and of marriage — and, even in primitive cultures, has been carried out with trappings intended to demonstrate the debutante's social position and wealth. Among certain tribes in New Guinea, fathers announce the marriageability of their daughters by throwing large quantities of coconuts into the sea — the richer the man, the more coconuts he throws. In Africa, there are tribes which ritually prepare their young women for their debuts by placing them in "fattening houses" where, for beauty's sake, their bodies are anointed with butter for weeks on end while the girls are stuffed with food. Again, it is the richest men who produce the fattest daughters. In most of these primitive ceremonies the girls wear approximations, or adaptations, of the wedding costume, just as American debutantes — anthropologically just a step away from their sisters in the savanna — today appear in their almost identical, though "one-of-a-kind" long white gowns, wearing bits of veiling, carrying bouquets, and stand in receiving lines like make-believe brides. Otherwise, today's debutantes retain few of the tribal practices of the Stone Age, but they have developed some equally interesting ones of their own. The father of a modern debutante does not toss coconuts into New York Harbor or San Francisco Bay, but he tosses considerable amounts of money in other directions.

There are, of course, many degrees of debutante parties, just as there are degrees of debutantes. Take, for instance, one of the largest and best-known debutante functions in New York, the Debutante Cotillion and Christmas Ball. Customarily given at the Waldorf-Astoria, where the grand ballroom is decorated in clouds of pink and silver fluff, pink tablecloths and twinkly lights, the Cotillion annually presents a hundred or more debutantes to "society." Around the dance floor, the tables are largely filled with members of New York business firms who have agreed to sponsor bits and pieces of the Cotillion and, from tiers of boxes above, parents and friends of the debutantes, plus patrons and patronesses of the Cotillion and members of the Cotillion Committee, survey the proceedings below. In the bar outside, white-tied young men press relentlessly toward a small band of perspiring bartenders, and it is clear that in the face of such a jostling, thirsty throng, the hotel has abandoned any pretense of seeking proof-of-age from the young drinkers. In the anteroom outside the ballroom, games of chance offer rewards ranging from color television sets to ladies' gloves to Waring Blenders to free photographs "By Famous Fashion Photographer, Irving Penn." Domestic champagne circulates in this area for two dollars the glass and, through an opening in the crowd, one may see a shiny new automobile being raffled off at one dollar the chance. If the New York Cotillion seems to have a faint odor of commercialism, to say nothing of Las Vegas, this perhaps can be forgiven, since the whole affair is for the benefit of the New York Infirmary, and all the merchandise offered as prizes in the lottery games has been donated. Just how much money the Cotillion makes for the Infirmary is not recorded as a rule, but, according to Mrs. Eugene W. Ong, a former Cotillion chairman, "The Infirmary could not keep its doors open without the Ball."

Within the ballroom the lights dim as the debutantes are presented from the center of the stage. The orchestra plays a tinkly version of "The Teddy Bears' Picnic" over and over again as, one by one, the girls step forward, grip their escorts' hands for wobbly support, and sink into a deep curtsy. A master of ceremonies intones each girl's name over the loudspeaker. Once presented, the young women and their escorts perform a series of Cotillion figures, after which, in somewhat thin and reedy voices, the girls sing "The Coming-Out Waltz" — the lyric of which was written by Mrs. Eugene W. Ong's daughter when she was a debutante:

> We're coming out tonight,
> We're having a fling!
> Debs dressed in yards of white,
> Waltzing we sing — 'cause —
> Beaux flock around tonight,
> Flowers are part of the scheme!
> Tomorrow may be just another day,
> But tonight we are part of a dream!

Which sums things up pretty well, at least during the early part of the evening.

Later on, it is possible for the mood of the evening to change. A young man in tails reels drunkenly down a staircase and, all at once, a small crowd gathers around a sobbing girl. It seems the young man, in passing, stepped on the hem of her huge white gown, and a large section of the underskirt has ripped out at the waist; as the girl's mother and friends surround and try to comfort the girl, the elaborate dress is daintily upraised revealing the puffs of petticoats, in layers, like the components of a parfait. "Look what some slob did to Marcia!" the girl's mother cries repeatedly to anyone who will listen, and others join the group and begin debating what to do. The cost of the dress is mentioned, and there is talk of legal action and insurance. Others suggest that the problem be taken into the ladies' room where, perhaps, the matron can supply needle and thread. Through it all, the debutante herself keeps crying, "Oh, Mother! Mother! Leave me alone!" her voice childlike and despairing.

Not all debutante parties should be judged by this one, however. For all the needed dollars it brings to the New York Infirmary, the Debutante Cotillion and Christmas Ball is not one of the more fashionable balls in the United States. In New York, the Grosvenor Ball, given at Thanksgiving time to benefit the Grosvenor Neighborhood

House, is far more exclusive; it not only presents far fewer girls, but it costs considerably more than the Cotillion. (To put a girl on the Cotillion's list costs only about one hundred and fifty dollars; the Grosvenor costs over one thousand dollars per debutante but, since it benefits a charity, much of this sum is deductible.) The Junior League Ball and the Junior Assemblies are also considered more important, socially, than the Cotillion, and the Assemblies are more important than the Ball. At all of these, one can feel surer of being presented to Real Society. As a New York social secretary explains, "I can almost always arrange for a girl to be presented at the Cotillion, and, sometimes, the Junior League Ball — using pull, that is. But the Assemblies and the Grosvenor she simply must manage for herself." A truly important debutante, of course, will be presented at all of these balls — the Cotillion thrown in, as if for good measure — plus a number of others, plus at a ball of her very own. "A girl who has a little dinner party in the Sert Room, and who has been presented at the Cotillion afterward — and *nothing else* — hasn't had much of a debut," another social secretary says. No, for not enough money has been spent.

Another way to gauge the importance, or realness, of a girl's debut is to consider at which point during her eighteenth year she makes her first, and therefore official, emergence. The Christmas-to-New Year's holiday season is perhaps the gayest and the busiest — with, in most large cities, several hotel-based parties scheduled each evening — but, within that period, there are subtle gradations of status. A girl whose debut is placed toward the New Year's end of the week has less to look forward to, and is therefore less favored. There are, however, three other distinct "little" seasons, and each of these has its own connotations. The June, beginning-of-summer coming-out season is probably the least fashionable; one associates June with impoverished, shabby-genteel families, with teas, and with unstylish Boston (where June is as fashionable as any other season). Then there is the Thanksgiving holiday season which, for its very brevity, was for many years considered the most fashionable coming-out season of all. But recently the most wanted season, in terms of everything that matters to a debutante and her parents, has been the somewhat longer fall "little season" between Labor Day and the start of school. In New York, this comes to a sort of climax with the Tuxedo Autumn Ball in Tuxedo Park. In other cities it is the scene of large and lavish private parties given at country houses and under tents. Looked at cynically, the fall season gives a girl a fine and early start on a long social season that will continue through Thanksgiving, move into full speed at Christmas, carry on through spring and wind her up, exhausted, in June.

There are other ways for a girl to come out than at a ball. In theory, she can come out at a luncheon, a tea, or at a dinner dance. But nowadays coming-out luncheons have virtually disappeared. Teas continue to be popular in a few cities — notably in the South — but each year sees fewer of them. (A debutante tea, of course, is not the one-lump-or-two variety; it is a "great tea" with champagne, an orchestra, dancing, and "the same guest list you'd invite to a ball — around a thousand.") As one debutante says, "Teas are too exhausting. They last only two hours, but a girl has to be on her feet the whole time, receiving." It leaves a girl too tuckered to enjoy any parties that evening. Dinner dances are also disappearing as coming-out media, and the reason for the waning importance of all these — leaving it a question of a ball or nothing — is that the *raison d'être* for the debut itself has changed gradually in the last fifty years. Formerly, a girl's debut was to introduce her to friends of her parents, and single men, if present at all, were as a rule older than she. Today, the reason is boys. Luncheons and teas are disappearing because, as one social secretary explains, "Boys don't like to go to parties in the daytime." Adults today are pushed into the background and, by their own admission, enjoy going to coming-out parties — even their own daughters' — far less than their parents did a generation ago. "I remember what a lovely time we all had in those days," a Boston grandmother reminisces. "When each of us in our set brought a daughter out, it was a chance for us all to get together. Now? I don't understand what they do at these parties any more. If a granddaughter of a *particularly* dear friend has a party, I go, put in an appearance, but I leave as soon as possible." Older people leaving a party as soon as possible can have consequences, at a large private ball, more severe than a ripped-out underskirt. It can result in a rented mansion being vandalized on Long Island or in any number of less publicized incidents. During the early morning hours at a recent Connecticut party, for instance, it was for some reason decided — by the time the guests had gathered at the swimming pool — to break all the glassware. For several hours afterward, guests danced and swam with bare and bleeding feet.

And so it has become a rule of thumb that to bring out a daughter properly she must have a ball of her own. (There was a time when small groups of girls would band together and, to share the expenses, give a joint ball; in the affluent 1960's, this has become according to one girl "the cheapie way" to come out.) That Society is now addicted to the private ball was nowhere more apparent than in San Francisco where the G. W. Douglas Carvers did the uncommon thing in buying their own ball-sized tent, instead of renting one, along with the glasses and the folding chairs, from a caterer. The Carvers point out that their tent is an investment. They have four daughters. Their tent also makes them popular with their neighbors. (The James Floods borrowed it for the 1966 debut of their daughter Elizabeth.) And the Carvers like to point out that theirs is, after all, only a small tent — just sixty feet in diameter. Larger San Francisco parties — like that of the William Wallace Meins for their daughter — must still turn elsewhere for tents. To canopy more than a thousand guests, the Meins had to import one from Los Angeles. San Francisco parties have gotten so large that Millie Robbins, a local Society columnist, has commented, "They'll soon have to bring the girls out in the Cow Palace — which might be rather appropriate!"

As the number and scale of private balls have climbed steadily since the Second World War, so have the possibilities for decorating, outfitting, and staffing them. When the Henry Fords spent a reported $50,000 on a party for their daughter, the affair made news and raised eyebrows here and there. But many American families, with names less well-known to those outside Society, today spend that much and more to bring out their daughters in what they consider the proper style. It has become unfashionable to have merely one dance orchestra on hand; to make their parties sure of success, many parents hire as many as three — one for dancing, one for jazz, one for folk-rock — and place each in a separate part of the garden so that young guests can traipse from one style of music to another. It is also unthinkable to hire one of the big Society bands — Meyer Davis's, Lester Lanin's, or Peter Duchin's — without its leader. Meyer Davis, though he has some ninety different orchestras, had, as of 1966, bookings to appear with his band up into the year 1985 which Davis, a man in his seventies, wryly suggests that the lawyers handling his estate will have to fill. Davis will not personally appear with his band for an evening for a penny under five thousand dollars. The good old days of unbridled spending on parties and such frivolity are not dead and gone. They are here.

Obviously, a debutante ball on the grandest possible scale is an enterprise to be undertaken neither lightly nor by the inexperienced and, in recent years, professional party-planners have found themselves in a lucrative business. These social secretaries, as they designate themselves, are for the most part women. Almost all are members of well-connected (or *almost* well-connected) families who, for various reasons (for the sheer thrill of it all, they say), use their social connections to help them make a living. They are nearly always gracious and charming and yet, at the same time, they are shrewd businesswomen who know how to come to quick terms with the most recalcitrant Teamster or member of the electricians' union should the occasion demand. The undisputed dean of all social secretaries was the late, great Juliana Cutting of New York, and New York's three most prominent social secretaries — Mrs. William H. Tew, Mrs. Katherine Palmer, and Mrs. Chester Burden — admit that they carry on in her illustrious tradition and clutch Mrs. Cutting's image, figuratively, next to their hearts. (Mrs. Tew, probably the grandest of the three, has actually allowed the myth to grow up around her that she decides who goes into the *Social Register* and who does not; this is untrue.)

A New York parent going to one of these three ladies will first be asked to select a date for the ball — and it is wise to do this as early as possible — literally when the child is a toddler. All three ladies have brought out their second generation of debutantes, and have dates selected for a third. A date, once picked, is immediately registered with the other social secretaries. The three are scrupulously honest; if Mrs. Tew has selected a date for a debut, Mrs. Palmer would never dream of giving it to a client of hers, nor would Mrs. Burden. They are competitors, but in ladylike cahoots. Not all social secretaries are as trustworthy; pirating of dates occurs, particularly in smaller cities, and it is a practice that plagues innocent San Francisco. When it happens, there is only one practical course for a hostess to take — make sure that her party is at least twice as lavish as her rival's. A San Francisco mother, hearing that her claim on a date had been jumped, rushed to the house of the usurper and, being told by the butler that the lady of the house was indisposed, seized a precious Chinese vase in her white-gloved hands, flung it to the marble floor where it shattered into bits, and cried, "Tell the bitch I know her for what she is!" and departed.

Social secretaries insist that the more completely they are allowed to plan and run a coming-out, the better it will be. One social secretary recalls a party where the hostess insisted on making her own arrangements for the orchestra. On the night of the party, did the orchestra show up? Of course it didn't, so there you are. Given *carte blanche*, a social secretary will arrange for all the catering, the liquor (champagne is recommended because, as one social secretary says, "It gives them a *pleasant* little bun on"), the music, tent, flowers, decorations, invitations, photographs, notices in the newspapers — right up to the clean-up crew the day after. "As a result of television," Mrs. Tew says, "everybody wants celebrities at their parties." Celebrities who, for a fee, have appeared and entertained at coming-out parties range from Victor Borge and Ethel Merman (of whom parents approve) to Elvis Presley and the Rolling Stones (of whom the parents approve less).

A social secretary selects a motif for each party and, looking back, will recall, "I did her in pink geraniums, and married her a year later in wisteria," or, "The family colors are purple and white, so we did her in lilacs and white crocus." But perhaps the most important ingredient that a social secretary supplies is her list. In New York, such a list may contain twenty-five hundred names — two thousand boys and five hundred girls. The boys' list is, of course, more important, and each secretary jealously guards and maintains her names. One social secretary keeps her list in her safe-deposit box at her bank, and will not even let her own secretary see it; the quality of her list is a social secretary's most precious asset, and social-climbing parents with ambitions for their sons must, in order to get anywhere at all, get their sons' names placed somehow on a social secretary's list. Actually, it is not all that hard, and the composition of the list is not much of a mystery. The names come from prep school and college catalogues, from the *Social Register*, from the pupils at private dancing classes, and from those who attend "junior" or sub-debutante dances and, in New York, particularly the Groton-St. Mark's Dance. This dance, given each year by the two schools, serves as a major clearing house for stags. The behavior of a sixteen- or seventeen-year-old boy at the Groton-St. Mark's Dance can determine his social career for years to come, and will decide whether or not his name will appear on a list the following season. At the dance, which is usually given at the Hotel Pierre, soft punch and sweet biscuit are the only refreshments served. Social secretaries post emissaries in the Hotel Pierre bar to take down names of boys who go there for sturdier libations.

There is one other reason why a boy's name may not appear on a social secretary's list. In New York and in other large cities, few Jewish boys are listed — or, more exactly, boys with Jewish-sounding names, since social secretaries have no access to facts about a boy's religion. It is at the debutante stage that what is known as "The Great Division" begins to take place, and Jewish and Gentile Society are parted like the Red Sea. In Jewish Society there is, of course, a similar list of boys' names, similarly carefully maintained, by Jewish social secretaries for Jewish debutantes; in New York, its backbone is provided by the pupils of the Viola Wolff Dancing Classes, the Jewish equivalent of Mrs. William de Rham's. But it is rare for a boy's name to appear on both a Jewish and a Gentile list; when this happens, it is assumed to be through an inadvertence.

Normally, a boy's name stays on a list for four years — from age seventeen to twenty-one. But the social secretary must be ever on the lookout for things that could disqualify him as a suitable stag. If he should become engaged for example, his name must be removed, or if he should commit some social misdemeanor such as failing to dance with his hostess, drinking too much, failing to reply properly to an invitation, or attending a party to which he had not been invited. Flunking out of prep school or college is not considered a social crime, nor, apparently, is expulsion from school for stealing. A young man of good family, dismissed from his school for theft in a case that even made its way to newspaper headlines, remained on the list and turned up at all the best parties the following season. Drinking of hard liquor has long been a commonplace of debutante parties; if it isn't provided at the bar — and it usually is — it turns up anyway. When a group of Darien, Connecticut, parents was arrested for serving liquor to teen-agers at a debutante party — after which a girl was killed in an auto accident — the parents understandably felt that they had been unfairly singled out. Other parents have been serving liquor to underaged boys and girls at other parties for years. The only rule governing liquor is the vague one that states that a young person should be able to "handle" it.

Alongside each boy's name on the list are his parents' names, his address, his school and his class and — in most cases — a meaningful blank space for "Remarks." One debutante, looking over the list for her party, wrote "Spits when he talks" under "Remarks." That boy's name came off the list. So carefully do social secretaries tend their lists that many debutantes, and their parents, allow the secretaries a free rein with the party invitations. As one social secretary says, "If a boy's name is on my list, he's guaranteed to behave."

While they all agree that there should be more boys than girls at a coming-out party, each social secretary has her own favorite proportion. Some prefer three boys to every girl; others say four to one is better, "the proportions of a good Martini." More than four to one is considered undesirable. "The boys gang together then, and shoot craps and talk about the Army," says one lady. Gate-crashing is a perennial cause for concern. Most ballrooms, private and public, have additional, little-known entrances, through kitchens and pantries where a boy can enter the party with the lobster Newburg, and the secrets of these are passed on from crasher-father to crasher-son, along with the studs and cufflinks. Social secretaries post members of their staffs — called "dragons" by the young men — at strategic spots to keep out the uninvited, and most dragons make it a point to know not only the names but also the faces of the men on their list. But the crashing problem, like the servant problem, is secretly a non-problem. As one social secretary confesses, "If a party doesn't have a *few* crashers, nobody thinks it's a success." For their thoughtful services — to which one social secretary adds, as a fillip of her own, a hot bath drawn for the mother of the debutante filled with special salts in which Mother is instructed to loll for an hour before the party — social secretaries either charge a flat fee of ten or fifteen per cent of the party's cost, or receive discounts from the caterer, the florist, the photographer, the orchestra, and the wine merchant. The ladies seldom quote the prices of their clients' parties, but most admit that they would be uninterested in tackling anything with a budget under five thousand dollars.

In New York it is now true that any girl can come out — not the best way, perhaps, but at least get out — if her family is willing to spend the money. It is not true in Philadelphia. By tradition, Philadelphia Society is restricted to members of "first Philadelphia families." Newcomers generally have a hard time of it. One Philadelphia "newcomer," whose family had been in Philadelphia only since 1860 and who recently sought admission to Philadelphia's coveted Assemblies, an institution that began in 1748, was, after considerable effort and with the help of many friends, finally allowed to attend — as an out-of-town guest. So stern are the Philadelphia Assemblies' rules against admitting divorced people that the John Ingersolls (and she a Cadwalader) were not permitted to attend the coming-out of their daughter, since Mrs. Ingersoll had once been divorced. Philadelphians take a superior view of their sister city to the north. "New York is pretty much come-and-go, isn't it?" asks a Philadelphia lady.

Unlike New York, Philadelphia has a single official debutante list, printed up by J. E. Caldwell & Company, a jewelry and stationery store, the Tiffany's of Philadelphia. Caldwell's employs an official debutante screener named George W. Rehfuss. A mother registers her daughter with Mr. Rehfuss five or six years before her debut and, from that point on, Mr. Rehfuss sees that no debutante's dates overlap with another's and that, somehow, each of the city's hundred to two hundred debutantes gets her rightful share of the important college weekends and of the sixty-eight days of the four debutante seasons. Upstarts who hope to make debutantes of their daughters face their initial barrier in the person of Mr. Rehfuss, and those who treat Mr. Rehfuss as an ordinary clerk or suspect that he will respond to bribery are disappointed. "If someone came to me whose daughter *shouldn't* be a debutante, I would know it," says Mr. Rehfuss.

Philadelphia's most powerful social secretary was the late Mrs. Edward J. MacMullan, a woman who lived to be, as the saying goes, a legend in her time. At her death in the summer of 1966, it was a shock to realize from the obituary notices that this striking woman — with her flaming red hair, aquiline nose, boundless energy and Irish temper — was seventy-eight years old. For over forty years she had been, as she herself liked to put it, "the ringmaster of the Philadelphia social circus." The secret of her ringmastery was her direct approach to problems. For years, Mrs. MacMullan was Mrs. Edward T. Stotesbury's personal arbiter *elegantiarum,* and one of Mrs. Stotesbury's great difficulties in life was a particular diamond and emerald tiara. It was so heavy with stones that whenever she wore it, it gave her a stiff neck.

Mrs. MacMullan said, "You deserve to suffer with that much jewelry on your head. Either attach a few helium balloons to it or wear it without complaining." The same tiara had a tendency to list to one side and fall over Mrs. Stotesbury's ear. And so Mrs. MacMullan stationed herself behind Mrs. Stotesbury at parties and, whenever the tiara began to slip, nudged it back into place again.

Her own background was humble — or so it is said; Mrs. MacMullan herself always preferred to keep her background out of the conversation. But for two generations the foremost families of Philadelphia Society regarded "Mrs. Mac" with something close to awe, and something even closer to dread. "Oh, she's a devil!" they would murmur, rolling their eyes, and there were catalogued instances where young men — dropped from Mrs. Mac's list for one reason or another — felt themselves so permanently ruined in Philadelphia Society that they left to start life over in other cities. Mrs. MacMullan herself used to laugh loudly at such assertions, but it was clear she enjoyed their being made. "My rules are simple," she once said. "Manners. Good manners. Rudimentary good manners are all I ask. There's little enough elegance left in the world. Are a few good manners too much to ask for? Take shaking hands. If a young lady is introduced to me, I expect her to take my hand. Naturally I go to all the parties I plan and, as the young men and women enter the room, I expect them to come up to me, say, 'Good evening, Mrs. MacMullan,' and take my hand. That's all. If they don't do that much, then they don't deserve to be in Society."

In addition to reportedly knowing the whereabouts of several well-placed family skeletons, Mrs. MacMullan's great success — and power — as a social secretary stemmed from the simple fact that she planned and ran very good parties. From her triumph at organizing the wedding of Ethel du Pont to Franklin D. Roosevelt, Jr., she went on to establish Philadelphia's Junior Bal Masque, the Piccadilly Dances, and the Headdress Balls — all now fixtures of the city's social life. Her inventiveness when it came to adding gay and sparkly side-show features to coming-out parties was endless. At one ball, a replica of a roadside diner was built just off the ballroom of the Bellevue-Stratford Hotel; from it, short-order cooks served hot dogs, hamburgers, and soft drinks to guests who sat on stools.

For the debut of Ella ("Tootie") Widener in 1946, a North Pole motif was selected. There was a real snowstorm, an aurora borealis overhead, and Miss Widener received from an igloo — which was heated, of course. With surprise, guests learned that it was not a Mac-Mullan party, but one designed by her competitor, Mrs. Wirt Thompson. "Trying to copy me, of course," sniffed Mrs. MacMullan. "Imagine! An igloo! I hear it dripped all over her dress."

Mrs. MacMullan was well aware of the hazards of drippage from overhead. She often used wildlife in her decor — releasing flocks of white doves or, in one instance, four hundred canaries. Beforehand, Mrs. MacMullan had thoughtfully fed the canaries a special seed mixture calculated to induce a mild constipation. Not all her schemes were successful. Once, a herd of peacocks was to parade magnificently across the ballroom, plumes fanned regally but, seeing the guests, the peacocks panicked and caused quite a disturbance. "One of the things came lunging at me, flapping its wings," a girl who was a guest at the party recalls. "Goodness, if I hadn't had so much champagne I think I would have fainted!" Flamingoes, it turns out, have considerably more aplomb. Philadelphians will never forget the ball where huge white paper cylinders were suspended from the ceiling of the tent. Everyone wondered what they were for until midnight, when the cylinders flew open releasing thousands of white butterflies. The butterflies came cascading down — all quite dead — killed, apparently, by the fire-preventative that had been sprayed around the tent. But, for all these mishaps, Mrs. MacMullan was a part of Philadelphia Society life. Who can possibly replace her is a subject of agitated speculation.

Boston is often likened to Philadelphia, but the two cities actually have little in common. "In Boston," says one Philadelphian, "you simply do not get enough to eat." This is certainly part of it and, compared to those in Philadelphia, Boston's coming-out parties are austere. For years, Boston debutantes were presented under simple marquees in their families' gardens; but with the rising costs of these affairs — costs which wouldn't make a New Yorker or a Philadelphian blink — more and more Boston girls are being presented at mass debuts, at the Debutante Cotillion held in June at the Sheraton Plaza Hotel, and the Debutante Assembly, held Thanksgiving Eve at the Statler. Before one of these parties not long ago, a debutante complained to a friend that the shoes she was planning to wear were too small and were uncomfortable; she doubted she could bear the pain of dancing in them all eve-

ning. "Why not wear sneakers?" her practical-minded friend offered.
"Under your long dress they'll never be noticed." She wore sneakers;
they were not noticed. At the same party, another un-style-conscious
debutante wore long woolen underwear under her ball gown, "because
it was cold."

Boston, like Philadelphia, has a Society that is generally chilly to the
upstart. "We don't snub them," a Boston lady says, "we side-step
them." Another city renowned for its impenetrable social barriers
against outsiders without connections and newcomers without portfo-
lio is Charleston, South Carolina. Although it is not a *"Social Register*
city," Charlestonians feel that it doesn't need to be. The city has a rich
and glorious past. Between the Revolution and the Civil War, it was
the capital of the Plantation System and the birthplace of all that is
considered gracious and elegant in the Southern "way of life." In
1762, Charleston's St. Cecilia Society was formed. Originally an amateur musical group, it was similar to and only slightly younger than
Philadelphia's Assemblies. For years, the St. Cecilia Society ruled
Charleston's social life; no girl could be a debutante in Charleston unless she was a daughter of a St. Cecilia's member. Recent pressure,
however, has broken down the system. Now about half of Charleston's
debutantes are from non-St. Cecilia families. They can do everything
except attend the St. Cecilia Ball.

In Dallas and other Texas cities where one might expect oil money
to have an exuberant influence on debutantes and their affairs, most
debuts are subdued and Eastern rather than Western in flavor. Eastern
social secretaries are often imported to arrange parties, and this fact
alone is enough to give a party great cachet. The same is true in the
motion picture colony of Los Angeles, where Society — like everything else about that billowing city-of-villages — is confusing and hard
to grasp. At one time there was a genuine Los Angeles Old Guard,
composed largely of Spanish land-grant families, many of whom clung
jealously to their ancient Spanish titles, and even spoke Spanish in
their homes. These were eclipsed, however, by suburban upper-crust
families centered around such towns as Pasadena and San Marino
where, if one was part of the circle, it was possible to believe that
nothing else was going on in Los Angeles at all. Such fixtures of Pasadena social life as the Los Angeles Country Club and the Las Madrinas Debutante Ball excluded, automatically, all movie people; the

"Pasadena crowd" and the "Beverly Hills crowd" literally never met. Gradually the great dividing line has begun to blur, and one of the first movie people to integrate with the Pasadena set was none other than the late Walt Disney. His daughter Sharon made Los Angeles social history as the first movie-colony debutante in the Las Madrinas Ball. The occasion even had a touch of Hollywood comedy. Realizing that he and Sharon were the same height in their stocking feet, and that when he led her in the first dance she would tower over him in her high heels, Disney went to his studio's wardrobe department and had his evening shoes fitted out with tall lifts. Sharon, meanwhile, had thought of the same possibility and so, on the evening of the ball, considerately wore flats. On the dance floor, a towering Disney lurched about with Sharon's head at waist level.

Debutantes have undergone some interesting personality changes in the last few decades. In the 1920's, they prided themselves on being brittle, animated, and witty, and were admired for their boyish gaiety, their ability to swing from chandeliers and to drink and mix cocktails. But in the thirties the movies were promoting the word "glamour," and debutantes let their hair down to their shoulders, became willowy, languid, and torchy. At the same time, they discovered show business. A debutante named Cobina Wright, Jr., was singing at the Waldorf, and Sally Clark, a Roosevelt relative, was at the Plaza. Eve Symington, a Senator's daughter, was at a West Side bistro called La Place Pigalle. Paragraphs in Society columns seemed less important than write-ups in *Variety,* photographs in the tabloids, and gossipy innuendos by Walter Winchell. "Café Society" became a phrase. The Old Guard was more amused than shocked. It all seemed very new and strange and, therefore, exciting. Much of the show business aspect of coming out remains. In 1951, when *Life* published a full-page picture of Caroline Lee Bouvier, now Princess Stanislaus Radziwill, commenting that "Society editors and arbiters" considered her the leading debutante of the New York season, she was besieged with fan mail. In one letter, a certain Boris Kaplan of the talent department of Paramount Pictures wrote the future sister-in-law of President Kennedy to ask her whether she would be interested in discussing motion picture work. Writing to her at Sarah Lawrence College in Bronxville, New York, Mr. Kaplan urged the rich and beautiful Miss Bouvier to call him at his New York office — "collect." She has underscored this suggestion, in red, and has placed the letter in a scrapbook with other invitations collected during her debutante year. A daughter of *real* Society cannot be bought for the price of a twenty-cent call, as Miss Bouvier later proved by launching herself as an actress on her own terms.

In every season there is a girl who might be called a superfluous debutante — a girl who, long before her debutante year, has received all the acclaim and admiration any girl could dream of, and for whom the ritual of coming out seems to add little of importance. She has been "out" for a long time. Sometimes this Ultimate Girl is a creation of the press. From the thirties one thinks of Brenda Diana Duff Frazier who, fresh from the genteel Miss Hewitt's classes in New York, became advertised as "America's Number One Glamour Debutante," with her long "debutante bob," her dark eyes, her pale skin and thin red mouth "more beautiful that Joan Crawford's." She was the Girl-with-Everything, and clever reporters were skillful at inducing dumb-girl quotes from her so that, long before her debutante year was over, she was hated by the Depression-poor American public, and had to face such ordeals as being hissed when she entered a restaurant. Some thirty years and two collapsed marriages later, Brenda Frazier lives in near-retirement, far from the Society into which she came. Then there was Gloria Vanderbilt, now also several times married, whose coming-out career was singular. Though labeled by the press the "Number One Debutante," she was never technically a debutante at all since she was never presented at a ball.

Then, periodically, there are the girls with helpful mothers behind them, pushing them into social prominence, and one recalls the blond and beautiful Joanne Connelley, Debutante Queen of 1948 who, less than ten years after her press-agented debut, was dead of a heart ailment induced by an overdose of reducing pills, and was survived by her ambitious, more robust mother. Of the same vintage as Miss Connelley was a dark-haired girl with a heart-shaped face named Jacqueline Lee Bouvier. Though her debut was *not* press-agented, she emerged a few years later as one of the most famous women in the world. Ten years later, a beautiful English girl named Henrietta Tiarks — and her mother — arrived on these shores. Henrietta Tiarks was already one of the most come-out girls in recent history. Her debutante career had begun in England when she was presented to the Queen and was heralded in the press as "the last of the debs." This was not strictly accurate. Royal presentation parties were being discontinued that year as being "out of keeping with the times," but debutantes have continued to proliferate in England nonetheless. Henrietta's presentation was followed by a series of luncheons, teas, cocktail parties, dinners, and "one or two balls every night." In between there were weekends at Oxford, May Week at Cambridge, polo matches at Windsor Great Park, the Henley Regatta, the Eton-Harrow cricket match, Ascot, and the Derby. She gave a ball of her own, in London, and it took up the entire ground floor of Claridge's Hotel; the party lasted until five, after which there was a trip to London Airport for breakfast.

Next came the "little season" in Scotland where, to make it official north of the border, Henrietta came out all over again, and attended "twenty-five or thirty balls." Then on to Paris, to come out there, and next to Madrid for the same reason. "Paris parties are fabulous," Henrietta said afterward. "They're all given in such beautiful houses. Madrid is wonderful, too, but fewer balls are given there." Arriving in New York, she was enrolled in Briarcliff College, in a horsey part of suburban Westchester, and her mother installed herself in a Manhattan apartment and busied herself keeping Henrietta's social calendar and pasting Henrietta's press clippings into big scrapbooks, "So her grandchildren may see what a wonderful year she is having." Briarcliff — often called "Debutante U." — could be little more than a place to go and rest between parties because, of course, Henrietta Tiarks was presented to New York Society at two balls and then plunged into the generally hectic Eastern social schedule. For good measure, she also made debuts in Boston, Philadelphia, and Washington, D.C., and went to balls in San Francisco, Los Angeles, and Chicago. How many balls, all told, did Henrietta Tiarks attend? She lost count somewhere along the way. "It was hundreds and hundreds. Looking back on it, it was all quite wonderful," she said when it was over. "But I'm glad it's only once in a lifetime. When the clock struck midnight, January first, I said, 'Hooray! I'm an *ex*-debutante!'" Her mother, meanwhile, had stuffed five scrapbooks full of photographs and clippings and cried, "I've still got drawers and *drawersful* more!" Such an elaborate coming-out season undoubtedly had its desired long-term result. The Tiarkses, though very rich (Henrietta's banker father was, among other things, one of the developers of Jamaica's Round Hill), did not have a title in the family. Now they do. A few years after her coming-out year, Henrietta married the young Marquis of Tavistock, heir to the Duke of Bedford.

But girls like these are the exception in a debutante season. Ultimate Girls are only rarely national or international celebrities. For the most part they are the pretty products of the Eastern boarding schools — Foxcroft, Miss Porter's, Westover, Madeira, Dobbs Ferry, Ethel Walker, Chatham Hall. The Ultimate Girl is an artifact of American prep school life, as persistent as the rumor that there is saltpeter in the gravy. She is selected not by a Cholly Knickerbocker but, in an informal election, by perspiring boys who sit sprawled on beds and cracked leather chairs in banner-decked dormitory rooms of such schools as Choate, Hotchkiss, Exeter, St. Paul's, St. Mark's, Lawrenceville, Groton, Taft and Hill, and in fraternity lounges of both the big and the little Ivy League. Selection is based on her ability to leave male heads dizzy with desire, grief, and frustration. Once picked, she is advertised by word of mouth. She is authoritatively reported to be both fast and frigid, in one breath a Magdalen and in the next a Medusa. Suddenly she receives dozens of invitations to every party there is and when she appears she radiates the "star quality" of a movie queen, with lesser debutantes, eager to share her light, hovering about her like handmaidens. But this Ultimate Girl is not necessarily doomed to a future of divorce, notoriety, alcohol, sleeping pills, and psychiatry. More often than not she simply finishes her debutante year, graduates from college, marries, moves to Scarsdale, has babies, joins the country club and the Junior League.

The Diana Barrymores, the Brenda Fraziers, and the Joanne Connelleys of the debutante world have given a somewhat lurid connotation to the word. And so coming out has become a point of some controversy in Society. Should one let one's teenage daughter step into these highly charged and perfumed waters? What are the real values of the debutante ritual, if any? There are many opinions. One handsome young New York woman says, "Daddy asked me if I wanted a coming-out party, and I told him flatly no, I didn't. To me it's silly to spend all that money just so that I could have a fabulous party. What's a party? When it's all over, what have you got but a ball gown you'll never wear again? I told him that if he had that much money to spend, he could put it in a savings account for me. Then, when I get married, it will help me buy a house or furniture or educate my children." Then she added, thoughtfully, "To me a girl who wants to be a debutante is basically insecure."

The late Mrs. MacMullan of Philadelphia would have agreed with this, more or less. But she saw in the system factors which, if a girl *was* "basically insecure," would cure her of all her emotional problems. "You may say I'm in a luxury business, that it's a lot of froth," she once said. "But, believe me, it's thrilling to see what her debutante year does for a girl! It can turn a shy, awkward child into a radiant, charming young woman. It teaches a girl poise and manners. Do you know there are girls nowadays who don't know how to perform an introduction properly? Much less pour tea! And think of the employment these parties give to caterers, florists, musicians, marquee men, photographers, and gown shops!"

The mother of a debutante says, "Why *shouldn't* I give her a little gaiety? These are perilous times. She'll have to face the hard facts soon enough." And another says, "It's a gracious tradition that ought to be preserved." And yet, when the guests at Fernanda Wanamaker Leas's coming-out party helped dismantle the house where they were staying, dragging mattresses out onto the Southampton beach, some of the graciousness of the tradition seemed to disappear. "What do they drag out mattresses on the beach *for?*" asks one mother. "That's what worries me." A New York father says flatly, "I'm not going to give a party so a lot of drunks and hopheads can rape my daughter." In a somewhat more restrained tone, a Boston grandmother asks worriedly, "Is it true that all the debutantes nowadays go the whole hog?"

In the Old Stone Age when a marriageable maiden was preened, fattened, buttered, and presented to the tribe, she was offered as a virgin — yet how many of her modern sisters offer an equivalent degree of virtue is a debatable point. The debutantes of 1966 generally take the view that girls today are no more, and no less, virtuous than they were in their mothers' generation. Others disagree. Obviously, firm statistics are not available but when, not long ago, an American girl traveling in England announced that she guessed that "at least fifty per cent" of American debutantes were virgins, this was greeted with widespread skepticism. "This would certainly not be true here," a London Society columnist commented, adding that in England "only a tiny per cent" were pure.

American parents prefer not to dwell overlong on such aspects of the rite, and instead try to see in it something worthwhile and reassuring. As one mother says, "I've heard all the talk about the Sexual Revolution, but I confess I haven't seen it. I mean, how *can* one see something like that going on if one isn't a peeping Tom? But I *have* seen the way college girls *dress* nowadays — with their scraggly hair and sloppy shoes and dirty raincoats. At least if a girl's a debutante she has to *look* like a lady!"

6

Playing the Game

ACCORDING to the best possible source — the Social Establishment itself — the most important college, socially, is unquestionably Yale. Princeton has a lot of glamour, but Yale is solider. Boston, naturally, has always favored Harvard, but it is only a particular part of Harvard — a Harvard centered around such clubs as Porcellian, Fly, and Spee — that is favored. (There are, in a very real sense, two Harvards. In the Porcellian Club, a one-way mirror on the dining room wall symbolizes the division; members, dining, can look out on the rest of the university as it passes by; non-members see only a reflection of themselves. The two Harvards, therefore, neither speak to, nor recognize, each other.) Though Philadelphia prefers the St. Paul's-to-Yale route, it still sends a number of its upper-class sons to its own University of Pennsylvania, an institution which Philadelphians blandly admit is "second-rate Ivy League," and which other cities place far down on their lists. For company and solace at the University, the well-born young of Philadelphia huddle together in three select fraternities — Delta Psi (St. Anthony's), Delta Phi (St. Elmo's), and Zeta Psi — and quite literally never meet anyone else. These three clubs are so selective and conservative that they have occasionally had years when they took in no new pledges at all; there was simply no one suitable to take in. New England's "little three," Williams, Amherst, and Wesleyan, are favorites of individual families, with the first two considered "better," from a social standpoint. Dartmouth has a rather raffish reputation, associated with hard drinking and long winter weekends. "A lot of Dartmouth men go into advertising," says one non-Dartmouth man. Also, a lot of them are Irish." (Nelson Rockefeller, Dartmouth '30, however, is neither Irish nor in advertising.) Notre Dame is not considered in the social running at all. Yale men are supposed to go into banking. (David Rockefeller, however, who is a banker, went to Harvard.)

A rough indication — and very rough — of the social standing of American colleges is the *Social Register,* which lists college and classes of the socially registered. The *Register* has standard abbreviations for all the colleges of the Ivy League — Yale, Harvard, Princeton, Brown, Dartmouth, Columbia, the University of Pennsylvania, and "perhaps Cornell." For years, however, it listed only two of the "little three" — omitting Wesleyan, though it long included the Massachusetts Institute of Technology, Trinity, and, somewhat mysteriously, Union College, Rutgers, Rensselaer Polytechnic Institute, Johns Hopkins, C.C.N.Y., and N.Y.U. For reasons equally mysterious, the only women's college honored with its own *Social Register* symbol is Barnard, although Smith, Vassar, and Bryn Mawr, of the "seven sister" women's colleges, are all a good deal more fashionable. And none of these may be as prestigious as certain of the women's junior colleges — Bennett, Briarcliff, and Colby. Recently, Wesleyan was recognized and given its own *Social Register* symbol, "Wes," indicating a possible improvement of its status. At the same time it has seemed to a few sensitive observers that Wesleyan is only partway into the *Social Register.* Though other collegiate symbols are translated in full in a key at the front of the book — "J Hop," for instance, is said to stand for "Johns Hopkins Graduate" — "Wes" is somewhat sneeringly dismissed as "Wesleyan Univ. Grad."

The *Social Register* makes allowances for graduates of both Annapolis and West Point, but has never recognized the United States Air Force Academy, and, of course, regional editions reflect local preferences. The San Francisco *Register* has symbols for Stanford and the University of California and, of the Eastern colleges, for only Yale, Harvard, and Princeton. The Washington book adds Georgetown and George Washington University, lists all the Ivy League except Cornell, and in another hard-to-fathom move, adds Hobart, which is in upstate New York.

There are other social "list" books besides the *Social Register* — though none considered as "reliable" — and a glance at their stand on colleges reveals that there may be a connection between the colleges and universities recognized and the alma maters of the lists' publishers. The *National Social Directory*, for instance, in its "The List of Society," gives the nod to all the colleges of the Ivy League and the "little three," plus — in an attempt, perhaps, to give the publication the appearance of national scope — four others: Northwestern University in Evanston, Illinois; Northeastern University, in Boston; Southwestern University (whether of Los Angeles or of Georgetown, Texas, the "List" does not specify); and Southeastern University in Washington, D.C. Still another list includes the customary Ivy League and "little three" and adds a few surprises of its own — South Dakota School of Mines and McNeese State College, which is in Lake Charles, Louisiana. Book editors are apt to be a class-conscious lot. A Harvard-graduated Boston editor, going over proof of a novel, objected to a line of dialogue that identified one of the characters as belonging to the Porcellian Club. "A fellow like that would never have been taken into the Porc," he announced. The author, suspicious, checked the editor's credentials and found him not to have been a member of Porcellian either, but of the Spee Club. He then changed the line to read, "Only a member of the Spee Club. Too bad it couldn't have been Porcellian."

Just as there are certain proper schools and colleges, so are there certain proper college sports. Being able to play the right game is as important a part of being a gentleman or lady in Society as using the right fork and the right accent. American Society, like English Society, has always been strongly oriented toward the out-of-doors, the saddle, the firearm, the wicket and the bat, but just as certain colleges — such as Wesleyan — have a way of going in and out of fashion, so do sports. In the early part of the century, for instance, no gentleman in Society could decently admit that he was unable to play golf, or "the golf," as it was somewhat flossily called. Golf brought with it the great era of the American country club, each surrounded by verdant acres of greens and fairways. Now, however, golf has become commonplace and is regarded as a middle-class sport. Few country clubs today could support themselves if they offered nothing but golf. Though there is admittedly a certain difference in cost, it is probably also significant of Society's changing athletic attitudes that a New York contractor, who used to be kept busy building such things, has not installed a private golf course — full-size or miniature — since 1926. He has no end of orders, however, for private tennis courts. And, on the campuses of the better Eastern colleges, the golfer finds himself toward the bottom of the social ladder, along with the long-distance runner, the swimmer, the wrestler, the basketball and baseball player and, the most *déclassé* figure on the college athletic scene, the cheerleader.

The "racquet" sports — tennis, squash, and court tennis — have long been mandatory upper-class pastimes, with the latter so "inside" that it has become almost obscure (requiring, as it does, medieval-style courtyards so elaborate that only a handful exist in the United States for the handful of aristocratic court-tennis players, all of whom know each other). Squash and tennis, suffused with an aura of easygoing good-fellowship, have a breezy, casual air about them that blends so perfectly with the Society manner. As a North Shore Long Island lady has said, "I'm always delighted to throw the house open to young men who come up to the Club for our Tennis Week — even if I don't know them. Of course I'd hardly want to throw the house open to a group of *golfers.* That would be quite different, somehow — I don't know why, but it would." And a member of Amherst's tennis squad says, "The nice thing about the racquet sports is that they look easy to play, but aren't, and that keeps the duffers out of the game." On Eastern college campuses, an argument can always be started over which is the most prestigious sport, tennis or squash. Squash, which is played indoors, is of necessity the sweatier sport, yet squash courts are among the most popular features of the best men's clubs — and this of course, is the essential difference. Squash is a one-sex sport, but tennis is a sport for both sexes and is associated with summer, youth, and love. As a Yale man says, "It's more important to know how to play tennis than squash because — well, you play tennis in the spring, which is the most important time of year to make a good impression if you're looking for invitations to June coming-out parties." In spanking clean tennis whites, a young man can make an excellent impression — even before swooping down on his opening serve.

College crew, until a generation ago, was in roughly the same position of importance that tennis is in today, and it used to be taken as an article of faith that anyone rowing on the crew of a decent college bore credentials that were socially impeccable. Those were the days when so much snobbery surrounded crew that the father of Princess Grace, John Brendan Kelly, was told he could not compete in England's Diamond Sculls because "A man who has worked with his hands should not compete against gentlemen." Kelly, as the world surely knows by now, was a contractor's son and, in the most noble purlieus of Philadelphia Society today, it is still said that Kelly "tried to use crew as a means to climb into Society." Of the same era was the Porcellian stroke of the Harvard crew of whom it was said — according to a persistent legend — "He's quite a democratic chap. He knows every man in the boat but the three up front."

At such schools as St. Paul's and Kent, crew continues to lure the sons of noted families but, at college, when athletic habits congeal, crew has had a considerable falling off. No one is quite sure why. The disintegration of the Yale-Harvard Regatta as a social event may be one reason. What was a chic affair in the twenties — involving private railway cars and all the largest steam yachts in the East — has turned into a general traffic jam that ties up all roadways, railways, and riverways around New London, Connecticut, and litters them all with empty beer cans. "Too many alumni got into the act," explains a Yale senior.

Another social sport that, like crew, has suffered recently from overcrowding is Rugby. For a number of years, Rugby failed to get an official athletic department recognition at major colleges, which gave its partisans — like the select few who make up college polo teams — the pleasant feeling of being insiders by virtue of being outsiders. Also, on most campuses, Rugby players were not really required to know how to play Rugby; the major talent for Rugby was the ability to muster round-trip plane fare to Bermuda for Rugby Week, the sport's annual rite of spring. Rugby Week or College Week was once cozy and gay and giggly and distinctly upper class, and mothers had no qualms about allowing their daughters to go, in groups, to attend the event. But slowly, the tiny Atlantic archipelago began noticing annual increases in the numbers of Rugby and non-Rugby playing guests at Easter time. Soon College Week was more crowded than the Yale-Harvard Regatta, more wild-eyed than Derby Day, Yale's famous (and now defunct) romp. College Week sat in the middle of Bermuda's sunny season like a drunk at a tea party. "I've gone to my last College Week," said a Princeton sophomore a few years ago. "You can't believe what it's like. The hotels are all filled, so guys sleep under rocks on the beach. If you're lucky enough to have a room, you're expected to share it with twenty other guys. The bar at the Elbow-Beach Club is packed three people deep and filled with armed Security Guards trying to keep order. And the girls! My blind date one night was a CPA from Chicago. For my money, the whole Rugby thing has gone way, way down." It was to go even further. Bermuda, displeased with the behavior of its visitors, made them increasingly unwelcome, and soon the young, and the ensuing disturbances, turned to the beaches of Florida, to Fort Lauderdale and then, a few years later, to Daytona Beach. All pretense at any connection with the sport of Rugby was abandoned, and College Week no longer has any Society overtones at all. Today, the holidaying college crowd tends to favor Puerto Rico and upper class mothers keep their daughters home — remembering, though, when it was all sweet innocence in Bermuda, with all those nice young Rugby players from the Ivy League. And where are the nice young men today if they are not playing Rugby? On the nearest ski slopes they can find.

Society fathers expect their sons to have learned, by the time of their maturity, to ride and respect horseflesh, to handle a firearm or a trout rod, to sail a boat, and to be kind to pedigreed dogs. Girls are expected only to be able to ride. From these areas of interest stem any number of specialist and rarified sports which are determinedly, perennially, and almost exclusively aristocratic; such as yacht-racing, fox hunting, polo, and beagling. These sports seem incapable of losing their upper-class gloss. But other sports, like Rugby, have suffered social reverses, and the most notable of these is Eastern college football which, for several decades, has undergone a long decline. Often called "King Football," the sport certainly is among the more enduring symbols of college life. For years, football games were the centers of huge, happy, sentimental, and generally well-bred gatherings. Saturday after Saturday, autumn after autumn, the packed station wagons threaded their way across the New England landscape toward the famous stadiums and bowls. And yet, though to an outsider all might have seemed well with college football, there were signs that it was sickening at its heart. It was not so much that Society boys no longer played football — there never have, really, been many Society football players — it was that the youngsters of Society were not *attending* football games with their old enthusiasm. The oldsters continued to flock to the games and to open the backs of their station wagons and spread out picnics with cocktails, chafing dishes, wines, and, in any number of cases, a white-coated houseboy in attendance to help serve. But they had not come to watch football being played as much as to pass around the thermos of iced Martinis, and to meet old friends at Portal Nine. After the game — or, more likely, before it was over, in order to beat the crowds — the oldsters left the stadium to wander over to Zeta Psi where a goodly number of football enthusiasts had already gathered for a drink and to inquire, in a bored and genial sort of way, about the victor and the final score.

During the games, cheering sections failed to materialize or, if they did, failed to cheer loudly enough to be heard across the field. Cheerleaders flopped about, calling for shreds of enthusiasm. Brilliant plays went unnoticed by larger and larger sections of the stands, and college newspaper editors editorialized halfheartedly about "lack of spirit" and "apathy." Friday nights were given over to listless pep rallies, and the social standing of football on the Ivy League campus slid lower and lower.

After World War II, when returning veterans — most of whom considered football kid stuff — flooded the campuses, football sank to its knees. Football players were openly and loudly kidded and lampooned. They became the butt of every joke. College humor magazines depicted them as bulky dimwits who were able to stay in college only if they took the simplest "gut" courses and received elaborate scholastic coaching from their friends. If a particular fraternity happened to attract mostly football players to its membership, it became known as "The Ape House," or "The Gorilla Cage," or "The Jungle Club," and Zeta Psi — which, on practically every campus it exists, is among the most exclusive — seriously discussed excluding football players from its Williams chapter. "They can give the house a bad name," it was said at the time.* College professors, rather than seem to be giving football players a break, often seemed to be giving them a harder time than other students, calling on them to recite excessively,

* Several years later, fraternities themselves were banned at Williams.

ridiculing them if they made mistakes. "Musclehead" and "meathead" became popular expressions of derogation.

In the twenties and thirties, days when the image of Princeton's great Hobey Baker hung in the sky, girls from Smith, Vassar, and Wellesley were the football hero's for the asking. In the late forties and fifties, the football player — a hero no longer — had trouble finding himself a date. "Quite frankly, they don't make *good* weekend dates," said a Wellesley girl. "At least not during the season. If they're playing, you have to go with one of their friends. After the game, if they're not banged up somehow, they're *tired*. Their training rules mean they don't have much fun at parties. They go to sleep, and there you are." During the week, too, life at the training table had the effect of isolating the football player from his fellow students. Lonely and neglected, he sought out the only company that was available to him — the company of other football players. Coincidentally, as the sixth decade of the century progressed, professional football increased enormously in popularity. Society turned on its television set or headed for the big pro games and, of all things, professional football became an upper-class spectator sport. At Yale today, the men who consider themselves the college's social leaders have never met members of the Yale football team. They indulge, instead, in a sport that would horrify their grandfathers — touch football.

Does this mean that Eastern college sports have gone all effete and namby-pamby — that future sporting events will be limited entirely to those which can be held under green-and-white striped awnings, where spectators, seated in rows of folding chairs, will show their appreciation of exceptional plays not with stomping or cheering, but with polite applause? Not exactly. Two fairly rough and tumble sports, hockey and lacrosse, have been rapidly moving up the social ladder to fill the gap left by college football. Field hockey, too, is becoming popular at men's colleges, as it long was at women's. "Do you know what I think the chic-est college sporting event in the entire East is at the moment, bar none?" asks a Bennington girl. "It's the annual Williams-Bennington field hockey game. You should see us out there in our little knickers!"

The Queen of San Francisco's younger set, Dolly Fritz

*Mrs. Adolph B. Spreckels in the drawing room of her
Washington Street mansion*

Alma Emma Charlotte Corday le Normand de Bretteville von Spreckelsen, otherwise known as San Francisco's Mrs. A. B. Spreckels, posed for this regal portrait on the royal throne given her by her friend Queen Marie of Rumania (Courtesy of Mrs. Spreckels)

In New York's Seventh Regiment Armory, a Knickerbocker Grey salutes the
ladies' committee who decide who will, and who will not, be a Grey

New York's Mrs. William De Rham and a young dancing pupil

Robert McGinley at the Lake Forest Horse Show

The Foxcroft School's headmistress, "Miss Charlotte" Noland

A pretty bouquet of New York debutantes before a ball

7

The Dirty Part

IN a large stone house outside Philadelphia, surrounded by acres of venerable lawn, at the end of a long graveled driveway that is raked so often that each car approaching leaves fresh furrows in it, lives a certain little old lady with servants and roomfuls of family photographs. At tea time, on designated afternoons, she receives her brothers and cousins, her nieces and nephews and little grandnieces and grandnephews, most of whom live nearby, and, as she pours from a large, heavily embossed silver service, the conversation is witty and cultivated and intimate and gay. "Gentle talk," she calls it. Mostly it is family talk, but often it ranges to art, the opera, the symphony, the local dances. Politics is a rare topic; so is the theatre — unless, of course, someone "knows someone" who has made the unusual move of "going into politics," or is "taking a fling" at going on the stage. The talk, in other words, centers around "people we know." When tea is over, the children kiss their elderly relative good-by and leave with parents or governesses, and a few adults stay on for cocktails and a few of these old members of the family may remain for dinner. At eleven o'clock, the great doors of the house close for the night.

This lady is a member of one of Philadelphia's oldest and wealthiest and most distinguished families. At eighteen, she was the city's most beautiful and popular debutante. Strangers ask why she never married. This is a subject that is not discussed much in the family any more; the reasons why no longer matter much. But, if pressed for an answer, close friends will tell the story of how once, when she was a young girl, she fell in love. The man she loved was out of her class, and was Jewish — either one of which circumstances might have been remotely tolerable, alone. But together they made the situation impossible. She never fell out of love, never fell in love again. Once, it is said, she asked her father for permission to marry the man. Papa, very gently, explained that it was out of the question. She bowed to Papa's wisdom. This story, in its classic simplicity, presents a classic truth: love, among the rich, can be cruel.

Love among the rich is different simply because the rich are rich, and for no other reason. (F. Scott Fitzgerald's sensitive observation about the rich that they are "different" from you and me and Ernest Hemingway's flat-footed rebuttal of it, that they have more money, reveals only that one man understood the power of money and the other did not.) "Power," states an old Chinese proverb, "is ancient wealth." And it is to this thinking that most American rich, knowingly or not, subscribe. The adjective here is most important. In order for the power — the influence, the prestige, the ability to control other people and shore up reserves against the world's inequities — to be at its fullest, the money must age. This is why the newly rich are very different from the anciently rich. Money, like a good strand of pearls, improves and grows more lustrous with each generation that wears it.

This, of course, explains why so much of the talk among the *very old* rich is family talk. Money is part of the bloodline, inextricable from it, celebrated along with it so that the two are tacitly considered to be the same. Family money is a thing that, from generation to generation, must not only be preserved, but must also be enriched and fed and nourished from time to time, from whatever sources are at hand, resupplied from other wells of ancient wealth. Otherwise, any family fortune — unless the strictest rules of primogeniture are adhered to — dissipates quickly through division, taxation, and simple spending. Marriage, therefore — the right marriage — is of prime importance. "Love" — taken to mean romantic love, or even sex — must be subordinated to that, or at least made equivalent to that. Among the rich, money and love and marriage go together like a horse and a pair of carriages — the money being the horse that pulls the caravan. In upper-class love, money is always raising its ugly head. Before the demands of love can be met, the demands of money must be. In marriage, money is definitely the dirty part; sooner or later all the implications of that five-letter word must be faced.

The rich in America are often accused of living in the past, but this is not really the case. The past, the family, and where the money came from provide a textured background for what goes on today, but the true concern of the rich is for the future: where the money will go. A child is more than a child. He is also the carrier of the money into the next generation, and the one after that. This is the reason for the unquestioning obedience and observance of ritual and tradition that accompany upper-class child-raising — a process that Wilmarth Lewis compares to the Oriental practice of foot-binding. This constrictive atmosphere is designed not to stifle romantic love, but to put it in its proper perspective, to help the young see love for what it is. The attitude is that love is cheap. Money isn't.

"Bringing up a child is so difficult these days," a New York woman sighed recently. "At schools and colleges, there is getting to be such a *range* of people." Of course. At the so-called "rich-boys' schools," it is increasingly difficult to be sure that one's son will meet only other rich boys, who are likeliest to have rich sisters. There are apt to be a few poor boys in these schools nowadays, and there are even more apt to be rich boys who are "the wrong kind of rich." This means that, to compensate for schools that "open their doors to practically everybody," more attention must be paid to what goes on in — and who goes to — the private dancing classes, the parties, and the subscription dances where little boys meet little girls. "I have to screen my list of boys' names so carefully," says Mrs. William Tew, the social secretary, "to see that someone who doesn't belong, or of whom parents would disapprove, is not invited." Parents themselves begin screening the list of their children's friends even earlier — from the first days of nursery school.

Why is it considered so important for the rich to marry rich? There are many reasons. "It's better that way," says a New York mother. "Then the young people will have the same interests, the same backgrounds." Oil and water don't mix. Also — always — there is the question of the money. When rich weds rich, there is less chance that one of the partners is a fortune hunter (though there is nothing to prevent a person with a fortune from setting out to bag an even larger fortune;

not all fortune hunters are poor). When money marries money, the union of wealth not only assures that the young couple will have few worries over household bills, and few arguments over who is spending too much of whose income, but it provides, for the generation following and the generation following that, an even greater financial cushion. There is less chance of the money's running out; instead, the wealth will grow more ancient, bringing even greater power and greater respectability, into perpetuity. This is why so many of the rich have a curious habit of growing richer. And, if there is one consolation for an old-rich-new-rich marriage, it is that, two generations from now, the money will all be old-rich.

Still, the marriage of two rich young people is less like a giant corporate merger than it sometimes seems from reading the newspapers. Instead, the money is joined in a kind of polite legal handshake. It is set up in this manner by attorneys and the trust officers of banks. The money is only married up to a point. Beyond that, against the unfortunate but very practical possibility of divorce, it is kept separate. In this way, when Thomas M. Bancroft, Jr., (whose mother was of the banking Woodwards, and related to the Astors) married Margaret (Peggy) Bedford, of a considerable Standard Oil fortune, it was called "a perfect marriage," and the Bancroft and Bedford fortunes joined hands. When the couple divorced, to allow Mrs. Bancroft to become Princess Charles d'Arenberg, the two fortunes slid apart and returned smoothly to their respective sources. Alimony is considered untidy, and, when both parties to a divorce are wealthy, it is quite unnecessary. In contrast to the Bancroft-Bedford arrangement was the $5,500,000 share of another Standard Oil fortune demanded, and won, by Mrs. Winthrop ("Bobo") Rockefeller in the 1950's — a tabloid hullabaloo that causes all Rockefellers to this day to turn pale when it is mentioned in their presence.

Often things go wrong when two fortunes attempt to disengage themselves in a divorce action. One California bridegroom, in a happy nuptial daze, put his signature to a number of legal documents in the process of taking a wife, without reading any of them carefully. A year or so later, in the process of a particularly bitter divorce suit, he discovered that one item he had acquired — for reasons that are still unclear to him — was half-ownership of a piece of real estate upon which his wife's parents' swimming pool reposed. To the distress of his in-laws, and to the dismay of their lawyers who could devise no legal way of excluding him, he came regularly to swim throughout the divorce proceedings, sometimes bringing large parties of friends but always, he says, "Being careful to swim only at my end of the pool."

In the East not long ago, a pretty girl whose homes are in New York City and Sands Point, Long Island, was more foresighted about divorce. While she and her young husband were honeymooning in Mexico they decided, after a particularly altitudinous evening on the town, to get a Mexican divorce. As she explains, "We were having such a marvelous, glorious time — a perfect holiday. We got the divorce for a lark, mostly. We were there, it was easy to get, and we thought — after all — we might want to use it *some* day." With their speedily obtained decree, the couple flew merrily home to New York, framed the document and hung it on their bathroom wall where, from friends, it provoked appropriate laughter. But, says the wife, "Later on we got to feeling rather funny about it. We didn't really know whether we were married or not. Some of our friends said the Mexican thing wasn't really legal, but others said it was. If we weren't married, it didn't seem quite right for us to be living together. So we sort of drifted apart . . ."

They have continued to drift. The young woman remarried, but she and her first husband are still "the best of friends," and the first husband continues to sail his boat out to Sands Point on summer weekends to visit his former wife's parents and to call on his former wife who is sometimes there for the weekend too. Sometimes, if the second husband doesn't happen to be in the vicinity, the former couple appear at parties together, "acting just like newlyweds."

There is always a good deal of clucking and headshaking about the morals of the rich. And it is true that when there is plenty of money a divorce can be both cheap and easy. But among a larger and less publicized group of American rich, divorces are not supposed to happen. Divorce is not considered respectable or practical. It casts an unfavorable light upon the families, and on the way they live, and on the money. It blurs, rather than strengthens, the bloodline. And, because the press pays more attention to divorces among the rich (HEIRESS SEEKS DIVORCE, scream the headlines) than it does to divorces among the poor, a divorce can be embarrassing. In this group, a marriage is supposed to last and last and last. It need not be happy, but it should last. Husbands and wives may stop speaking to each other, but they should not separate. American Society has, in fact, erected for itself a few bulwarks — flimsy, perhaps, but bulwarks nonetheless — to try to see to it that its marriages do last. One of these is Philadelphia's antique rule against divorced people attending its Assembly Ball. And, in Philadelphia, when one of the well-placed Ingersolls told his mother that he was getting along poorly with his wife, his mother sympathized and said, "Then I think you should take a mistress, dear."

Caring for the wealth and caring for the bloodline, and seeing that each reaches a not only ripe but indestructible old age, go hand in hand, but — in assembling the perfect marriage — concessions can be made in one direction or the other. An ample helping of Old Family and less money, on one side, can usually be brilliantly matched with a smaller amount of family, and *more* money, on the other. And a great family name — of the magnitude of Adams, Talbott, or Howard — can make up for almost anything, even total poverty. An Englishman, who had been visiting in Philadelphia, said recently, "I think that if a rich, social Philadelphia girl married an aging alcoholic homosexual in a wheelchair without a penny to his name — if the name were Cadwalader or Ingersoll or Biddle or Drexel or Roberts or Wister or Chew — everyone would say, 'What a marvelous marriage!' "

For though a divorce may be awkward it is as nothing compared with the disaster — and the cost — that can result from a *mésalliance*. When the late William Woodward, Jr., married Ann Eden Crowell, a former actress and model, and the daughter of a Middle Western streetcar conductor, his parents were models of stiff-upper-lip behavior. And, when young Mrs. Woodward later accidentally shot and killed her husband, Mrs. Woodward, Sr.'s lip was the stiffest anyone had ever seen. "Bill Woodward would be alive today, if he hadn't married that actress," says one of the elder Mrs. Woodward's friends, and certainly no one can refute that statement. The Woodward shooting illustrated a couple of tangential points — that the young Woodwards were doing the customary upper-class thing in maintaining separate bedrooms, and that shooting one's husband does not get a woman, no matter how lowly born, removed from the *Social Register*; the younger Mrs. Woodward retains her place in its pages, along with her membership in the exclusive Piping Rock Club.

More recently, when the son of a wealthy Chicago manufacturer insisted upon marrying a pretty California girl of simple origins, the wedding was described by a guest as "all minks and Mr. John hats on the groom's side of the church, and all little cloth coats and bonnets on the bride's." It was hard to decide, this guest confessed, which side of the church looked more uncomfortable. The young husband, in an attempt to tone up his new in-laws in the only way he knew how, gave them a sizable gift of money. His in-laws then did something that, it seemed, they had always dreamed of doing should a windfall ever appear. They bought a pick-up truck and an enormous house trailer. When they drove this caravan to Chicago and parked it, complete with butane tanks and chemical toilets, on the sweeping drive of their son-in-law's parents' estate on the North Shore, the fiber that held the young marriage together began to weaken. Another cash gift was tried — it went for plastic awnings and window boxes for the trailer — before the young man headed for the divorce court, another unhappy reminder of the importance of "sticking to our kind."

"I've told my daughter," says one mother, "that if she wants to have a fling with a stranger she should for goodness' sake *have* it. But not for a minute is she to entertain the thought of *marrying* him." But runaway daughters are a recurring Society phenomenon, and look what finally happens to them. Popular candidates for these girls' partners seem to be chauffeurs, cowboys, ski instructors — with fewer chauffeurs than cowboys and ski instructors because so few people keep chauffeurs any more while, as Mrs. Tew says sadly, "Everybody skis, everybody goes West . . ." A Chicago debutante of a few seasons back ran off and married her cowboy. When last heard from she was in Wyoming, trying to raise money through her family and their business connections, to get her husband a ranch of his own. A San Francisco debutante, selecting a ski instructor, was last heard from in the mountains trying to raise money to buy *her* husband a ski lodge. Moving up fast to fill the spot being vacated by chauffeurs are service station attendants. Why? So many girls these days are being given little sports cars as graduation presents. Sooner or later, each little car needs gas. Will such marriages last? Hardly ever, in the opinion of Society. Furthermore, when the novelty of such a mixed marriage has worn off, when it is time for the knot to be untied, it cannot be untied without cost.

Several years ago, Patricia Procter, heiress to a Procter & Gamble soap fortune (and a distant relative, through a complicated series of marriages, to the runaway Gamble Benedict) decided to marry Thomas Greenwood, the good-looking son of a London greengrocer. There was the customary consternation in the New York social world in which Miss Procter moved. In fact, her peppery grandmother (a curious parallel, ten years earlier, to Gamble Benedict's grandmother, for Mrs. Procter was also her granddaughter's legal guardian and controlled her inheritance), expressed more than consternation. "Granny," as Mrs. Sanford Procter was called, was so put out with the whole situation that, when arguments and blandishments and entreaties failed, she refused to attend the wedding, a relatively flossy affair with a reception following it at the Colony Club in New York. Guests at the reception bravely tried to ignore Mrs. Procter's conspicuous absence, but as one guest put it, "Granny was everywhere in that room!" (Leaving the reception line, after politely chatting with the young bridegroom, another guest moaned, "Oh, God! He even has a Cockney accent!")

Things seemed to go well enough for the young couple after their marriage, but friends soon became concerned when the Greenwoods moved into an apartment at The Mayfair House on Park Avenue, a couple of floors away from Granny's apartment, and when the groom began to seem more interested in the prompt delights of room service than in going to his job as a car salesman in New Jersey, an employment he suddenly appeared to find decidedly dull. Trouble, of a predictable variety, was not far off. There were quarrels, a separation, a reconciliation, more quarrels, and all the while Granny was right where a good granny should be, just a short elevator hop away. Soon the affair erupted unpleasantly in the newspapers. Greenwood was suing Granny for alienation of affections. Mrs. Procter, Greenwood testified, "through her great wealth," had systematically gone about breaking up the marriage. But what Greenwood wanted, it seemed, was not his wife's love back. He wanted money. There was a public scene in which Granny, a small and erect figure in aristocratic black, made a dramatic appearance in court. Love letters, and the opposite of love letters, were hauled out of dresser drawers where they should have stayed, and were read, and terrible accusations — many too spicy even for the tabloids — flew shrilly about. In the end, Greenwood lost his case, and disappeared. The couple were divorced. Patricia Greenwood, a sadly disillusioned young grass widow, withdrew from New York social life. Mrs. Sanford Procter continues to winter in Manhattan and summer at her farm in Massachusetts, which is called "Fish House," * where virtually every stick of furniture and item of decoration is in the shape of, or bears the stamp of, a finny creature — as though a reminder that a fish cannot survive outside its water.

Of young Mrs. Greenwood, her friends say, "She should have known. After all, the difference in their backgrounds. . . ."

* Not to be confused with the ancient Philadelphia men's club of the same name, and of which more will be said later.

8

Lovely, Lovely Ladies

ONE Sunday morning a couple of years ago, devotees of the New York *Times* crossword-puzzle page found themselves confronted with the following problem and partial solution:

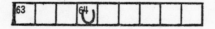

While, manfully, doers of the big weekly puzzle tried to find a nine-letter word to fit the definition, members of the Junior League themselves, girlfully, tried to make the solution be "volunteer." But try as they might, "volunteer" would not mesh with the vertical words around it. Less parochial puzzle-workers came to the correct solution more quickly — which, alas, was "debutante." So distressed were members of the Junior League that many letters were written to the *Times* about it, and an entire article on the subject appeared in the Junior League magazine.

That Sunday crossword, and the trouble the Leaguers had with it, illustrates the curious dichotomy that exists within the Junior League today. League members are, indeed, volunteers. A specific amount of weekly toil and endeavor in behalf of some approved good cause is a requisite to continuing membership. But League members are also, to a large extent, debutantes and former debutantes. In smaller cities that do not have organized debutante balls, joining the Junior League is the accompaniment, if not almost the equivalent, of coming out. Still, Leaguers do not like to be known as "just debutantes," because, as one Leaguer puts it, "That makes us sound as though we're dilettantes who are afraid to get our hands dirty." Nor do they like to be considered "just volunteers." That, as the same lady says, sounds "pretty dreary," as though Leaguers' hands were wrist-deep in mud most of the time. In other words, Junior Leaguers are unwilling to give up completely either half of their disparate organization, though the two halves do not seem to blend very comfortably, if at all.

This problem is currently reflected, in other forms, all across the pastel-hued landscape of American Society: should "society" be written with a capital or lower-case s, for example? Most people who are "in Society" today would seem to want to have it a little of both, but such a compromise would call for a new kind of typography. "In 1904 and 1905, when I came out in New York, Society was still written with a capital S," says Mrs. Corinne Robinson Alsop Cole, a niece of President Theodore Roosevelt, very definitely a member of the New York Old Guard and (by her first marriage to the late Joseph Wright Alsop) the mother of columnist Joseph Alsop and *Saturday Evening Post* editor Stewart Alsop. (Mrs. Cole, from the bastion of her farm in Avon, Connecticut, is also, along with such formidable figures as Mrs. Winthrop Aldrich and Mrs. Alice Roosevelt Longworth, one of the towering *grandes dames* of the entire East.) "It was a period of an elite Four Hundred," she says, "the last year of Mrs. Astor's great balls. The list of debutantes was small. Forebears, not fortunes, gave the 'open sesame' to parties at the great private houses."

In those days, Mrs. Cole recalls, a young woman who made her debut was simultaneously made aware of the great and pressing obligations that family and social position imposed upon her. Society was a serious business and upon entering it a girl lifted her share of the city's poor, beleaguered, and untidy masses upon her fragile and well-bred shoulders. The community's unfortunate — its sick, its blind, its orphans, and its unwed mothers — became a burden that would be hers for life. As a result, says Mrs. Cole, coming out was not so much "a debutante party" as "a terrifying ordeal." In those days, a girl was "polished" rather than educated, and part of the polishing instructed her as to her responsibilities to those less well-off than she. "The word 'charity' was not in disrepute then, as it is now," says Mrs. Cole. "We *all* had our charities. We had local families whom we considered deserving, whom we cared for. And if a project seemed worthy we supported it with time and money. But we did it on a personal basis." Society was, for the young Corinne Robinson, "the small group of people we knew," and, in her debutante year, Miss Robinson joined a smallish organization established by a group of her friends and contemporaries called The Junior League for the Promotion of Settlement Houses "for the benefit of the poor and the betterment of the city."

Just three years earlier, in 1901, two well-connected young ladies — Miss Mary Harriman (the daughter of railroad king E. H. Harriman, and the sister of New York's ex-Governor Averell Harriman) and Miss Nathalie Henderson (later Mrs. Joseph R. Swan) — were driving down Riverside Drive in a snappy four-wheeled sulky behind Gulnair, Mary Harriman's trotting horse. On that excursion, Nathalie Henderson Swan later recalled, Mary Harriman said (in the somewhat stilted phrases Mrs. Swan has attributed to her), "There is an exceptionally large number of debutantes coming out our year. What can we do to make it a particularly good year, and to show that we recognize an obligation to the community besides having a good time?" Miss Harriman promptly answered her own question. She had heard about the College Settlement House on Rivington Street, and said, "We will work for the benefit of the College Settlement." The Junior League was born.

That year, a little entertainment was presented at the house of another debutante, and about $1000 was raised — not a large sum, perhaps, considering the wealth of the young ladies involved (E. H. Harriman alone was presumed to be worth a good $200,000,000), but, when one considers that this was in an era when young women were not supposed to handle money, and that the $1000 must have represented the girls' carefully hoarded piggy-bank cash, it is impressive. The idea (after all, there had never been anything quite like a debutantes' *organization* in the perfumed world of the Four Hundred) spread like wildfire. Debutantes clamored to get into the League, and other cities, hearing what New York was up to, raced to start leagues of their own. Boston came next and then, in quick succession: Brooklyn; Portland, Oregon; Baltimore; Philadelphia; and Chicago. "We had made it amusing," said Nathalie Henderson Swan modestly, "and also *chic* to belong."

This helps explain some of the problems that today surround the Junior League — why, particularly in the largest American cities, it is felt to have lost some of its status. It became too amusing, and too chic. Everybody and her sister wanted to belong. Today, there are more than sixteen hundred members of the New York Junior League. The Boston League has over fourteen hundred, and the San Francisco League has eleven hundred-plus. All together — busily manipulating puppets, restoring historic houses, manning mobile museums, pushing book carts through hospital corridors, singing Christmas carols to shut-ins, planning children's concerts and zoo trips, putting on operettas, plays, and films, organizing educational television stations, teaching arts, crafts, science and language courses, leading nature hikes, telling fairy stories to orphans, brightening the twilight days of the elderly by hanging pictures in their hospital rooms, stuffing envelopes and licking stamps, dancing their feet off in Junior League Follies, cheering the wounded and uplifting the imprisoned — there are more than eighty-five thousand Junior Leaguers in over two hundred cities in the United States, Canada, and Mexico. Over them all the mother-hen Association of Junior Leagues of America — with headquarters located chic-ly in a suite in New York's Waldorf-Astoria — keeps track of all the scattered League chickens, and attempts to impose a centralized system and discipline. To those who knew the Junior League in the drawing-room era, these figures and growth are "fantastic," "incredible," and "really rather frightening." "I simply cannot believe," says one woman, "that all those thousands of young women are *really* in Society today." Though Mrs. Cole is loyal to her old organization, she does not quite seem to believe it either. But, rather than admit that the Junior League has changed, she prefers to say that Society has changed.

Nowhere are the difficulties of big-city Junior Leagues more apparent than in the Pine Room of the New York Junior League clubhouse in East Eightieth Street where, at lunchtime, the ladies gather for a pre-luncheon cocktail served by a white-coated bartender, and where trays of Bloody Marys circulate. (The Bloody Mary, says one member, "is sort of the traditional New York Junior League drink — and they make yummy ones here.") The clubhouse, formerly the town house of

Vincent Astor, is handsomely paneled, furnished with French Provin-
cial furniture, and features a splendid curved staircase ("perfect for
wedding receptions") and a cuisine so exceptional that even the husbands of League ladies enjoy coming there for dinner. But the League
ladies themselves are fond of speaking of their mansion as though it
only offered shelter of a sort most Spartan and austere. "But this place
is *nothing*," they remind wide-eyed visitors, "compared with the old
clubhouse in East Seventy-first Street. *That* had a marvelous big ballroom, an indoor swimming pool, squash courts, and its own hairdress-
ing salon. But during the war it just seemed *wrong* for us to have a big
place like that, and we moved over to this little place in 1949." At the
same time, lest anyone accuse the League of living too plushly even in
the *old* clubhouse, Junior Leaguers hurry to point out that, contrary to
"that persistent rumor," the Seventy-first Street place did *not* include
a nurse and baby-sitting service for members to free them for good
works. "It's ridiculous to think we'd need the League to provide us with
sitters," an older League member says. "Why, in those dear, golden
days we all had servants and nannies of our own."

It is in the Pine Room that the arguments most often arise over just
what today's Junior League *is*, as well as what it isn't, and what it
means to the world outside, and what it doesn't. "We're often thought
of as a purely *social* organization," said one Bloody-Mary-sipping member at a gathering the other day. "People who aren't in the League
don't realize the tremendous amount of work we do. We're considered
snobs." Others agreed that it was other people — "outsiders" — who
brand the League snobbish. Those in the League don't consider it
snobbish at all.

"But isn't *everything* snobbish, really?" said another lady. "I mean,
we're like a sorority. We want people in the League who are *nice*, and
share the same interests, and get along with the other members."

Several others agreed that everything was, in a way, snobbish. "For
instance," said one woman, "I live in the heart of Yorkville and there's
a Hungarian social club right around the corner. Now, if my husband
decided to drop into that Hungarian club for a drink some Saturday
night, do you think they'd admit him? They would *not!* They'd throw
him right out on his ear — as he *should* be thrown out."

"Yes," agreed another. "The Junior League isn't snobbish — just selective."

"If," said one, "you asked someone like a taxi driver what the Junior League meant to *him,* he'd say, 'Yeah, the Junior League — a rich girls' hangout.' But we know differently."

"On the other hand," said another, "we do come from a higher economic bracket, and Junior League affairs do rate Society-page attention."

"But don't we want to get *off* the Society page?" put in one woman. "Isn't that our trouble?"

"Well, yes," agreed the first. "But we don't want to get off the Society page *entirely,* do we?"

"I think," said one woman with finality, "that similarity of *education* is the greatest equating factor in the League — and similarity of interests."

"But we wouldn't hold it against a girl if she went to school in Europe," put in another.

"To me," said one lady, "the Junior League is simply one of several pleasant clubs in New York City." And so it went.

Of the many pleasant women's clubs in New York City — which include the Colony Club, the Cosmopolitan Club, the River Club (a family club), and such hereditary ladies' societies which exist, for the most part, without clubhouses, such as the Daughters of the American Revolution (the Daughters use the Junior League clubhouse), the Colonial Dames of America, the National Society of Colonial Dames of America in the State of New York, the Daughters of the Cincinnati and the Daughters of Holland Dames — only one enjoys top social prestige and top Society patronage, and that is the Colony Club. In Boston, the Colony Club's equivalent is the Chilton Club; in Philadelphia, the Acorn Club; in San Francisco, the Francisca Club. When invited to lunch "at the Colony," a New York lady is expected to tell — by the tone of voice and inflection — whether her hostess means the Colony Club or the elegant but slightly more flashy Colony restaurant. In the sedate and serenely still rooms of the Colony Club on Park Avenue are considered to gather New York's noblest and best women. And it is typical of the Junior League's ambiguous and uncertain position that there should be considerable internecine warfare between the League and the Colony over which is the "more social" or the "more important" club. And this is a little odd because the two clubs have little in common but the sex of their membership and their formal interior decor.

The Junior League's stated *raison d'être* is "a desire to participate, through volunteer service, in the community's health, education, welfare, and culture." The Colony Club has no such lofty aims and is a social club, pure and simple. Yet the battleground between Sixty-second and Park and Eightieth and Lexington is strewn with the aspersions the two clubs cast back and forth about each other.

Membership in the two overlaps rather little. The Colony seems to select its members almost exclusively from the pages of the *Social Register;* the League no longer does. As a result, Colony Club members smile sadly and say that the Junior League has gone "terribly, terribly downhill," and "just isn't what it used to be." Junior Leaguers counter by saying that the Colony Club is "stuffy and dull," and is filled with "very, very old ladies." ("They say things like that about the Colony," says a Colony member, "simply because they can't get in." Replies a Junior Leaguer with a brittle laugh, "But who'd *want* to get in?" "Sour grapes," insists the Colony.)

A newcomer to New York from Austin, Texas, made her first social move in the city by transferring her Austin Junior League affiliation to New York. The New York League likes to say that it "isn't always easy" to transfer from one of the minor Leagues out of town to the big-city League, but the Austin woman accomplished it without difficulty. She soon realized, however, that a more significant social goal still lay ahead of her — the Colony Club. Lunching with a Colony member who she hoped would propose her name, she cited, among her qualifications, her League membership. The Colony member gasped and said, "Good heavens! I wouldn't mention *that* if I were you!" (The Austin lady kept mum about the League, got into the Colony, and now snubs the League.)

The situation is different in other, smaller cities — cities which New Yorkers loftily lump together and call "the provinces." In such places as Knoxville, Mobile, Spokane, Great Falls, South Bend — even Austin — the Junior Leagues are composed of women who feel themselves to be from the very top drawer of local Society, and it is unwise to treat them otherwise.

A New York woman had this demonstrated to her forcefully when her husband's business required that the family move from New York

to Oklahoma City. Being a member of one of New York's proud families, she was promptly rushed by Oklahoma City Society, and was invited to join the Oklahoma City Junior League. But, according to a
friend, she made the naïve mistake of saying, "No thank you. In New
York, you see, the best people don't join the League." Great beyond
description was the wrath of the Oklahoma City ladies, and the new
arrival soon found that she had been placed in the social deep-freeze
by everyone in the town who mattered — a circumstance which, besides making her lonely, caused her husband some embarrassment in
his business relationships.

It did not take the lady long to see her error, but it took a longer
time — and a series of blandishments, persuasions, letters from family
and friends across the country, and from one particular friend from
New York (who had been smarter when *she* had moved to Oklahoma
City) who actually threatened to blackball every new member the
Oklahoma League wanted to take in if her repentant friend were not
accepted — before the League grandly deigned to include the hum-
bled and contrite woman in its ranks.

Just what is "wrong" with the League in New York, and why "the
best people" eschew it, is a complicated question to answer. There are
several answers, actually, and they apply not only to New York but to
Boston, Philadelphia, and San Francisco as well, for in all four cities
the League occupies a social position somewhat below the top. Naturally, no loyal Leaguer in any of these cities will admit that there is
anything wrong, but a few disloyal ones will. One New York woman
who is "really much fonder" of the Colony Club maintains a dilatory
Junior League connection because, as she puts it, "The League *makes*
you do things that you probably should do, but probably wouldn't do if
there weren't something like the League around to make you do them,
and that's good." She inveighs against the run-of-the-mill Leaguer,
however, for the following reasons: "I hate to sound snobbish, but
those League women just don't *do* things the way we do. For instance,
they start calling you by your first name too quickly. My name happens to be Caroline, and I was no sooner introduced than everybody
started calling me Carol. I think I dress simply and nicely, but *really*
— those women are so *over*dressed. They wear cocktail dresses for
lunch. And the hairdos! I went to a meeting the other day in a woman's house, and it could not have been grimmer. She served curry —

for lunch! You could smell it in the elevator lobby. We all had to fill our plates and then sprinkle different things on our food from a lot of little pots. And her apartment! Over the mantel she'd put some hideous ornament that I'd seen at Altman's for eleven dollars and ninety-five cents, and all the women *raved* about her apartment. She confessed that she'd decorated it herself. Do you see what I mean?"

To see what this woman means, to understand the crimes of first names too soon, of overdressing, of decorating your own apartment with department store figurines, and of serving curry for lunch — you have only to appreciate the hazy but still palpable line which, in big-city Society, separates "our kind" from "not our kind." This explains the persistent comparison in New York between the League and the Colony Club. The Colony draws the line firmly. It — and its comparable clubs in other cities — is felt to be peopled by *real* Society. The Junior League, to a greater or lesser extent, is populated by climbers. And climbers, of course, are the most snobbish souls in the entire Society picture.

The Association of Junior Leagues of America is cautiously vague on the subject of membership requirements. They murmur such generalities as "Members should be compatible," and "Members should be interested in the community," and "Members should meet Junior League standards." What are Junior League standards? "If a woman is judged to be Junior League material, she is considered to have met Junior League standards." Just as each city sets its own dues — which range from ten dollars a year up to one hundred dollars, according to the community — so does each city decide for itself whom it will take in, and sets up its own mechanics for doing so. In some Leagues, members are voted in by a simple show of hands; in others, an elaborate sorority-house ritual of secrecy is followed, and new members are informed of their acceptance with girlish cries of "Surprise! Surprise!" and are expected to shed a few tears of joy at the news. Because the League likes to keep the emphasis on the *junior* part of its name, no woman can vote or hold office after she reaches the age of forty. She is then called a sustaining member, and is considered "a trained volunteer, active in her community." Of course, women being the way they are about age, this rule is a delicate one to enforce and, often a woman will be tactfully treated as an active member while, secretly, her name is placed on the sustaining list. As for women who refuse to reveal their ages, one woman says, "Every now and then we hear a member say, 'You know, that rule about becoming inactive at forty is *silly*. Let's change it.' That's a dead giveaway that that girl's fortieth birthday is just around the corner."

In growing to its present size, the Junior League has accepted a number of Jewish members — particularly in the larger cities. This, too, startles the Old Guard. On the other hand, the Jewish membership is still significantly small and, as one member candidly puts it, "Most Leagues just take in a token number of Jewish girls — enough so they won't be called anti-Semitic." At the same time, many Jewish girls — recalling the state of affairs a generation ago when the League was unquestionably discriminatory nearly everywhere — refuse to belong to the Junior League when invited. As far as is known, there has never been a Negro League member.

Meanwhile, nobody denies that the Junior Leagues make important contributions in a number of areas. In Raleigh, the League sponsors a cerebral palsy clinic. A nursery school is League maintained in Kansas City. In Evanston, the Institute for Language Disorders is sponsored by the Evanston League in conjunction with Northwestern University. Also in Evanston, a now famous Mothers' Milk Bank was a League brainstorm, hit upon when a League member discovered a shortage of this commodity in local hospitals. Now, according to the League, new mothers in the organization put their babies immediately on formula or hire wet nurses so that they may donate their own milk and, if the picture of well-bred young women hurrying to the hospital on schedule to be milked seems a trifle grotesque, it is nonetheless said that these women fill a vital role. The Mothers' Milk Bank has been widely copied elsewhere.

In Tulsa, a children's medical center has been developed by the League. The list goes on and on. The AJLA reports that some five hundred specific health and welfare projects are being kept afloat by Leagues across the country, and that as many as a hundred and twenty-five thousand volunteer jobs for various other community organizations are tackled by Leaguers in a busy year — and these figures do not include the tens of thousands of ladies who volunteer for special fund-raising jobs, year in, year out.

New York City's Commissioner of Welfare has nothing but admiration for the work done by the New York Junior League, which he considers an important force in the city's life, and other organizations that have sought help from the Junior League pronounce themselves "astonished and delighted" with the cooperation and efficiency of the Leaguers, and are impressed with the thoroughness of the groundwork and training in welfare operations that the League gives its young members in the provisional training course.

True, there are moments when the Junior League seems to go off the track a bit in its zeal for doing good, as happened awhile back at a fund-raising party in Philadelphia. At the party, chances a dollar each were sold for door prizes. The prizes had been donated by Leaguers and their friends, and many of them had considerable value. Too late, apparently, it was discovered that there were more prizes than chances, and one guest at the party reports that he won — for an outlay of one dollar — a handsome pair of Sheffield silver candelabra, a radio-phonograph, a Waring Blender, and a woman's silver-fox muff. It was later estimated that, though $1500 had been raised for the worthy cause at hand, the prizes given away to Junior Leaguers and their friends had been worth close to $15,000 — a philanthropic circumstance that might boggle the imagination of a Harvard economist.

Another dilemma, this one of a moral rather than a financial nature, was faced by a well-to-do young Leaguer from New Jersey who must remain nameless. At *her* Junior League function, it was decreed that door prizes should be articles made by the Junior Leaguers themselves. "I kept trying to think of something I could make," says this untalented but well-intentioned lady, "and I couldn't think of anything. And I kept putting it off. At the last minute, I knew I had to turn in *something*. So I dashed into New York and bought a pair of artificial lemon trees made out of wire and ceramic fruit at a darling little shop on Second Avenue." The handmade lemon trees, imported from Italy, cost her three hundred dollars. "Then," says the lady, "at the party the most awful thing happened. My lemon trees — which I'd *had* to say I made myself, you see — were the absolute hit of the evening. People kept saying they never dreamed I was so clever, and several of my friends asked me if I'd please make some little lemon trees for *them!*" So far, the poor woman has bought two more pairs of lemon trees at the Second Avenue shop. She is the best-known lemon-tree-maker in her section of the state — all to support the Junior League's reputation for integrity. If she keeps it up, according to one friend who is aware of the costly deception, she may soon have to apply to the Junior League for aid herself.

But, for all the Junior League does, it cannot seem to solve its personality problem — whether it should be wholly chic, or wholly dutiful, whether it is a collection of snobs or social workers, post-debutantes or do-gooders. So it continues to be a little of each. Nowhere is the schizophrenia more apparent than in Bridgeport, Connecticut. The Bridgeport Junior League starts out with a special problem — its very name. "Bridgeport," says Mrs. Bradley Johnson of that League, in a minor miracle of understatement, "isn't really the most *attractive* city in the world." And, she quickly points out, "Most of the League members, of course, live here in Fairfield." Why, then, can it not be called the Fairfield Junior League? Well, Fairfield is a wealthy commuter suburb, quite short of folk needy enough to require the ministrations of a Junior League. So Bridgeport, a name redolent of brassworks and ferocious air pollution, it must be.

One of the most important operations of the Bridgeport League is its Thrift Shop, which the Fairfield ladies operate. The Thrift Shop is located "in a very run-down section of the city" — Bridgeport, that is — but it is in that sort of neighborhood that thrift shops find their customers. As the Fairfield ladies say, rolling their eyes as if envisioning rapists and purse-snatchers, "At least it's near a bus stop." It is hard work manning — or womaning — the Bridgeport Thrift Shop. "We get all kinds coming in for bargains — people from the lowest walks of life." Work there can be "depressing," but, when a shopper's face lights up at the sight of a true bargain, it becomes "rewarding." "They tell us all their problems," says Mrs. Johnson, "but, you know, I really don't think they know one of us from another. I mean, to them we all look alike! I suppose it's like what happens when an American goes to China and thinks that all Chinese look alike. But don't misunderstand. The League is *not* snobbish." (Later, a more candid member of the Bridgeport League added, "She says the League isn't snobbish. Well, it is.")

Junior Leagues everywhere — and the AJLA itself — are aware that the League has "image" problems, that it is often regarded as a group of rich women whose chief activities are socializing and being exclusive. Such well-publicized events as the New York League's great Mardi Gras Ball may actually add to this reputation. (The Mardi Gras

Ball is often televised and, when it is, it earns excellent ratings.)* The
Ball nets as much as fifty thousand dollars for the League's welfare
work. But its glamorous, dressy, and champagne-sipping aspects are
what the public notices. "The League has *many* areas of interest," says
a New York Leaguer. "Is it wrong if once a year we turn out for a little
fun? The rest of the time we try to help — wherever we feel our volunteers can make a real contribution. The purpose of the League is
volunteer service, and each year our members contribute more than
three hundred thousand hours to New York City!"

"You see only one side of the League here in the Pine Room," one
woman added, sipping her Bloody Mary.

"We may not be drudges, but we get a lot accomplished," said another.

"And, furthermore, the women who belong to the New York
League are — well, just lovely, lovely people. Lovely ladies."

And it's true. The Junior League today continues to embrace the
same double purpose that Mary Harriman and Nathalie Henderson
conceived for it in 1901 — to toil honestly and well for worthwhile
causes, and yet to be "amusing" and "chic" at the same time. Filling
those three hundred thousand woman hours in New York are, among
others, the Junior League Puppeteers — a beloved group that has become a League institution — who present such favorites as *Hansel and
Gretel* and *Nestor, the Talking Horse* to the young in hospitals, settlement houses, and child-care centers. Other volunteers work with
Puerto Rican and other immigrant youngsters to help them improve
their reading and mastery of English. ("In this program," one Leaguer
explains, "we've found that one of the tricks is to give a child reading
matter that relates to his surroundings. 'Farmer Brown went out to
milk the cow' means nothing to a city child. So our texts say things
like, 'The bus roared down Columbus Avenue.'") The League also
trains junior high school boys and girls as junior aides in after-school
day-care centers and play centers for smaller children. Though most
Leaguers confess that they're fondest of working with children, the
New York League also works with the Swope Community Center, a
housing development for the elderly, and the League pays the salary of
a professional director of the program. The League has also offered a

* In 1960, for instance, the Mardi Gras Ball pulled an "Arbitron" rating of 25.2,
compared with 7.8 for Jack Paar in the same hour on a competing channel.

series of English-language courses to exceptionally well-educated for-
eign-born arrivals in New York, and Leaguers with language skills
teach these classes themselves at the clubhouse. "We've been criticized for offering these courses only to those who have had superior
educations or backgrounds in their own countries," one woman says
— facing up, once again, to that old unpleasant word — "but the reasons are *not* snobbish. *Really*. It's just because we feel that these superior foreign people will learn English faster and, when they do, will be
able to fill more important roles in the community."

"Still," said another woman, "we get some awfully peculiar-*looking*
people in here at night, even though they're supposed to be superior.
Not to sound snobbish, of course."

A tray of whiskey sours came bobbing across the Pine Room, and
someone exclaimed, "Look! Whiskey sours! Who are *they* for?"

"They must be for the New Jersey Leagues," someone said.
"They're having a meeting downstairs."

"New *Jersey!*" said still another woman. "What on earth are *they*
doing here?"

"Well," said the second woman, "they asked to use our clubhouse,
and, after all, they're Junior Leaguers *too*. We couldn't really refuse
fellow Junior Leaguers, could we?"

"But New *Jersey*," the first woman persisted. "New *Jersey* . . ."

Perhaps the saddest Junior League story of all involves a newlywed
young woman whose husband's job required that the couple move
from New York City to Bluffton, Indiana. In New York, the bride had
been a member of the stately Colony Club, and she was certain she
would not find anything approximating its equivalent in Bluffton. She
decided, therefore, to settle on the Junior League — if there was one.
She had been in Bluffton only a few days when she received a caller
representing the Welcome Wagon. While the Welcome Wagon lady
was telling her all about Bluffton's shops and services, the newcomer
interrupted to ask, hesitantly, "Is there Junior League in Bluffton?"

The Welcome Wagon woman looked briefly uncertain, then
brightened and said, "Well, honey, I know they've got a Little League
and a Midget League — but a *Junior* League? To tell the truth, honey,
that's one I've just never heard of."

9

The Club Convention

NOT long ago, to their dismay, the heirs of a prominent Philadelphian read in his obituary notice, "Mr. —— was a member of the Philadelphia Club and the Racquet Club." The deceased's son picked up the telephone, called the editor of the paper and demanded a retraction. "He was a member of the *Rabbit,* not the Racquet Club!" the son explained. When the editor apologized and added, "But does it really make all that much difference?" the son exploded, "But it makes a *world* of difference! A *world!*"

The difference between the exclusive Philadelphia Racquet Club, and the ultra-exclusive Old Philadelphia Rabbit Club is clear enough. The Rabbit has only eighty to a hundred members, compared with the somewhat more inclusive Racquet. But the Rabbit itself plays a weak second fiddle in Philadelphia to the redoubtable Fish House or, as it is officially called The State in Schuylkill. Social historians often point out that men's city social clubs in the United States are modeled on their counterparts in London. But Philadelphia's Fish House has been able to work it out the other way around — so that London, in fact, was copying Philadelphia. The Fish House calls itself "The oldest formally organized men's social club in the Anglo-Saxon (which is to say civilized) world." The important qualifier in this claim is "formally organized." Such famous London clubs as White's, St. James's, and Boodle's would, according to most standards, seem actually older, but Fish House members point out that the London clubs were not private clubs, but public coffee houses, until White's became "formally organized" in 1736. The Fish House, therefore, which formally organized in 1732, squeaks under the longevity wire. The Fish House membership is limited to thirty, plus a tiny handful of "apprentice" members, and so, though it is often said that "Nearly all Fish House members also belong to the Rabbit," all the members of the Rabbit do not belong to the Fish House. The Rabbit, by the way, is a relative stripling among Philadelphia men's clubs — founded and "formally organized" in 1861.

Both the Fish House and the Rabbit are, of all things, cooking clubs. If the Fish House specialized in cooking fish, and the Rabbit in rabbit, it would be simple enough, but the Rabbit is called the Rabbit because its original clubhouse stood on Rabbit Lane. Philadelphians nourish their parochialisms and eccentricities, and so the fact that these two clubs have no exact parallels in the Anglo-Saxon — or other — world is exactly as Philadelphia Society prefers it to be. In the Fish House, for instance, for over nine generations distinguished Philadelphia men who normally would not enter their own kitchens from one month to the next have put on long white aprons and strange wide-brimmed straw hats which members call "boaters" (but which look more like Chinese coolie hats* than traditional boaters) and, with ladles and saucepans and other implements of cuisine, prepare such delicacies as boola-boola soup and planked shad. The Fish House meets thirteen times a summer, from May to October, and at each of its lengthy and somewhat bibulous luncheons — Fish House Punch is the club's invention and its traditional specialty — each course is the responsibility of an individual member. Thus every member gets a try at several dishes during a season.

The "State in Schuylkill" aspect of the club is equally quaint, and even more tradition-bound. The club began as a "Fishing Company," one of several groups that gathered along the banks of the Schuylkill River (after a morning of fishing, members cooked their catch for lunch), but somewhere along the line the group that has descended as the Fish House got off on a novel tack. It decided that it was an inde-

---

* The similarity to coolie hats has been remarked upon by others, and so Fish House members make it a point to say, "These hats are of a pattern brought from China . . . early in the last century, and were worn by a high mandarin caste."

pendent Colony, with a separate government, its own laws, and its own officials. What justification in fact there was for this assumption is dim indeed. Nevertheless, the State in Schuylkill continues to this day to pretend that it is a separate state "in Schuylkill," even though it moved from Schuylkill in 1822 and, in 1888, moved from the Schuylkill River altogether to the banks of the Delaware where it now reposes. In 1781, the club formally joined the United States of America — even though the United States has never acknowledged its membership — but it continues to call its members "citizens," and among its elected officials are a Secretary of State, a Secretary of the Treasury, a Governor, Counsellors, Sheriff, and even a Coroner. Its headquarters — the club-house — is called "the Castle." When national Prohibition was imposed in the 1920's, the State in Schuylkill remembered that, though it was indeed a state, it had never ratified the United States Constitution. Prohibition, it argued, was an infringement of states' rights, but once again the Federal government seemed not to hear. If members of the Fish House approached these matters with tongue in cheek, that would be one thing, but they do not. They take them with intense seriousness, and any guest at the Fish House, confronted with its incorruptible ritual, is ill-advised to snicker. For example, meals traditionally begin with the toast, "To the memory of General Washington," followed by a second, "To the memory of Governor Morris." (Samuel Morris, Jr., was Governor of the State in Schuylkill from 1765 to 1811.) After past Governors have been toasted, there is a toast "To the President of the United States." During the Presidency of Franklin Delano Roosevelt, however, this part of the ritual was conspicuously omitted. The Rabbit, though newer, observes very similar rites, and complements the Fish House in that it holds its meetings — with meals, again, prepared by members — during the winter. The Rabbit can be said to surpass the Fish House in at least one matter. The recipe for Fish House Punch was leaked to the public around 1900, but the formula for the Rabbit's sacred grog is still a closely guarded secret. All that is known about Rabbit Punch is that it is brewed for twenty-four hours in "leather firkins," and is served hot.

Obviously, all men's social clubs are designed in part to allow men to remove themselves for a little while from the company of women, and doubtless one of the joys of a men's cooking club is that it challenges feminine domination of the kitchen, at least symbolically. Probably a very similar anti-woman feeling spawned San Francisco's famous Bohemian Club where, lest it be supposed that the ladies of Society controlled such cultural bailiwicks as music, theatre, and the dance, the gentlemen proposed to mix good fellowship and wine with a bit of antic art. The Bohemian Club has never claimed to be its own state of the Union, but it has more cause to than the Fish House; in addition to a spacious clubhouse on Nob Hill, which includes a theatre seating seven hundred and fifty, the club maintains a twenty-eight-hundred acre "Grove" in the Sierra Nevada mountains where, once a year, Bohemian Club members and their carefully chosen guests (President Eisenhower was one) gather and "encamp" for two weeks. Typical encampments include lectures, poetry readings, musical productions, spectacles of *son et lumière,* concerts by the club's own seventy-piece symphony orchestra and, of course, revels of a more alcoholic sort. Each Bohemian encampment opens with a campfire ceremony called "The Cremation of Care," and proceeds from there, with all entertainment designed, directed, and performed by members themselves. For years, the location of Bohemian Grove was — or so members solemnly insisted — a secret, and no one of the female sex was allowed to set foot on the territory (though ladies were admitted to the clubhouse in the city). As a result, lurid tales circulated about Bohemian Club encampments during which, it was said, primitive and erotic rites were celebrated by men from the *Social Register* and ladies, in Rubenesque disarray, of slightly lower social standing. Such tales — though club members naturally did little to put an end to them — were apparently exaggerated. Nowadays, though not admitted during the encampment period, wives and families of members may visit the Bohemian Grove for picnics. Most agree that it is a pretty and unsinful-looking spot.

The Bohemian Club is one of several descendants of New York's Century Association, the first "artistic" men's club designed, according to its founders in 1847, for "authors and artists," as well as for "gentlemen of any occupation provided their breadth of interest and . . . imagination make them sympathetic, stimulating, and congenial companions in the society of authors and artists." How closely this policy has been adhered to is a matter of debate, but the Century Association idea has been both durable and popular. In addition to the Bohemian, other clubs founded along the same artist-and-writer lines include the

Players, the Lambs, the Lotos, and the Coffee House in New York; St. Botolph's in Boston; the Franklin Inn Club in Philadelphia; the Cosmos Club in Washington, D.C.; the Cactus Club of Denver; and the Tavern Clubs of Boston and Chicago. Each maintains its own rules and rituals — such as the rule at the Coffee House that members, who sit family-style around circular tables, must not "talk shop," and that guests, furthermore, may not be introduced to members. As a result, a guest at the Coffee House is often in the dark as to the identity of his luncheon companions unless his host resorts to some such tactic as, "Well, if it isn't Woody Broun!" when a member appears at the table.

The no-ladies-allowed rule in men's clubs was, needless to say, one of the earliest to be challenged. Long before Lucy Stone, the women of American Society wanted — out of sheer curiosity and jealousy if nothing else — to have equal access to their husbands' hideaways. Every club, as a result, has its favorite story of this or that prominent Society woman who dressed as a man in order to gain entrance, and who, as the case may be, may or may not have succeeded. And, one by one, the barriers began collapsing. Interestingly enough, the conventional men's clubs — that is, the non-artistic — were the first to relax their rules. Boston's Somerset Club, from its very early days, had a ladies' dining room where women were admitted for the evening meal — though at lunchtime it is still strictly a male affair, and wives of members who may call for their husbands are unceremoniously placed on a horsehair sofa in a dimly lit waiting room. The Philadelphia Club, in contrast, was a long holdout. The Club insists that it was not until its centenary ball in 1934 that a female foot set foot on the premises. Now, however, women may come to the club for dinner on all but certain nights. In New York, the first club to admit ladies at the dinner hour was the Harmonie, a club of the city's German-Jewish elite. The Union Club, New York's oldest and grandest club of the Gentile elite (though, from its earliest days, it had a few Sephardic Lazaruses and Hendrickses among its membership, plus at least one German Jew, Adolphe Ladenburg, and, of course, August Belmont who "passed") soon followed suit. It is supposedly at the Union that a member, noticing a certain lady enter the club one evening, commented wryly to the doorman, "Is it now permitted for a member's mistress to enter the club at dinnertime?" To which the doorman is said to have imperturbably replied, "Only if she is the wife of another member, sir."

In Washington, women crept into the Metropolitan Club floor by floor starting, naturally, at the bottom. First the ground, and then the second floor of the clubhouse felt the imprint of the spiked heel, and presently a sign was posted at the foot of the third-floor staircase, reading: NO LADIES ALLOWED ON THE THIRD FLOOR FOR ANY PURPOSES WHATEVER. The ladies themselves made such fun of the way the sign was worded that soon, in embarrassment, it was removed, though ladies are still enjoined not to mount to the sacred floor and, so far at least, they have been obedient. The Harvard Club of New York, meanwhile, quaintly separates the sexes by making ladies use a separate entrance located barely an arm's length away from the crimson-painted main entrance. Inside the clubhouse, ladies and gentlemen are permitted to join one another. The Pacific Union Club, in San Francisco, though not as old as some of its counterpart men's clubs in the East, is said to have the cleanest record in the country when it comes to excluding women. The only concession the Pacific Union makes to the opposite sex is in one by-law which states that if a member should be stricken while in the clubhouse, and should be considered "in extremis," he may be permitted to have "one female nurse" in attendance.

While the women of American Society were busily and systematically invading their husbands' clubhouses, they were also forming clubs of their own — to the equal consternation of the men. New York's Colony Club (founded in 1903 by such as Mrs. John Jacob Astor III, Mrs. W. S. Rainsford, and a sister-in-law of the Junior League cofounder, Mrs. J. Borden Harriman) was designed to be as sexually exclusive as the Union, the Knickerbocker, and the Brook. Male clubmen were scandalized, and said flatly that the only reason a group of women would wish such an organization was to have a place to conduct clandestine love affairs, and to receive letters from their lovers — which gives a fair indication of the use some of the men of Society were putting *their* clubs to. The ladies airily replied that, as a matter of fact, having an extra letter box *was* one of their reasons for establishing the club. These were the golden years before the First World War when such controversies were as serious as any that arose. The idea of the women's social club caught on, and many others were established across the country. In New York, one of the most interesting was the Cosmopolitan Club, which is now roughly the feminine equivalent of the Century, drawing its membership largely from ladies who, though gently born and bred, toil in literature, music, and the arts. In the Cosmopolitan Club's first years following its founding in 1911, it had nowhere near such an intellectual cast. It was known, in fact, for its wild, night-long "revels" to which no men were admitted, and where the lady members, costumed according to the theme of the evening — a night in Rome, in Hong Kong, or in Araby — carried on with every bit as much alcoholic abandon as any camper in the Bohemian Grove. "At dawn, the halls and public rooms were strewn with wilted ladies," wrote one diarist of the time. Naturally, when word of such carryings-on reached the men, they were as anxious to get inside the women's clubs as the women had been to get inside the men's and, true to form, rumors began to circulate of men dressed as women, who had gained admission to such clubs as the Colony and Cosmopolitan. Clearly, the walls that separated the sexes were about to come tumbling down.

While all this was going on, another force was at work — eating at the single-sex club structure from within, as it were. This was the jealousy, rivalry, and competitiveness that has always characterized American Society. No sooner were there men's clubs in American cities than everyone was arguing over which one was the "best." The American club scene became a social battleground as it never was in England. Just as the Junior League and the Colony Club today spar over which is the more "important," so, in the old days, did the Cosmopolitan make it a three-sided battle in New York with members of various clubs snubbing each other, dropping each other from their guest lists, and blackballing each other from their clubs. The idea of "exclusivity" — of keeping people out — became the backbone of club life when, as sometimes happens, a club can also be oriented toward the more positive goal of taking people in. The men's clubs bickered and called each other names, and members were always stalking out of clubs never to come back again. Clubs splintered into other clubs. In New York, the Union League was founded by a "league" of ex-members of the Union Club who departed, angrily, at the time of the Civil War protesting that, despite its name, the Union had merely allowed a pro-Confederate member to resign, instead of expelling him bodily. The Knickerbocker Club — named after the patron saint of

New York City — was another Union Club spinoff, protesting that the Union was taking in too many members from out of town. When one of J. P. Morgan's friends was blackballed by the Union, Morgan simply built a club of his own — the Metropolitan.

Often the clubs squabbled over which had the better food and service, but the heart of the matter was really which had the higher social standing. The Harvard Club became renowned for its popovers — and still is. (When dining there, it is part of protocol to admire the popovers.) The Union League, so said its members, could not be outdone when it came to johnnycake. At the Racquet and Tennis Club, the *pièce de résistance* of any meal was the rice pudding. ("Would you join a club for its rice pudding?" sniffed members of other clubs.) The Brook Club was known for the overall excellence of its cuisine, as well as for its slippered and unobtrusive service (members are never presented with checks to sign; a soft-spoken servant follows each gentleman around, seeing to his needs), and also for the general grandeur of its operation. Guests of members of the Brook, for instance, are first escorted to the downstairs "Stranger's Room," where they may peruse an ancient edition of *Barron's* while waiting for their host.

Still, for all the clubs' attempts at elegance, there were perennial complaints and dissatisfactions. At the Knickerbocker a member complained that a waiter had "touched" him. He would say no more. The man's fellow members were puzzled, not knowing whether the waiter had made an inappropriate sexual advance, or had asked to borrow money. At last, however, it turned out that the waiter had tapped the member on the shoulder to call him to the telephone.

The battle of the sexes — in this case to be in on each others' doings — and the battle of the clubs themselves are certainly two factors which have brought both men's and women's clubs to their present somewhat diminished state of social importance. The day when such a club as the Union League could successfully abide by its rule of four — "no women, no dogs, no Democrats, no reporters" — has passed. The Club Idea — as it was conceived in the nineteenth century — can only survive when everyone in Society agrees that one club, and one alone, is the one that matters. College fraternities and sororities, another nineteenth-century invention, have fared about as men's and women's clubs have, and are quietly disappearing from one after another of the best campuses. And yet, at Yale, there exists a club institution that continues to seem indestructible.

There are two ranking senior societies at Yale, Skull and Bones, and Scroll and Key — known affectionately as "Bones" and "Keys" — which occupy similarly sinister and mausoleum-like structures on the New Haven campus. Membership in either club is a portentous matter, and is said to cast a mystic influence on a man's affairs throughout his life. Of the two, Skull and Bones, founded in 1832, is the older and definitely the grander. Even Scroll and Key men admit that. A Bones man, hearing his club's name spoken aloud by an "outsider," is supposed to get to his feet and immediately leave the room. A Keys man, whose club was founded ten years later, can boast of no such strictures. To Skull and Bones have belonged such men as Averell Harriman, Archibald MacLeish, Robert A. Taft, and Henry R. Luce. On the other hand, Scroll and Key, by not *claiming* the grandeur and distinction of Skull and Bones, by not protesting its importance quite so much, often comes out a social notch or two ahead. To Scroll and Key have belonged John Hay Whitney, Dean Acheson, Newbold Morris, and any number of Rockefellers, along with many old-Society Browns, Delanos, Potters, and Auchinclosses — a membership list hardly to be sneezed at. And yet, when asked, a Scroll and Key member will *always* insist that his society is less important than Skull and Bones. Scroll and Key, having always, and with such perfect modesty, accepted second place, inevitably emerges occupying a place considerably in front of first. It is a fact that infuriates Skull and Bones, but there is nothing they can do. If the grown-up world of big-city Society could have learned the lesson taught by Scroll and Key on a college campus — that those who don't seem to care about being Number One are usually those who make it — Society might have developed a true Club Elite. But it never did.

And, in any case, while the city clubs were fussing over members and fighting with each other, America was changing. The countryside was opening up. Travel was easier. Resorts were building, people were on the move, and country houses were going up. While men's clubs in the city were grudgingly letting down their bars and admitting women, and women's clubs were doing the same to men, a country club Society — with plenty of room for both sexes — was developing on the rolling, wooded hills outside of town.

Rehearsal before Chicago's Passavant Cotillion at The Casino. At left, Philip Armour III with his escort, Miss Katherine Buchanan

"Austere" Boston's Debutante Cotillion includes young men in white tie, black tie, and just plain tie.

The Waltz persists in Boston

*Post-debutantes Patsy Pulitzer, left, and Fern Tailer at the
April in Paris Ball in New York*

Part Two

HOW MONEY LIVES:

A Nosegay of the Best Addresses

10

The Riches of Westchester

"I'M sure you have been told," a faultlessly tailored Scarsdale woman said to a visitor the other day, "that Scarsdale is the wealthiest community per capita in the United States." She smiled a smile of inner satisfaction which that identical knowledge brings to residents of Bryn Mawr, Chevy Chase, West Hartford, Lake Forest, and Beverly Hills. The "wealthiest-town-per-capita" legend has been circulated about Sewickley, Pennsylvania; Clayton, Missouri; Wellesley Hills, Massachusetts; Palm Beach, Florida; Bloomfield Hills, Michigan; and Burlingame, California. In each town where the legend flourishes, it has been impossible to put down. Actually, the title in the wealth race of American suburbs is said to belong to Shaker Heights, Ohio, a complex of villages that sprawls wealthily outside Cleveland. (Shaker Heights has its claim backed by the United States Census Bureau, which assumedly has ways of discovering these things.) Residents of other towns across the landscape of American Society have read about Shaker Heights's imposing per capita wealth — and have ignored it, in favor of a certainty that their own towns are secretly richer. And, of course, the trouble with Shaker Heights is Cleveland. If Cleveland were a socially more important city, and Ohio a socially more important state, the claims of Shaker Heights might be taken more seriously. It's too bad, in other words, that Shaker Heights is where it is. Too bad it isn't in, for instance, Westchester County, New York.

There are easily a dozen towns in Westchester in addition to Scarsdale — including Mount Kisco, Pound Ridge, Katonah, Larchmont, Rye, Bronxville, Irvington, Bedford, Harrison, and "our particular part of Pelham" — whose residents are convinced are not only the richest towns in the country, if not the world, but also the nicest. These beliefs account for Westchester's particular air of solidity and style. After all, to live wealthily — among other wealthy people — was Westchester's original reason-for-being. Wealth is one of the things about these towns which their residents want to preserve. "There are no poor people at all in Bronxville," a Bronxville woman sweepingly states. "They come in, by the day, to work here, but they go somewhere else at night — mostly to Tuckahoe." The poor people in Rye go home to Port Chester.

Every city in America has at least one "nice" residential section outside it, where it is fashionable to live, and New York has several score — many of them in Westchester — but Westchester's social genesis was rather different. It was not originally colonized by New Yorkers to be anything like the clutch of suburban commuter towns it has become. It was colonized for grandeur. Almost from the beginning, in fact even before New Amsterdam was rechristened New York, the area attracted men who wished to live on a large and noble scale. The true "first families" of Westchester include the De Lanceys, the Van Cortlandts, the Philipses, the Pells, the Van der Doncks — all names linked inseparably with the early days of the little colony at the mouth of the Hudson River. It was these families who launched, beginning about 1680, the great era of patroonship and manor building in Westchester County, an era which may be said to have lasted until the Wall Street crash of 1929.

Shortly after the Civil War, grandeur in Westchester was given a new twist. It became a Society resort. In the days when the New Jersey Shore and the Adirondacks were fashionable, and when Society paid stricter attention to "seasons," when the shore — and sea air — were for July, and the mountains — and mountain air — were for August, Westchester County began to have two "little" seasons of its own, spring and autumn. At the outset, Westchester was a controversial resort. Critics pointed out that it had no good beaches, no lakes of any size, no mountains of particular splendor. But its defenders pointed out that it had hills and streams and ponds and, most impor-

tant, views; it was an era when admiring the landscape was more popular than it is today, and in scape of land the area excelled. It had rolling,
sweeping vistas. It was a park, a garden.

Before the middle of the nineteenth century, when railroads began
to open up the grain centers of the Middle West, Westchester County
was literally a garden, the East's granary, its fields yielding rich crops
of wheat and oats and corn. Between the fields were stands of virgin
timber, and the "Westchester rocks," a curious topographical feature
of the county, protruded everywhere in cliffs and crags jutting almost
perpendicularly from the ground. In the woods, deer and rabbits leapt
and over fifteen hundred varieties of wildflowers grew. Even the
county's location was park-like, swept on both sides by majestic, if not
beach-lined, bodies of water — the Hudson River to the west, and
Long Island Sound to the east, which together give the county some
sixty-four miles of coastline. As New York Society began coming to
Westchester, the hills and cliffs began to be covered with castles. The
wildflower-woods were buried under golf courses and *en tout cas* tennis courts, and the littoral sprouted yachting marinas. Westchester's
fate was sealed.

Soon Westchester was castle-poor. "The average size of a Westchester estate," it was announced in the elegant eighties and the gay nineties, was sixty-five rooms. Banquet halls extended to ninety feet in
length, then ninety-five. As they always do when they stake out a new
preserve, the members of Society became competitive. At "Carrollcliff," the home of the late General Howard Carroll in Tarrytown —
an imposing hilltop replica of a Rhine castle from the heights of
which, on clear days, can still be viewed both the Hudson and the
Sound, as well as the Manhattan skyline — old Westchesterites can
remember when the great baronial dining hall was thrown open
regularly for as many as eighty guests, with a liveried footman stationed behind every second chair. "I don't think all the footmen were
from the regular household staff, though," one guest has recalled. "I
think they brought in a few people from the grounds staff." Not long
ago, one of the linen tablecloths from "Carrollcliff" found its way to a
hospital, where it was cut up to make sheets for twenty beds. The huge
American flag that flew from "Carrollcliff's" top mast had stars somewhat larger than most tea trays and weighed, folded, forty pounds. It
was in this same post-Civil War era that John D. Rockefeller's house

was built in Pocantico Hills in North Tarrytown, staffed by servants whose wages ran to thirty thousand dollars a year.*

Not all the attempts to rearrange nature in Westchester were successful. At "Ophir Farm," the seven-hundred-and-fifty-acre estate in Purchase which later became the home of newspaper-publisher Whitelaw Reid, the original owner, Benjamin Holliday, wanted to create what he called "a private prairie." To obtain the desired effect, he imported a sizable herd of elk and an even more sizable herd of buffalo. But the elk jumped over his fences, and the buffalo broke them down, and the neighbors, understandably, complained. Similar complaints plagued the first owner of "Belvedere," now the property of Samuel Bronfman, the liquor magnate. The builder installed several thousand sprinklers to water the commodious lawn, and the sprinkler system did an excellent job of keeping the lawn green. The only trouble was that, when it was turned on, the system reduced the water pressure of Tarrytown to practically zero. But the owner of the sprinklers was considerate. Though his gardeners liked to run the sprinklers early in the morning, he made sure that the water would not be turned on during the hours when his friends on neighboring estates were shaving.

Not far from "Belvedere," the late Jay Gould built "Lyndhurst," a seven-hundred-acre estate with a mansion copied from a French château. After Gould's death, the estate passed to his daughter, Mrs. Finley J. Shepard, and, after *her* death, to another daughter, the Duchess of Talleyrand, who not only maintained the great place but erratically and unpredictably enlarged it, buying up land and houses in the vicinity as soon as they became for sale, and then letting her properties fall into disrepair. Since the Duchess's death, however, "Lyndhurst" has been preserved, and is now one of the few nineteenth-century Westchester palaces both standing and open to the public.

Equally unpredictable and just as colorful and wealthy were the Wendel Sisters, Ella and Rebecca, whose country place was also in Tarrytown, hard by "Belvedere" and "Lyndhurst." The Wendels, maiden ladies who shared their home with an aging unwed brother,

---

* Today, the village of Pocantico Hills and the name Rockefeller are synonymous in Westchester. The family estate contains, in addition to the homes of Laurance, David, Nelson, and John D. III, a two-hundred-acre farm in full production, and the Rockefellers are considered the largest individual landholders in the county.

J. G. Wendel, always dressed alike — in dusty and patched black dresses whose hems trailed in the streets, and in matching black sailor hats secured to the ladies' heads by elastic bands beneath their chins. Despite their disreputable appearance, the sisters were decidedly "Old Family" — listed in the earliest editions of the *Social Register* and its predecessor, the *Elite Directory* — and were large owners of New York real estate. The Wendels were fond of horses, and each sister drove her own team, with a groom seated at her side. Yet such was their penuriousness that once, when a friend who had not seen the sisters for a long time asked them what they'd been up to, the ladies — who often spoke in unison — replied, "Why, we've been busy mending the saddle blankets for the last six weeks!"

Long after their horses had died, and after more modern means of transportation had become common, the Misses Wendel refused to replace the horses, and would permit no other system of transportation to be used on their property. No automobiles were permitted within the gates of the Wendel estate. Horseless visitors were required to negotiate the long drive on foot, and the Wendels themselves walked wherever they went. Once, Miss Ella Wendel was seen coming down her graveled drive in a state of agitation, her small dog, Tobey, cradled in her arms. When a groundsman asked her what the trouble was, Miss Ella said that Tobey had a piece of gravel in his foot. Removing the stone from the affected paw, the man commented that if Miss Ella would have her drive paved in concrete it would provide a more comfortable canine walking surface. "Excellent idea!" cried Miss Ella and, within days, a contractor had been called and the job was done. When the contractor presented his bill to Miss Ella — it was for $20,000 — she promptly opened her purse and paid him the full amount, in cash.*

A feature of turn-of-the-century social life in Westchester was "the afternoon drive" down Broadway in Tarrytown, a ritual frankly copied from similar promenades in Newport and Saratoga. All Westchester Society turned out in full regalia for these drives, behind coaches-and-

---

* In 1929, Tobey, a flagrant mongrel whose appearance was as unprepossessing as his mistresses', made national headlines as "the world's most expensively maintained dog." The Union Club had offered the Wendel sisters $5,000,000 for their town house at 442 Fifth Avenue in order to build a new clubhouse. The sisters turned the offer down and, when asked why, explained that the house was not important to them, but the back garden was — as a run for Tobey. At the time it was rumored that the ladies kept a cow in the back garden too, but this has never been proved.

four equipped with silver harnesses and driven by blue-coated coachmen with silver buttons, high hats with black or red cockades, white
gloves, white trousers, and patent-leather boots with blue or pink tops.
On these splendid drives, Vanderbilts and Fields, Schwabs and Rockefellers, and Archbolds and Whitehouses smiled and bowed at one another. Mrs. Jennie Prince Black, who wrote a chatty book about Westchester of those perfumed days, recalled seeing Alexander Hamilton II
daily during the afternoon drive. He always sat alone in the rear of his
barouche — "a small figure wrapped in a gray plaid shawl . . . He
never seemed to notice anyone or to change his expression of solitary
boredom." Mrs. Black also noted the presence of "an interesting visitor" from England, Winston Churchill, "the novelist."

There was, to be sure, a certain amount of commuting to New
York in those days, but it was commuting of a special sort. "My father
had a hundred-foot steam yacht, *The Gracemere,* named after his
house," Mrs. H. Stuart Green of Tarrytown recalled not long ago. (She
was a Browning, of a retailing fortune.) "At eight o'clock in the morning, on days when he went to New York, he and a few friends would
gather at the pier. They would have a leisurely breakfast on the boat
while they sailed downriver to their offices."

"Oh, those were days like none that will ever come again," said Mrs.
Harold Scott, a senior resident of Irvington, not long ago. Mrs. Scott's
father was Dr. Charles Brace, who made millions in the drug business
in the days before income taxes. At Irvington, overlooking the Hudson, he built an enormous house out of Westchester granite quarried
on his property — "a house built to last a thousand years. It's gone
now." Mrs. Scott remembers, "At Father's house, dinner was at seven.
And that meant not two minutes *after* seven, but *seven.* If you were
early, you waited outside the door until the clockstroke. The gentlemen wore white tie, and the ladies long gowns. The ladies took their
wraps to the downstairs cloakroom, and the gentlemen took theirs upstairs. In the gentlemen's cloakroom, white envelopes were arranged
on a silver tray, with a gentleman's name on each envelope. Inside was
a card with a lady's name on it — the lady he was to take into dinner.
That way, you see, a lady never knew which gentleman would escort
her, which made it exciting. The ladies and gentlemen gathered again
downstairs and there were cocktails, but none of this 'What'll-you-have-
to-drink?' business. Father liked a Jack Rose cocktail, and so that was

what was served. The butler came in with the tray — one Jack Rose for each guest. He was followed by the parlormaid with a tray of canapés — one apiece. Nobody would dream of asking for a second canapé, much less a second drink.

"In fifteen minutes, dinner was announced." No one would think, either, of carrying an unfinished cocktail to the dinner table. "There was always sherry with the soup. At the table were printed place cards and menus, outlining the courses through the appetizer, soup, fish, meat, salad, cheese and fruit, dessert, and coffee with, perhaps, a sherbet course somewhere in the middle. Dinner lasted at least two hours. Really, I don't know how we managed to eat so much! It was a day of gracious living, and when you look at the way people do things now! Cocktail parties! Father would have died of horror if he'd ever seen a cocktail shaker in the drawing room. It was a kitchen implement."

It was an era so accustomed to lavish and imperturbable entertaining that once, in a mix-up of social invitations among the Browns (there were several millionaire Browns in Westchester, and it was hard to keep them straight), Mr. and Mrs. Frank A. Vanderlip (he was President of the National City Bank) who had been invited to dinner at the Franklin Q. Browns' in Dobbs Ferry, arrived instead, in full fig, at the Walston H. Browns' or perhaps — as survivors of the date admit — it was the other way around. In any case, the Browns who were expecting the Vanderlips waited fearing accident or, worse, a snub, while the Browns who were not expecting the Vanderlips, and who were enjoying a quiet evening by the fire, were unfazed by the arrival, promptly at seven, of their elegantly attired and unexpected guests. Murmuring politely that dinner would be *en famille*, Mrs. Brown, perfect hostess to the last, led the Vanderlips into her dining room where they were served, faultlessly, a six-course dinner with four wines. After the Vanderlips had left, Mrs. Brown still did not understand what had happened. "I must have invited them and forgotten about it," she remarked to her husband.

Today, everyone in Westchester insists, there is no longer such a thing as "Westchester County Society." Instead, each community in the county is considered to have its own. But it is not really quite so simple. On the map, Westchester looks like a fat Christmas stocking cinched tight at the ankle. The cinch divides the county horizontally into two sections — northern Westchester and southern Westchester — and there is a social division between the two halves as well. But within these two halves, social dividing lines have tended to run vertically, almost as though they followed the spiny ridges that extend through the county from north to south, and the rivers that flow between the ridges, and the main north-south highways, and, of course, the tracks of the railroad commuter lines. Though it is less true today than it was a generation ago, a Larchmont couple is still more likely to go to parties in Rye, to the north, or in New Rochelle, to the south, than to venture westward to Irvington. A Tarrytown boy is more apt to marry a Dobbs Ferry girl, on his same vertical axis, than one from over the hills in Harrison.* There is always talk about which side of the county is "nicer" — the east or the west. "Of course the real start of things was over *here,*" a third-generation Ardsley resident insists. "All that, over *there,* came much later." Ardsley is on the east, or River side. "Oh, but the families over here are much more thoroughly grounded," insists a Rye resident, on the Sound side. "Those River people, you know, are all rather *nouveau.*"

If there is any actual social difference between the two sides of the county, it is that the River side has seemed to attract bigger, flashier "names" — Vanderbilt, Rockefeller, Duke, Biddle, Gould, and the like. "But," says a Rye woman, "don't forget that the Rockefellers were *nouveau* when they came here." And Roger Sherman, also of Rye — a many times direct descendant of the Declaration of Independence signer — once said, "We never chose to mix much with the Vanderbilts. We all considered the old Commodore nothing but an ex-ferryboat captain. I met the Vanderbilt boys at dancing classes, but that was the extent of it." Such families as the Shermans and the Wainwrights, on the Sound side, were perhaps less colorful, but more august, than their rivals on the River. (The Wainwrights produced noted Army officers, including General Jonathan M. Wainwright.) But through all the controversy — and confusing it somewhat more — runs the assertion that, eastern and western Westchester regardless, northern Westchester is nicer than southern Westchester — on the theory

---

* When a young man from Hastings, on the Hudson River, recently announced his intention of marrying a girl from Mamaroneck, on the Sound — and of moving to her side of the county to live — his father exclaimed in dismay, "But that means you'll have to commute on the New Haven!"

that the farther one lives from New York City the richer one must be.

Wealth continues to be apparent in Westchester, where building lots — considerably smaller than the seven-hundred-acre tracts of the old estate builders — can, depending upon location, cost as much as half a million dollars each. Money nowadays, however, is not so much spent upon gigantic houses as it is on landscaping and interior decorating. A collection of good paintings carries more weight, socially, than a private squash court, and an electronic kitchen and air-conditioned garage ("So much better for the car," one resident insists) can mean more than a ninety-foot banquet hall. To be sure, the more city a man builds into his "country place," the less "country" it becomes, and, in Westchester, nature has been systematically subdued, rearranged, clipped, manicured and, in many cases, forced to do an about-face. Brooks have been made to reverse their courses, mountain laurel and dogwood have been coaxed to yield outsize blooms, and boxwoods have been japanned with plastic sprays to give their leaves a hard green gloss.

A number of Westchester residents have radiantly heated driveways to melt the winter snow. A woman in Ardsley has installed a specially built vacuum cleaner to dust her shrubbery. A house at the edge of the Sound has an ingenious watering system designed to launder the grass; salt spray from the Sound was being unkind to the lawn. A special filtering device removes the salty taste from the swimming pool water. James Russell Ashley of Scarsdale built, in his backyard, not only an outsize swimming pool with a sandy beach at one end, but a brook and waterfall, and what Mr. Ashley christened "an underground cave above ground" in which to have parties. At night, concealed floodlights simulate moonlight. Nor does the era of great estate building appear to be completely over. Only a few years ago, the Edgar Bronfmans — he is the son of the liquor potentate — built a sprawling, handsome Georgian house that might have been lifted right out of the last century, and surrounded it with all the traditional estate trimmings, including pool, pool house, tennis court, and — to be up-to-date — had the whole house air-conditioned.

For the last twenty-five years, Westchester Society has been polarized around the institution of the country club and, as this has happened, many of the old Sound/River dividing lines have become blurred. River-side families now journey across the county to the Sound in order to sail at the American Yacht Club in Rye which, in the opinion of its members, is "the most fashionable club in America." Members of the Apawamis Club, on the Sound side also, come from both sides of the county, too, and think that *it* is the most fashionable club in America. ("The Apawamis *used* to be nice," one Yacht Club member says, "when it used to be all bankers and lawyers. Now they've started taking in a lot of advertising people. I'm very fond of advertising people. But most of them are Irish, you know.")

Another club that "used to be nice" is the Coveleigh Club in Rye. Now, for mysterious reasons, it is not considered so. "They started taking in so many Australians," one woman explained not long ago.*

The Ardsley Club, on the River, was established with but a single thought in mind. It was to be the be-all and end-all of clubs. Founded in 1896, eight years after the first appearance of golf on the social scene in the United States, it had on its founding board of governors John D. Rockefeller, J. Pierpont Morgan, Cornelius Vanderbilt, and Chauncey M. Depew. Many Sound people feel the Ardsley Club never quite came off, but others insist it did and travel cross-county to play golf there today.

There is also a large and wealthy Jewish population in Westchester which many people feel composes a Society of its own. "They live in a different world," one Westchesterite says. "They isolate and ghetto-ize themselves by their sheer wealth." But it is not that simple, though there are large communities — such as the Green Haven community between Rye and Mamaroneck, and a large portion of the town of Harrison — which are Jewish almost to the point of excluding, or at least appearing to exclude, non-Jews. "It started with clubs that excluded Jews," says a prominent Westchester Jewess. "Naturally, the answer was Jewish clubs. Until recently, a Jew couldn't set *foot* on the Apawamis Club golf course, and Jewish sailors — even when they were competing in races at the American Yacht Club — weren't allowed inside the clubhouse, not even if they *won!* So, at our club, the Century, we've been just as exclusive in return. It's a vicious circle."

But it is not even *that* simple. At the Century Country Club, certainly the elite Jewish club in Westchester, it is rather apparent that

---

* The only known Australian member of the Coveleigh Club laughs at this and says, "It doesn't take many of us to make our presence felt."

the membership consists of German Jews and, furthermore, of the German-Jewish families from the Wall Street investment-banking community "plus," as one Century member says, "a few token Gimbels from retailing." Jews from "Eastern Europe" — meaning Russian and Polish Jews — find the walls of the Century very difficult to scale. The Sunningdale Country Club, meanwhile, in Scarsdale, is called "The club for Jews waiting to get into the Century." And still another Jewish club, the Old Oaks Country Club, is "The club for Jews waiting to get into Sunningdale." In view of the complexity of this situation, it is easy to see why most people in Westchester feel it is unlikely to change.

An old bit of doggerel runs:

> *Here's to Westchester County,*
> *Society's uppermost shelf,*
> *Where Scarsdale speaks only to Bronxville,*
> *And Bronxville just talks to itself.*

Poor Scarsdale. It is the butt of all the Westchester jokes. "It's an unpretentious little scent," said a cartoon saleslady at a perfume counter in an old *New Yorker* cartoon, "called '*Evening in Scarsdale.*'" No one knows why Scarsdale has come to stand for all that is banal in Westchester. Perhaps it is because Scarsdale's appearance is possibly the most clipped and manicured of all the county's towns. The edges of walks and driveways in Scarsdale are pared with almost knifelike precision; it is another of those towns in which there appear to be no poor people, where affluence beams from every Tudoresque facade. Or perhaps it is because, like many Westchester towns — Pleasantville, Briarcliff Manor, Hawthorne, Hastings-on-Hudson — the name "Scarsdale" has a starched and stuffy ring to it, a sound of phony-English elegance like an olde tea shoppe. But for all the fun-poking, Scarsdale is an interesting community because it contains both large Jewish and non-Jewish elements, and the two groups live in singular civic accord. Scarsdalers, accustomed to snickers from outsiders when they mention the name of their town, take it all in good grace, and even with a sense of humor of their own. "I live in Scarsdale, the cliché suburb," says one woman with a smile. "But, like all clichés, it's familiar and it's useful and it's comfortable."

Bronxville is something else again. Bronxville is an extraordinary

place. Its location is not auspicious — tucked in the southern toe of the
county, almost equidistant from the two bodies of water, just a few
short miles from the teeming tenements of the Bronx. Yet there it is,
an insulated, isolated pocket of wealth. One feels Bronxville should
have a high wall around it and, in a sense, it does. The town has many
admirers, in addition to the people who live there and who wouldn't
live anywhere else, and among them are such hard-to-please critics of
city planning as Lewis Mumford. An English city planner, visiting
Bronxville not long ago, said, "Here is the answer to suburban planning." Bronxville streets are narrow and winding, curling picturesquely
among the hills past large, impressive houses. As a result, unnecessary
traffic is discouraged, and speeding is virtually impossible.

The man responsible for this felicitous layout — indeed for the
whole town — was also an extraordinary figure, the late William Van
Duzer Lawrence. Lawrence moved to New York from Canada after
making an immense fortune with two pharmaceutical products, and,
according to one member of the family, "When the taxes on his house
on Fifth Avenue got to be $36,000 a year, he decided to move to the
country." The spot he chose was the sleepy, bosky hamlet of Bronxville, and the taxes on the house he built there would now be well in
excess of $36,000 a year if it were still used as a residence. The Law-
rence estate is now a part of Sarah Lawrence College which he gave in
memory of his wife after her death in 1926.

Beginning with roughly a hundred acres (before he had finished he
had added another three hundred), Mr. Lawrence decided to build a
town. When his contractor asked him where to put the streets, Lawrence looked at the cow paths meandering up and down the hills and
said, "Why not make the streets follow the cow paths?" And so, following the rules of bovine common sense, there the streets are for Mr.
Mumford to admire.

Though not personally involved in the world of art and letters, Lawrence was swept by its romance. He decided to populate his town with
"creative" folk — poets, sculptors, and writers. He selected many of
the artists personally. He did not get talents of the first magnitude —
perhaps because successful artists were perfectly happy where they
were and saw no reason for moving to Bronxville — but he did get a
number of people who were, more or less, figures of the day. He got,
for example, a romantic poet named Edmund Clarence Stedman; artists

Otto Barker, Will H. Low, Edward Smedley, and William Howe (beloved for his rural scenes); and Violet Oakley, whose murals decorate the state capitol building in Harrisburg, Pennsylvania.

He built houses to order for each of these people, and charged them minimal rents — which they must have appreciated — since it was his stated notion to "create a congenial community of talented people." Many of the houses Lawrence built must certainly have been far beyond the average struggling artist's wildest dreams. (Perhaps this is why so few of them are occupied by creative people today.) Lawrence was a successful businessman, and he built houses for successful businessmen, though each artist's mansion had a token concession to art — a top-floor studio with an enormous skylight facing north. The more he built, the more elaborate his houses became, and we begin to sense a man fulfilling an ancient dream of childhood to cover an entire beach with towering castles, with moats and avenues and causeways running between. Most of his great playthings, furthermore, are still standing.

"He did it mostly as a hobby," his son, Dudley Lawrence, said not long ago. "But," the younger Lawrence added with a little smile, "my father was not a man who felt a thing was worth doing unless, in the long run, it would be financially successful."

In the long run, it *was* financially successful, to say the least. Today, Lawrence Properties, Inc., owns, leases, or otherwise controls a large portion of Bronxville real estate. Though the Lawrences have generally avoided involvement in local politics, the family's interest in the town has been steadfast. The Lawrence hand has been firmly businesslike (for a while, all persons leasing apartments in Lawrence-owned buildings were required to buy stock in the Lawrence corporation as insurance against failure to pay rent), and the family's influence has been benign. Good causes — from Boy Scouts to unwed mothers — have received their bountiful support. In addition to giving Sarah Lawrence College, the family has performed such large-scale civic deeds as the establishment of Lawrence Hospital, which William Van Duzer Lawrence built and endowed at a cost of half a million dollars in 1906.

Today, Mr. Lawrence's granddaughter, Mrs. Donald K. Clifford, a slender woman with silver hair, lives in a hilltop house overlooking the town her grandfather built. Two other Lawrence granddaughters —

Mrs. Charles Sperry Andrews and Mrs. R. Ridgely Lytle — live nearby. Mrs. Clifford's house is new, built on the foundation of an older, much larger house that was her grandfather's wedding present to her parents in 1898 and which burned just a few years ago. Though Mrs. Clifford is devoted to Bronxville, she has some reservations about the village and its Society that are unusual for a woman of her position. (For instance, when she married "out" of the *Social Register,* she insisted that her own name be removed from the little book.) She is distressed by suggestions that Bronxville is snobbish and "stuffy." "I have always found the people here very serious-minded," she says, "and much more dedicated to community activities and civic work than to social life and gaiety."

Bronxville was for a long time one of those Westchester communities in which — by vague "common consent," and impalpable "gentlemen's agreements" — racial and religious restrictions prevailed in the sale or rental of houses and apartments. Prospective buyers in Bronxville were assured that "the one Jew in town," a retailer, "goes home to Yonkers at night." Though the restrictions no longer technically exist, Bronxville continues to have a reputation for "not welcoming" Jews and Negroes — a reputation which disturbs many Bronxville people, including Mrs. Clifford. "How could a whole town of seven thousand people be guilty of prejudice?" one woman asks.

Another unanswered question is how much, or how little, has Lawrence Properties, Inc., the largest real estate concern in town, had to do with this?

There are some who feel that Mr. Lawrence's town, his multi-million-dollar toy, has become "a bit of an anachronism." "It's a queer little island here," one woman says. "A mile-square residential area isolated right in the center of one of the most thickly populated parts of the county. I sometimes feel the world outside is not beating on our doors to get into Bronxville, the way we used to feel — but is simply passing us by."

Bronxville seems particularly anachronistic in its ways and outlook when one remembers that it is a suburb of New York City, a metropolis where Jews have provided such a rich and heady infusion to both civic and social life. Louis Auchincloss has spoken of "the curious deadness and dryness that sets into any group" in New York the moment Jews are excluded from it. Some of that deadness and dryness is perceptible in Bronxville.

Bronxville seems inappropriate to Westchester County. In other parts of the country, on the other hand, the "Bronxvilles" of America are at home, and even commonplace.

11

By the Shores of Lake St. Clair

TO those who have never been to either place, Grosse Pointe, Michigan, is often considered hand in hand with Lake Forest, Illinois. ("Isn't Grosse Pointe just sort of a *rich* Lake Forest?" a New Yorker asks humorously.) No comparison could be more inexact. Lake Forest is rolling and spacious, many miles north of Chicago. Grosse Pointe is flat and compact, and one of Detroit's closest suburbs — a sliver of privilege barely six miles long and hardly more than a mile wide. The outer edge of this strip of real estate curves along the shores of Lake St. Clair — which might be called a satellite of Lake Erie — and its southern corners brush untidily against a woebegone sector of the metropolis, a maculose region of auto courts, funeral parlors, and dim cafes. Within the strip are tucked "the Grosse Pointes," no less than five towns named (reading from south to north) Grosse Pointe Park, Grosse Pointe City, Grosse Pointe Farms, Grosse Pointe Shores, and (tucked behind the Shores) Grosse Pointe Woods. Here, in an area roughly the size of Block Island, Rhode Island, live some fifty-five thousand people, compared with Block Island's seven hundred and thirty-two. The Grosse Pointe complex may not be "the wealthiest community per capita in the United States," but it may well contain the densest concentration of rich people in the world. Also, according to Mrs. John M. S. Hutchinson of "the boating group," "We have more sailboats in Grosse Pointe than Cleveland, Chicago, and Detroit combined."

Though its approaches, from the Detroit side, are unpromising, the minute one crosses the Detroit-Grosse Pointe line one is plunged into cool green shade. Next to its profusion of fine old trees, one notices the tight concentration of Grosse Pointe's houses. They are fitted so closely together, on such relatively small lots, within such neatly squared-off blocks, along such arrow-straight streets, that one tends to lose a sense of scale. The houses appear small. When one gets inside them, however, one discovers that many of them are very large. A city ordinance forbids fences between Grosse Pointe houses, and one can see its point: with fences around them, Grosse Pointe houses, on this level terrain, might look like so many large brownish eggs in a crate. But as it is there is an hysterical appearance to the place; the houses seem to jostle one another, each guards its square of land so jealously. Where windows peer directly into one's neighbors', one is swept with a sense of caution rather than security, even of alarm.

There are certain differences between the five Grosse Pointes. Grosse Pointe Farms is certainly the choicest address. It has one of the largest areas, the smallest population, and is zoned exclusively for single-family residences. Running a close second to the Farms is the Shores, the smallest both in land area and in population. Here, too, all residences are single-family except for one or two lonely-looking multiple dwellings. People in Grosse Pointe Park would certainly argue as to whether their town was second- or third-best; it is largest in both area and population, and it is over ninety per cent single dwellings. Grosse Pointe City would argue with Grosse Pointe Park as to whether it deserved third or fourth place, but nobody would argue much about where Grosse Pointe Woods stands — at the bottom of the social ladder. It is, among other things, the only one of the five towns that possesses no lakeshore; it is the most populous and crowded; and it is the fastest-growing. In the last ten years, the Woods population has nearly doubled; it has fallen prey to the developer's spade and ax and, belying its name, much of the Woods is now bleak and bereft of trees. The Woods is also full of apartment houses. "Very *nice* apartments, though," one woman says. "Many of our nice young people start out there when they're first married — moving into one of those cute little garden apartments on Vernier Road. They wait, then, until they can

afford to move into a nicer part of Grosse Pointe." Still, there have
been mutterings in the other four towns to the effect that Grosse
Pointe Woods does not really deserve the cachet of the name "Grosse
Pointe" and should change its name to something else.

Of course Grosse Pointe "isn't what it used to be." Everyone agrees
to that. What it really used to be, in the years after Antoine de la
Mothe Cadillac established his fort on the banks of the Detroit River
in 1701, was farmland. The French settlers built what are now called
"ribbon farms" — each farm with a few dozen yards of lake front, to
provide water, and extending inland, sometimes for several miles, into
the plain. These farms ran in neatly parallel strips perpendicular to the
shore and, today, Grosse Pointe streets follow the boundaries of the
ribbon farms. But the loss of the French farms is not what Grosse
Pointers mean when they talk about how the place was changed.

In the late nineteenth century, when Detroit became a city and an
important port for Great Lakes shipping, fortunes were made: in shipping, banking, real estate, and — importantly — in the timber and
mining lands of northern Michigan. Detroit Society was born, and
families with such names as McMillan, Joy, Newberry, and Alger
(still considered the Big Four "old" Detroit names) labored to create the
impression that they were just as grand as slightly older families in the
East, and arranged themselves in gingerbread palaces along Jefferson
Avenue, on the riverbank. As the city grew, Society moved farther and
farther out along Jefferson, toward Grosse Pointe — the "fat point" of
land the French settlers had named — and, presently, was building
elaborate summer residences there. Then, because the growing city of
Detroit pushed harder than Society could push back, Society found
itself in Grosse Pointe altogether. The summer places became year-
round homes, and there were more and more of them. Detroit is still
pushing. McMillans, Joys, Newberrys, and Algers are plentiful in
Grosse Pointe today, but under somewhat more crowded circumstances. The genesis of Grosse Pointe, in other words, was similar to
that of Westchester, but on a smaller scale.

"It was lovely to be a girl growing up in Detroit," said the Countess
Cyril Tolstoi not long ago. The Countess is a McMillan relative, the
widow of a nephew of Count Leo and, though a grandmother, is as
slim and chic as a fashion model. "Jefferson Avenue was a beautiful
street. There were huge elms on either side, and their branches met in

the middle overhead. I remember coming out here to Grosse Pointe for parties and dances. We came in private trolleys — it was the fashionable thing to do. It was the era of the private trolley-car party. Once, my escort took me to a party in a trolley that he'd hired just for the two of us! This place used to be my grandfather's farm — his property ran all the way down to the lake. We'd cut across wide, wide lawns and through woods to the place next door. Now, I look up and down this street and realize I hardly know anybody. I occasionally go to parties and find there's not a human being there I've ever *heard* of." The Countess's butler served her an impeccable Martini and, as though to punctuate the Countess's remarks a Good Humor truck tinkled its merry way down the street outside her windows.

In the early days, there was another important residential street in Detroit besides Jefferson — Woodward Avenue. Woodward Avenue was where "the other people" lived. "We didn't know the people who lived 'up Woodward,' as we used to say," said the Countess. "I'm sure they were nice people. But we just didn't know them." And, between that golden day and this, there was a development that spelled the end of, among other things, the trolley-car party: the invention of a vehicle that ran on gasoline. If there is one thing that irritates an Old Guard Grosse Pointer it is to have Grosse Pointe considered purely the product of the automobile industry. Lest there be any doubt about where *her* family's money came from, the late Mrs. Henry B. Joy drove, until 1958, a 1914 electric car. "Grosse Pointe was fashionable *long* before the automobile," said the Countess Tolstoi. Then she added with a little smile, "The first Henry Fords lived 'up Woodward.' We didn't know them." As for Bloomfield Hills, Detroit's other select suburb, "*That's* the town that automobile money built." Bloomfield Hills is far up, almost at the very end of Woodward, where, as far as Grosse Pointe is concerned, it belongs.

Whether Grosse Pointe was fashionable before the internal-combustion engine or not, it is automobile money, more than anything else, that has turned the place into what it is today. A man doesn't have to be in Grosse Pointe long before someone asks him, "What kind of car are you driving?" To drive a foreign-made car is to fly in the face of Grosse Pointe convention, good manners, good taste, and — one gathers — morality. A woman, ordering her car brought round by the doorman at the Detroit Country Club in Grosse Pointe Farms does not ask for a "yellow Oldsmobile." She asks for a "Sahara Sand Super-88." According to one Grosse Pointe man, a lawyer, "The automobile industry has such a terrific effect on the economy of Detroit that no businessman, whether he's remotely connected with the automobile business or not, can afford to ignore it. Each fall, when the new models are introduced, everybody holds his breath. Depending on how well the new cars go over — that's how well we'll all eat during the coming year." What's good for General Motors is definitely good for Grosse Pointe.

As automobile fortunes created a new clutch of millionaires, the millionaires moved their families into Grosse Pointe. "Naturally," says one woman, "they wanted to *be* Society so the first thing they did was to move to where Society was." Motor money built Loire-inspired châteaux along Lake Shore Road next to the châteaux, castles, and manor houses that were already there. As property values and taxes have risen, many of the proudest Lake Shore houses have come down, and "old money" houses and "car money" houses have suffered about equally. The Truman Newberry house, "built of the most beautiful rose-colored brick" (and lumber money) has been razed, and some of its paneling and fixtures repose in newer car-money houses. The Roy Chapin mansion (he was president of the Hudson Motor Company) still stands, but probably would not if Henry Ford II had not bought it a few years ago for his own home. Mrs. Joseph Schlotman (pre-automobile money) still owns an imposing Lake Shore estate, but is resigned to the fact that it will be torn down and subdivided after her death. Mrs. Russell Alger's house is now the Grosse Point War Memorial. Mrs. Joy's property is the Crescent Sail Yacht Club. The Seabourn Livingstone house ("Grandfather cornered the wheel market — for buggies, that is," according to his granddaughter, Helen Livingstone Howard) recently fell to the wrecker's ball. Mrs. Horace Dodge, Sr., still keeps "Rose Terrace," her huge house on the lake, and her two hundred and forty foot yacht, *Delphine,* lies in wraps at the pier at the foot of her lawn. The *Delphine* contains, among other delights, a $10,000 pipe organ; she requires a twenty-seven-man crew, and she has not stirred from her berth in years. (In fact, according to boating experts, the *Delphine* no longer *can* be taken out; her hull is said to lie encased in lake-bottom mud like a frankfurter in a bun. There she may stay forever, a plump reminder of a grander, more naïve time.)

Lake Shore Road has been labeled "Widows' Row." Of those who still occupy the great houses, most are widows. "The other day, having nothing else to do," said Mrs. Joseph Schlotman, "I made a list of all my friends. I wrote down a hundred and twenty-five names — all women, all widows. We entertain each other — back and forth. We play cards, have teas, and little dinners. We watch rather a lot of television. If a man's face ever appeared at one of our tables — why, we wouldn't know what to do! Sometimes — I wonder. Why has this happened? Did we women work our men too hard?"

Nowadays it is hard to tell where pre-automobile money leaves off and automobile money begins. "We all lent money to old Henry Ford," one woman says, "and he gave us stock in his little company. Who ever dreamed he'd be so successful?" So, many non-automotive families made automotive fortunes whether they liked it or not — and there is no evidence to show that they did not like it. But if the sources of some families' wealth are no longer clear-cut, one name must stand as an exception — Ford. Fords are so integrally a part of Grosse Pointe, and Grosse Pointe is so obsessively conscious of Fords, that scarcely a waking hour passes without some mention of them. "That's Mrs. Robert Kanzler," someone may whisper. "Her husband is Mrs. Edsel Ford's sister's son." Just as customers in English pubs gather and talk about the Queen, so do guests at Grosse Pointe cocktail parties gather and talk — and speculate, and gossip, and exchange the latest bit of news — about the Fords. It is a persistent, though unproven, tale in Grosse Pointe that the rector of one of the local churches not long ago let his tongue slip and said, "Now let us bow our heads and praise the Ford."

As a new arrival to Grosse Pointe soon realizes, however, there is not one important Ford family in existence but three — none of them remotely related — and sorting out the Fords is a newcomer's first social chore, not an easy one. The richest Fords are, needless to say, "the car Fords" as they are called, represented by Mrs. Edsel Ford, her three sons, Henry II, Benson, and William, and her daughter, "Dodie." Then there are the John B. Fords and the Emory Fords, known as "the salt Fords" because their family enterprises include the Wyandotte Chemical Company (built on Wyandotte's rich salt beds) as well as the Libbey-Owens-Ford Glass Company (soda ash from the salt beds is an ingredient in glassmaking). Finally, there are "the old Fords," who include Mr. and Mrs. Frederick Clifford Ford; he is a retired investment banker. These last Fords are not wealthy by the standards of other Fords, but their name has the patina of age. Mrs. Ford, an amateur genealogist, has traced the family right back through the Plantagenets to Alfred the Great in the ninth century. "Lord knows how we got mixed up with Alfred the Great," Mrs. Ford says, "but there he is — right in the book." In this tracing, she did not encounter a single automobile manufacturer or buggy-maker. Mrs. Ford was a Brush and Mr. Ford's mother was a Buhl — both "first-cabin" families in Detroit. The original Buhl was given a land grant by King George III in the 1760's, and when one of the Buhls was selling some property recently an elaborate search was made into his legal title to it — a search that never was successful. "Damn it," said Mr. Buhl finally, "there *isn't* any title to that land. The Buhls just took it."

To confuse Ford matters further is the fact that, while the Frederick Clifford Fords are old Fords, the Frederick *Sloane* Fords (no kin to Alfred P. Sloan of General Motors) are salt Fords. Also, the Frederick C. "old" Fords' son, Walter Buhl Ford, married "Dodie" Ford, daughter of Mrs. Edsel "car" Ford. She is therefore twice a Ford, and she, her husband, and their children are known as "the Ford-Fords."

Each of the three Ford families occupies a special niche in Grosse Pointe life, and each has carved for itself its own area of community endeavor. The car Fords have generally taken over the "glamour" charities — the Detroit Institute of Arts, the Detroit Symphony, the Opera, and the various museums. As a result, Mrs. Edsel Ford is without doubt the grandest *grande dame* in Grosse Pointe Society. So surrounded with servants and secretaries and other "protectors" is she that telephone calls to her have become heroic feats. Getting "put through" to Eleanor Ford can consume an afternoon and, whether she herself is aware of this state of affairs is a matter of perennial conjecture. When she appears at a private party — seldom — or at an important public function — less seldom — a great hush falls upon the room which she does not seem to notice either. A pleasant-looking white-haired woman with no particular sense of fashion, her appearance would not inspire awe in any other city. Her conversation is chatty and housewifely — she always wants to hear about her friends' children — conducted in a down-to-earth manner in a Middle Western accent. "Now don't you go off and go home without me, hear!" she called to her escort at a museum opening not long ago. Yet, at her entrance, crowds part like the waters of the Red Sea.

The salt Fords have tended to concentrate their labors on such social-welfare causes as the Planned Parenthood Federation, the United Fund, and the local hospitals. The old Fords enthusiastically — and appropriately — support the Grosse Pointe War Memorial Center, the historical society, and the Episcopal Church.

Each of the three Ford families stands for a certain set of values for a certain group of Grosse Pointers. "Every class of society has its royalty image," says the painter Clifford West (whose wife is a salt Ford), "the image of the people it would most like to *be* like and be accepted by." Grosse Pointe has at least three such heads of state, all named Ford. To Grosse Pointe's new millionaires (not surprisingly, since Henry Ford's is the most spectacular success story in the annals of American business) the car Fords represent the apex of society, and Henry II, Benson, and William are the kings. Oscar L. Olsen, for example, has become enormously wealthy in what his wife calls "the steel and plastics business," but what he enjoys calling "the toilet seat business." (Olsenite Toilet Seats, with Mr. Olsen's slogan, "Tops for Bottoms," are among his products.) He says, "To me, Mrs. Edsel Ford is *the* great lady of Grosse Pointe. Do you want to know *what* a great lady she is? Well, sir, my wife sent her an invitation to a charity ball with a little note saying she hoped Mrs. Ford would come. And do you know what that great lady did? She *picked up the phone* and called my wife to tell her she couldn't come! That's what I call a great lady!"

The car Fords also represent the sort of large-scale fun that can be had with large amounts of money. When the Henry Fords threw a coming-out party a few years ago for their daughter Anne — a party reported to have cost in the neighborhood of a quarter of a million dollars, the affair was lampooned in several national magazines, and was criticized generally in the American press. Among the new millionaires in Grosse Pointe, however, the party and its cost were vigorously defended. "Why, when you stop to think that the Ford Foundation gives away an average of half a million dollars a day, why shouldn't the Fords have fun with what they've got left? Old Henry never had any fun with *his* money. Why shouldn't young Henry have a little fun with his?"

A less spectacular group of Grosse Pointers would argue with this.

To them, the salt-Ford kind of wealth is more acceptable. It is older money, and it is quieter money. It has more generations behind it to give it temperance and tone. Still others would point to the old Fords as symbolizing the gracious way of life — in their comfortable and modest house, surrounded by comfortable, well-used things and family heirlooms and portraits.

It is the people who subscribe to the salt-Ford set of values who speak most frequently of "all these new people — who *are* they?" And who bemoan the fact that the *nouveaux riches* are robbing Grosse Pointe of its original character. On the other hand, says Mrs. F. C. Ford, "Everybody was *nouveau* to begin with, wasn't he? This place was built by the *nouveaux* of different generations, as far as I can see. The only difference is, we used to feel we knew everybody in Grosse Pointe. Now we don't. But the change is good. I get so tired of people at parties who say, 'I don't know anybody here!' "

"Grosse Pointe is a friendly town, don't you think?" a hostess asked her guest the other day, a trifle anxiously. Her guest agreed that it was. There is a kind of openhanded generosity and kindliness about the place, a take-me-as-I-am quality that greets the visitor, a quality that is particularly Middle Western. "We love visitors," another woman says. "We love anything that gives us an excuse to have a little party." Visitors are scooped up, taken on a jolly round of parties and entertainments, invited to play golf, and in general are given a warmer welcome than a similar visitor would expect to get in a suburb of Philadelphia or Boston or, for that matter, New York or San Francisco.

Grosse Pointe wants terribly to be liked. This is not to say that the friendliness is forced, but Grosse Pointe has achieved a poor national "image." Everyone in Grosse Pointe is aware of this, but not everyone is certain what to do about it. "The trouble is," one woman says, "that Grosse Pointe seems to have 'arrived' somehow — it's on the map now, and it's become a symbol of something it really isn't — or is it?" Another resident says, "Whenever I go anywhere and say I'm from Grosse Pointe, Michigan, I get a funny look — a look that says, 'Well, where're your emeralds? Where's your Cadillac?' "

Grosse Pointe has become a symbol of wealth, but of wealth with pomposity and very little taste. The revelation, not long ago, that

Grosse Pointe realtors operated an elaborate "point system" designed to keep Jews and other "undesirables" from the area did not help the community's reputation. Then, to add insult to injury, there was a television broadcast which noted that several members of Detroit's infamous "Purple Gang" had established themselves in flossy, heavily guarded residences in the Windmill Pointe section of Grosse Pointe Park — which left the impression that, while it did not welcome Jews or Negroes, Grosse Pointe did not mind a mobster or two. It has been called "Gauche Pointe," and "the last stronghold of tailfin culture." But to tick off Grosse Pointe as any of these things is to miss the point, or Pointe.

More than anything else, Grosse Pointe is nervous. Under its facade of good-natured geniality run ripples of anxiety. The community is nervous about Negroes. ("There's a real kind of fear here about that," says Mrs. F. C. Ford.) Detroit's Negro population has climbed to about thirty per cent of the total — a larger percentage share than in New York or Chicago — and the 1967 riots were terrible proof of a long-explosive situation. Grosse Pointe is nervous about its own expanding Negro population, even though it relies on Negroes almost exclusively for domestic help. It is nervous about appearing anti-Semitic, and it is also nervous about Jews. The so-called point system did operate — though most Grosse Pointers insist they were unaware of it — and there are those who say that it still does. At the same time there is a feeling which one woman expresses with marvelous candor: "There's no religious prejudice in Grosse Pointe. We've seen to that. There's never been anyone here to be prejudiced against." There is nervousness about gangsters. "We have gangsters living across the street from us — I think," one Grosse Pointe Park woman says. And then adds, "At least they keep to themselves." The parent of a Little Leaguer in this same section of town was startled to hear his son say, "I'd better not strike out today. If I do, the captain of the team says he'll have his father bump me off."

Grosse Pointe is nervous about the role religion is playing in the community, and theological arguments lately have had less to do with whether God is dead than with whether or not He is being misused as a social-climbing device. Traditionally, community life has been strongly centered around Grosse Pointe's three churches — Christ Church (Episcopal), Memorial (Presbyterian), and St. Paul's (Roman Catholic) — and joining one of these churches is a traditional first step for newcomers to take if they hope to be accepted in the town. But Mrs. Alexander Wiener, a prominent Episcopalian, expressed distress not long ago by the way her church, at least, is being used as "an avenue to status and respectability. People are using the church to help them jockey for social position." Prominent Catholics and Presbyterians, meanwhile, worry that their respective churches — always considered a notch or two down, socially — may lose followers because of this.

Though it likes to think and talk of itself as a steady, settled community, Grosse Pointe is in fact relatively young as suburbs go. It has grown up fast, shot out of its clothes, and some of the nervousness may be laid to suburban adolescence. Clifford West says, "There's always been a kind of raw-boned quality about Detroit. The first generation were young and vigorous go-getters. They went to Grosse Pointe and became custodians of a kind of culture. But now the old castles are coming down and, at the same time, the Detroit slums are being renewed. Everything is different. The third generation is young and vigorous, too, and eager to learn. They know that the rich are supposed to become idle and decadent — but they're determined not to. They're searching, instead, for some kind of mission of their own."

Mrs. Raymond Dykema, of the older generation (she was a "one-*l* Russel," also a first-cabin family), says, "There was a feeling of *importance* as I grew up, watching the ships go by in front of our house, knowing that my father built them — a feeling of belonging to the city, of helping shape it." And James Earl, of the younger generation, says, "There's a philosophy that the young here have — which is that *I* am my only asset. My body, my being, my mind, my self — Me. And, as long as this 'me' is making money, I'll spend it, by God!" This comes close to pinpointing Grosse Pointe's special flavor, its boyish, coltish, high-stepping, sometimes awkward behavior. If one closes one's eyes for a fraction of a second, one can almost see the shade of young Sam Dodsworth at the country club dance. Grosse Pointe is not Zenith by a long shot, but the spirit of Sinclair Lewis's wealthy, bumbling hero is everywhere.

If, while it is restlessly looking for "some kind of mission," the young generation of Grosse Pointers has nothing else, it has money — a lot of it. There is endless talk of money in the community — not smug talk, or envious talk, but frank and excited talk. New or old money, the theme is the same. Money is fun — to spend and to make. It also offers a kind of nostrum for nervousness. "Whenever I get depressed, I remember that I make $100,000 a year," one young man — barely out of his twenties — said. "If I make that much money, I've got to be good, don't I?" ($100,000 a year is the yardstick for success in Grosse Pointe; anyone making less than that is considered a failure.) Oscar Olsen is apt to buttonhole an acquaintance of no more than a few minutes to say, "Come on down to my office — I want to tell you about a deal I've got going that's going to make ten million." In the living room of the Walter B. Fords' (the Ford-Fords) hangs a Picasso head of a woman who appears to be gazing at an oblong slip of paper. Jokingly, to friends, Ford says, "That's a picture of Dodie writing a check," and one gathers that it would not be too difficult to persuade him to reveal the present balance in her account.

To an Easterner, bred in the polite and powdered ways of Philadelphia or Boston Society, such openness about money might seem more than slightly vulgar. On the other hand, one transplanted Eastern woman says, "I was startled at first. Then I decided that it was rather refreshing. After all, if you're rich, why not be honest about it?"

If a new family moves to Grosse Pointe and cannot get "in" socially, the cause is likely not to be that its appearance or its manners are lacking but that its money-spending is insufficient. "Is it easy to be accepted in Grosse Pointe?" Helen Howard asks rhetorically. "Well, yes and no. A college friend of mine moved here from the East with her husband a while ago. My Grosse Pointe friends really knocked themselves out for those two — entertained them all over the place — for a while, at least. But my Eastern friends just couldn't hold up their end, financially. Look, if a couple is attractive, and likes sports, they have an easier time. But let's face it: more than anything else, they've got to have the scratch."

With singular determination (perhaps fearing that too much luxury may make them soft), Grosse Pointers hurl themselves into athletics, and Grosse Pointe is one of the most sports-minded communities in the country, specializing in activities somewhat different from those considered upper class in the East. Paddle tennis is enormously in vogue — "Nothing like paddle tennis for a hangover," says one woman —

and, to help Grosse Pointers work off their nervous energy, there are golf, swimming, sailing, speedboat races, riding, field dog trials, and sports car races for both sexes (one young wife helps her husband in the mechanics' pit at the track wearing a "pit suit" of gold lamé). In winter, there are skiing, skating, ice-boating. Grosse Pointers fancy sports in which there is an element of danger, and sky-diving has become a fashionable pastime. On weekends, in season, the men are off to their private marshes and duck blinds and fishing streams. ("My husband used to rent eight miles of salmon," Mrs. Joseph Schlotman recalled not long ago. "He had to rent. It seems you can't *buy* a river.") The women hunt, shoot skeet, fence, and bowl.

Much of this activity centers around the various Grosse Pointe clubs — the Country Club of Detroit, the Grosse Pointe Club (called "the little club"), the Grosse Pointe Yacht Club, and the Hunt Club. But a number of adventuresome Grosse Pointers have established sporting outposts in horsey Metamora, Michigan, southwest of Detroit, where there are two clubs: on the northern shore of Lake St. Clair, where there is a club called "the old club" ("a hunting, fishing, and oh-hell-a-bit-of-drinking club," according to a member); and in Gaylord, Michigan, a five-hour drive to the north, where there is a private ski club.

Grosse Pointe has also made a "sport" of traveling. When not planning hunting, sailing, or fishing trips to northern Michigan and Canada, Grosse Pointers are departing for grouse-shooting expeditions to Scotland, skiing trips to Austria or Chile (depending on the season), skin-diving trips to the Aegean Islands, and safaris to East Africa. "We always say Grosse Pointe is a nice place to be *from*," says Helen Howard, adding that to be constantly "from" somewhere requires "scratch" too.

Sam Dodsworth was an outdoorsman and, if there had been television in his day, he would doubtless have been a TV fan too — as Grosse Pointe is, to a man and to a woman. Television is one of Grosse Pointe's favorite forms of relaxation and, not surprisingly, the sports programs are the most popular. On Sunday afternoons in autumn, the golf courses are deserted and Grosse Pointers are in their houses, with their friends, with their eyes fixed on the colored screen. This is not to say that Grosse Pointe has forsaken the social tradition of the Sunday afternoon cocktail party; on the contrary, it has merely expanded upon it so that the cocktail party includes television-watching. Sometimes several sets are put to use so that several football — or World Series baseball — games can be watched simultaneously; the announcers' voices describing plays provide a muted backdrop to cocktail party conversation.

"We're all nuts about pro football here," one man says. "If you call a friend up and ask him over on a Sunday, the first thing he asks is, "Which game are you watching?" " Grosse Pointe is similarly nuts about pro football players. "They're much nicer than professional baseball players," says one woman who often has a quarterback or two at her parties. "You can be sure they've had at least four years of college *some*where." One of the easiest ways to be accepted by Grosse Pointe Society is to be a member of the Detroit Lions team. (One Grosse Pointe woman is such a Lions fan that she had a diamond wristwatch made to order with the letters D E T R O I T   L I O N S representing the twelve digits on the dial.) The all-time record for the number of television sets going at a single party may belong to Ray Whyte, the ebullient head of several million-dollar electronics businesses. ("I'm president of seven companies. I've had a lot of luck.") Once, at a gathering at his house, it took twelve sets to keep the guests informed of the scores. His wife Celeste always travels with her own TV so that she may never be more than a button's-push away from a Lions game.

These attitudes are in sharp contrast with those encountered on the North Shore of Long Island at the summer home of the Denniston Slaters. Not long ago, before he retired, Whitey Ford dropped by the Slaters' for a visit, and Slater excitedly telephoned neighbors and friends to say, "Whitey Ford is here! Come on over!" Slater says, "They all came, of course. But half of them thought that Whitey Ford was a bandleader, and the other half thought it was Henry."

"I couldn't stand the physical set-up of Grosse Pointe," says Mrs. Clifford West who "escaped" to Bloomfield Hills — some twenty-five miles to the northwest of Grosse Pointe physically, and even farther away emotionally. "It was so close. I felt there was no air. I couldn't *breathe!* But look at what we've got here." She gestured out the window of her large, rambling house toward a long expanse of rolling lawn and an ancient willow tree standing like a fountain at the edge of a shaded pond. "I also didn't approve of the way they bring up their children there — the coming-out parties and all that, and the *lessons* the children are forever taking! French lessons, riding lessons, sailing lessons, swimming lessons, tennis lessons, skating lessons, dancing lessons, fencing lessons. Things are much more relaxed and less *organized* here."

And yet Mrs. West takes her children often to visit her aunt, Mrs. Schlotman, the salt Ford. "I do want them to see what it was like," Mrs. West says, "because Aunt Stella is one of the last ones to live on that enormous scale — in her huge house with the elevator to the ballroom, with a score of servants. I want them to see it before it goes — and to know that it really *wasn't* vulgar, but had such dignity, such manner, such taste, and such *integrity*."

Other Bloomfield Hills residents consider their town the "answer" to Grosse Pointe. "We're not stuffy, not inbred, not old-fashioned the way they are in Grosse Pointe," says a Bloomfield Hills man. "We're a community of individuals here. In Grosse Pointe, they do everything together. They belong to the same clubs, go to the same parties — see the same old faces, year in and year out. When they travel, they travel together, in packs, and wherever you see a Grosse Pointer in Europe you can be sure there are at least a dozen other Grosse Pointers in the same hotel."

And yet it is this "family" feeling that buoys Grosse Pointe up and holds it together. Families who were friends in one generation find that their children are friends in the next, and this gives Grosse Pointers a comfortable, cozy feeling of unity and continuity. When, as sometimes happens, a son — gone East to prep school and college — announces his intention of moving permanently to New York, the news distresses all Grosse Pointe, for the community wonders whether the tight fibers that bind it may be flying apart. A Grosse Pointer does not object — indeed, sees nothing wrong — that his house stands shoulder-to-shoulder with the houses on either side. The disadvantage of crowding has become an advantage. "You never need to be *afraid* in a community like this," says one woman — a community where, if you need one, you can reach out and touch a friend just a few feet away. Congestion here breeds contentment. A good many years ago, an edition of the *Social Register* was published for Detroit. It languished and died from lack of interest. "We didn't need it here," one woman explains. "A Grosse Pointe address has always been enough to tell us who belongs here from who does not."

Relaxing at Society's favorite Eastern ski resort, Sugarbush

Alice Topping practices the hula hoop in Palm Beach

As the population of Grosse Pointe has grown within its seven square miles, the one-big-happy-family feeling has intensified. The knots that secure the relationship of one to all have become stronger. When the day comes — which would not seem too far off — when there is simply no more room in the five towns for large brick houses, Grosse Pointe will not be upset; the family circle will then seem complete. As Grosse Pointe has grown, it has grown inward upon itself, and away from the city of Detroit. With its own shops and golf courses and churches close at hand, it is increasingly unnecessary for a Grosse Pointe woman to venture outside her town, except when she goes to and from the airport; Detroit is the men's city. The most important city, as far as the women are concerned, is New York; it sets their style. "We go to New York," one woman says. "Never to Chicago, never to Cleveland, never to Pittsburgh."

Grosse Pointers don't like Detroit much, either. "It's such an *ugly* city," one woman says. Another says, "The nice thing about Grosse Pointe is that when you're here it simply doesn't seem possible that Detroit is ten minutes away." Still another says, "I had to go to Detroit the other day — and I had to drive right by one of those plants when all the workers with their lunch boxes and tool kits were coming out. It was scary!"

Several prominent Grosse Pointe women, including Mrs. John Mc-Naughton ("Her husband's sister is Mrs. Benson Ford") and Mrs. Kirkland Alexander have journeyed to Detroit to work with the Detroit Artists' Market in the center of town — a nonprofit gallery for local artists, staffed by volunteers. But women like these are the exceptions. The Detroit Symphony, too, has its "set" of supporters in Grosse Pointe, but opening nights are nowhere near the social events they are in New York, Boston, Philadelphia, or San Francisco. Subscription seats are seldom more than partially filled. "No, we didn't go," one woman said of a recent Symphony opening. "There were riflery lessons at the club that night." Similarly, the large charity balls given in hotels in downtown Detroit are well-subscribed to by Grosse Pointers, but scantily attended by them. No one goes to Detroit for restaurants or nightclubs — "There aren't any." If, as one young woman explained, "there's nothing going on at the club, there's always Al Green's" — Grosse Pointe's own restaurant-nightclub. It is not that Grosse Pointe is uninterested in the arts. "Practically every woman here goes to her painting class — it's the thing to do." Paintings done at these classes run heavily to views of Grosse Pointe. As for the Symphony, "Grosse Pointe now has its *own* symphony orchestra."

As Grosse Pointe has turned its back on Detroit, it is perhaps not surprising that Detroit, in return, shows little cordiality to the suburb. "I did some volunteer work downtown once," one woman says. "When they learned I was from Grosse Pointe, the secretaries in the office stopped speaking to me. They were actually hostile. They hated me. I was the enemy."

Around itself, Grosse Pointe has built an invisible wall. The brawny, violent city seems to heave against it. So far, the wall has seemed secure and impregnable. If it ever comes tumbling down, of course, all Detroit will come tumbling in. One Grosse Pointe man, a long-time resident, says, "You know, there's so much *potential* here. There's so much essential *decency*. Most of them *are* nice people, and there *is* a great deal of wealth and power. If only — some day — in some way — this potential could find a means of expressing itself in some important way. Then —" His voice trailed off.

Meanwhile, Grosse Pointe floats among the restless seas outside.

12

The Main Line Eternal

WHILE the social attitudes of Grosse Pointe seem to be in a state of nervous flux, those of Philadelphia's Main Line seem to have come serenely to rest.

Not long ago a guest from out of town was rushed late at night to the emergency room of the Bryn Mawr Hospital for treatment of a sudden and mysterious intestinal complaint — the result, it turned out, of a heavy and gravied Main Line dinner. While the doctor was quieting the lady's stomach, she supplied a nurse with the vital statistics hospitals require — patient's age, place of birth, and so on. This done, the lady asked the nurse anxiously whether she thought everything would be all right. "Oh," said the nurse, "since you weren't *born* here you couldn't possibly *die* here. We wouldn't permit it."

This is not to say that none of the inexorable rules of time and tide, which plague such places as Grosse Pointe and Westchester, do not apply to the Main Line. But in the jagged-edged seventeen-mile-long stretch of townships that together make up the Main Line (townships which, on the map, follow a broken line leading out of Philadelphia), there are actually *two* Main Lines. There is the visible Main Line — the various and burgeoning suburban spread with its new highways, tract houses, and, recently, the discreet invasion of some light industry. Its population is mixed — white and Negro, poor and well-off, old and young; some residents have moved to the Main Line recently, others have lived there all their lives; some are executives, some are laborers; some are permanent, some are transient.

But there is also the old, or inner, Main Line — the legendary rampart of Philadelphia Society, composed of families who have been there and have known each other, as they will tell you, "always."

But the situation is not really so cut and dried. For one thing, quite a few people of the outer Main Line would like very much to be taken in by the inner — and, just possibly, they could be. The outer Main Line is divided, according to one woman, "between people who take the Main Line seriously, and people who don't give a damn — between people who *believe* in the Main Line, and people who just live here because of the good schools, the fresh air, and the quick commute to Philadelphia. Some people are here because it's a suburb, but some are here because it's *the Main Line,* and it stands for something they want to have. What do they want? Eventually, it's dinner with the Cadwaladers — *any* Cadwaladers. Me, I don't give a damn."

The don't-give-a-damn Main Line is the real Main Line.

Still, it isn't *that* simple. The inner Main Line knows well who its members are. But just who, or how many, of the outer Main Line would like to be inner is hard to say. The Philadelphia *Social Register* lists some two thousand families with Main Line addresses, but the *Social Register* has never been a reliable guide, and is even less so in Philadelphia. Many are listed who do not "deserve" to be. "It's a telephone book," says Mrs. Samuel Eckert, who very much belongs in it (her father was a Longstreth, an old Quaker name). "Still, it's better to be in it than out of it," she adds. Better for what? "Just — better." Polarized around Main Line Society, there are many groups at varying distances from its magnetic core. Some of them are in the *Social Register,* and some are not. There are some who think they have joined the inner group, but in reality have not. There are those who once did not care about joining, but now are beginning to somewhat. There are those who could never get in, but nonetheless go right on trying. On the Main Line, Society is like a lovely but stern old grandparent of whom everyone is a little frightened, but whose vagaries and peccadilloes everybody smiles at, and whom everyone in the long run respects and admires. Society here is such a solid and imposing affair that it may sometimes seem as though its pinnacle must be scaled because, like Everest, it is *there.*

People talk of how drastically the Main Line has changed — for the worse, needless to say — particularly people who have been away from it for a while, and have returned. "I just can't believe it," one young man said. He had been born and raised on the Main Line, and was visiting it again after a few years' absence in another city. "It's terrible. All the big estates have been broken up, or turned into schools or convents, or rest homes. There's hardly a tree left on Lancaster Avenue — nothing but apartment houses and subdivisions and shopping centers, nothing I remember any more." On the other hand, William Mirkil, a successful young real estate man from Ardmore who has not been away from the Main Line, looks startled at such a suggestion. "Of course the Main Line hasn't changed," he says. "What's more, I don't think it ever will change. The *tone* of the place has been preserved better than in any other area in the country." And a woman, also of the old Main Line, says, "But Lancaster Avenue never *was* a good address!" To those who believe in the Main Line, the more it changes, the more it remains the same.

Unlike Grosse Pointe, the physical look of the Main Line is not readily apparent. One certainly cannot see it from a window of the Paoli local as it clatters its way westward from Philadelphia, carrying all those commuters on whom the line loses so much money. All one can see from the train is the succession of railroad stations with their painted signs of red and gold. "Old Maids Never Wed And Have Babies, Period" is the phrase one must memorize to keep track of the first few station stops — Overbrook, Merion, Narberth, Wynnewood, Ardmore, Haverford, Bryn Mawr, with "period" standing for Paoli at the end of the line. Between Bryn Mawr and Paoli, the phrase makes less sense: "Really Vicious Retrievers Snap Willingly, Snarl Dangerously. Beagles Don't." (Rosemont, Villanova, Radnor, St. Davids, Wayne, Strafford, Devon, Berwyn, Daylesford). But there are those who say that those communities themselves don't make much sense. The Main Line breaks a number of rules, among them the rule that suburban addresses generally become "better" the farther away from the city one goes.

Nor can the Main Line be seen from Lancaster Avenue, the wide street that runs roughly parallel to the railroad tracks through most of the above communities. It is along Lancaster that the developer's hand has been the most savage and arbitrary, and a rigid corporation style has been imposed. One passes automobile showrooms, the tall and prison-like apartment houses, the motels giddy with glass and gassy with neon, the bunched gas stations — often engaged in furious price wars — and the ubiquitous shopping centers. As is the unerring way of such "centers," they have not been placed in the real centers of the towns at all, but out along the highway. While the new centers create a traffic problem, the real centers show the economic effects of this deployment, and look shabby and discouraged and embarrassed. "And the diners," says Mrs. Hugh Best, a relative newcomer to the Main Line. "Don't you think we have *beautiful* diners? We have them in every shade of chrome. When I first came here from California, I drove out to see what the Main Line was like. I got to Ardmore, which I'd heard was nice, and it was hideous. I drove on to Bryn Mawr, which I'd heard was even nicer, and it was worse. I couldn't imagine what all this 'Main Line' talk was all about."

To find what all the talk *is* about, one must venture off Lancaster Avenue for a little distance. Here you can find yourself in a trim suburb with clipped hedges and manicured lawns, with houses showing a Pennsylvanian regional fondness for brick and local stone. Or you can find yourself in a landscape of rolling, wooded hills, green fields dotted with lakes and ponds (dotted, in turn, with ducks and swans), where roads wind narrowly in and out of shadowy ravines, past old rail fences and stone walls, across ancient bridges and beside cascading waterfalls. It is in these boskier regions that the rich of the Main Line live, and it is easy to understand why this has been called one of the most beautiful residential areas in the United States. Spring and early summer are the loveliest seasons here, when azaleas, rhododendrons and roses offer their abundant blooms, when the sun warms the stone or white-painted brick of the low, rambling, Pennsylvania Colonial, Federal, and Georgian houses (many are actually old, and many more have been built to look old); and when even the newer, split-level houses of redwood and glass seem to blend comfortably into the terrain. Through these sections, the tree-lined lanes twist, turn, change direction so precipitately — and change their names so abruptly — that it is very easy to get lost. One route sign blandly informs drivers that they are, at that point, going both north *and* south, and newcomers admit that several months of painful experiment are required to learn to navigate the area. (Old Main Liners find their way around with a kind of Main Line radar, honking their horns authoritatively as they approach tight corners and blind intersections.) But it *is* delightful to the eye, and none of it, as everyone who lives there will soon reveal to the visitor, is more than twenty minutes from the heart of Philadelphia on the new Expressway, or more than ten minutes from the mud-colored shopping centers of Lancaster Avenue.

"The edges of Main Line towns all run together," says one woman, and so they do, "and all the Main Line towns are pretty much alike, so it doesn't matter where you live. It's all Main Line."

This — like so many other things Main Liners are apt to say about their environment — is not exactly true. There are subtle differences between certain communities, and some that are not so subtle. The most important thing to remember about the Main Line is that it could have only happened in Philadelphia, and Philadelphia is a city with a habit of making up myths about itself which it knows are myths and yet believes. One learns, for instance, not to argue with a Philadelphian when he refers to Philadelphia as "the second largest city in the United States," even though it is only fourth largest. Philadelphians seem to believe that if they repeat this non-fact long enough it will become true. Philadelphia's notion of its population is equally surrealistic. It is almost always referred to as "a city of four million," even though the latest United States census figures indicate only 2,002,512 — a decline in population, actually, from the figure of ten years before. Philadelphia is also fond of pretending that everything in the city was founded by Benjamin Franklin — if not by some Cadwalader, Wister, Morris, Ingersoll, Biddle or Roberts a century or so before Franklin. The names of Franklin, George Washington, William Penn, and General Anthony Wayne are so liberally applied to Main Line banks and insurance companies — to say nothing of roadhouses, motels, and diners — that it is easy to suppose that these great men actually lived here. One can also get the impression — so pervasive is the train of thought — that the city of Philadelphia was founded by the Main Line and not, as was the case, the other way around, and that the Main Line has been what it is, where it is, exerting the social force it does, since the dawn of American history.

Actually, the Main Line as a social suburb is not even a hundred years old. The area was conceived, designed, and developed by the Pennsylvania Railroad as a real estate venture in the 1870's and '80's when the railroad was pushing its tracks westward and was hoping to stir up freight and passenger business along its route. The railroad built a chain of resort hotels along this "Main Line of Internal Improvements of the State of Pennsylvania," and declared that these hotels were fashionable. When the hotel venture was not immediately successful, the line added houses and when these, too, failed to sell well, it decreed that all railroad executives of stature must build large estates there — a thing many railroad men, and their wives, were not at all eager to do. At the time, Philadelphia Society lived either on Society Hill, in the city, or in Chestnut Hill (though Chestnut Hill has always looked like a suburb, it technically is not since it is within the Philadelphia city line), or in the Whitemarsh-Penllyn area — all of them on the opposite side of the Schuylkill River from the Main Line. Germantown and West Philadelphia were not, in those days, to be sneezed at either.

Since the Pennsylvania Railroad was a social force in itself to be reckoned with, its executives and large stockholders reluctantly did as they were bidden, and the railroad helped out with financing the estates it wanted. It is the only suburb known to have been made fashionable by force.

For the next fifty years, like Grosse Pointe, the Main Line was considered largely a summer resort. It was not until the 1920's that the Main Line began to be what it so solidly is today, an area with a year-round population including, perhaps, the densest concentration of the upper class in America.

There is some justification for the preponderance of Main Line towns with Welsh names, just as there is a reason for the French in Grosse Pointe. A colony of Welsh Quakers had farmed the region before the arrival of the railroad. But many of the communities — such as Bryn Mawr, Narberth, and Radnor — were given their names Welshly, and rather spuriously, by none other than the railroad. Since then, private builders, developers, city planners, and estate owners have contributed to the Welshification process with names of their own devising, until now almost everything on the Main Line that does not commemorate a member of the Continental Congress has a name that at least *sounds* Welsh. It was apparently too late to do anything about "Paoli," an incongruous, winy whiff from the shores of Corsica.

As wealth moved to the Main Line, the position of Chestnut Hill declined. But Chestnut Hill has never for a moment felt that it was socially eclipsed by the upstart creation of the locomotive. Chestnut Hill continues to insist that it is where "the real power" of Philadelphia lives, and it enjoys quoting a somewhat elderly (1940) statistic showing that seventy-eight per cent of Chestnut Hill families are in the *Social Register,* a figure the Main Line can nowhere near approach. Chestnut Hill dismisses the Main Line as "mostly *nouveau riche* — those railroad builders, you know, were hardly gentlemen," and calls the Main Line, "Philadelphia's answer to Long Island." Chestnut Hill people like to say, "No one but Welsh peasants lived on the Main Line until the railroad came along and built it up." A certain way to start an argument in Philadelphia is to ask whether Chestnut Hill or the Main Line is better.

The railroad, and the railroad men who moved there, also decided that the north side of the tracks was the nicer side. Today, the illusion persists, though there is no basis for it in fact. The wealthy, and the *old* and *good* Philadelphia families have established well-tended outposts in both directions. But south-siders are still apt to say defensively, "*I* live on the south side, and *I'm* not ashamed of it." Others point out, "After all, the Merion Golf Club is south of the tracks." The famous and somewhat more splendid Merion Cricket Club, on the other hand, is on the north side.

And one's address does matter on the Main Line. Bryn Mawr and Villanova are the two most fashionable places, and Haverford runs a close third. Poor Narberth, however, is at the bottom of the status ladder. "Narberth just never *did* have any style!" one woman says. Bala-Cynwyd still contains pockets of wealth, but has lost a lot of its once rural charm; now much of it appears to be an extended shopping center. Radnor is considered "very nice." ("Very nice," says one man, "is the Main Line way of saying 'filthy rich,'" and perhaps even a little vulgar.) Paoli is "more horsey." Wynnewood is "a very nice young community." So is Penn Valley. But Penn Valley has a heavy cross to bear. It must use "Narberth" as a mailing address. The Post Office Department not long ago dealt a similarly cruel blow to a corner of Wynnewood; *its* mail, it was announced, would afterward be addressed — of all things — "Philadelphia, Pennsylvania, 19151." Devon is fortunate. It has the famous Devon Horse Show to give it the prestige it might otherwise lack. Wayne is a problem. Wayne's houses are large and substantial, but Wayne is not considered a good "social address." Wayne is beloved by the people who live there, who call it "the friendliest place on the Main Line" and Wayne people do seem to see a lot of one another and to have relatively few non-Wayne friends. It is considered "a nice *family* sort of place," and one Main Liner who owns a chain of movie theatres in the area, says, "It's mysterious. A Walt Disney movie — and I mean a real lousy Walt Disney movie that's done terrible business everywhere else — will break all box office records in Wayne." One reason may be that Wayne's comfortable old houses appeal to young couples with small children.

As for Gladwyne, "Gladwyne," says one woman, "can be either-or." The late Mrs. Edward MacMullan, Philadelphia's historic social secretary, once said, "People who live in Gladwyne who have chauffeurs use Bryn Mawr as their mailing address — the driver, you see, can be sent to the next town to collect the mail. But if you have to have the postman bring the mail to your door, then, of course, you have to use Gladwyne." Interestingly enough, the greatest amount of Main Line wealth is concentrated in Gladwyne, but in Philadelphia, of course, it is not just money that counts. And Gladwyne, as Main Liners caution the visitor, "is just a little bit Jewish."

But more interesting than the stratification of the various communities is the way Main Line Society — and the satellite members of would-be Society — has formed little groups or sets. The only way to get into Society here is to get into a set. Near the top of the scale, socially, is the "Arty Set," a term which in Philadelphia does not mean what it means in Greenwich Village. Mrs. John Wintersteen, trustee of the Philadelphia Art Museum, who lives in Villanova with her definitive collection of Picassos, is the *doyenne* of this group — even though, as she modestly says, "I'm only a first-generation Philadelphian." Her brother, Henry McIlhenny, when not away at his castle keep in Ireland, is the male leader of the Philadelphia art world, and around him are such art — and Society — figures as Ernest Biddle and Emlen Etting, both painters. Art has long been Philadelphia's number one cultural pursuit, with music, the dance, theatre, and literature following in that order down the ladder of acceptable endeavors. One Main Line newcomer who was working on a committee for the local library, was asked by a bemused *old* Main Liner, "The Library? *What* Library?" "The Bryn Mawr Public Library," was the newcomer's reply, to which the other woman answered, "How very interesting! I never knew Bryn Mawr had a public library."

At the same time, the Main Line is proud of its *own* authors, and numbers among them Catherine Drinker Bowen, the biographer, who, as a member of the oldest Main Line Society, is known as Mrs. Thomas McKean Downs of Haverford.

"The surest, quickest way to be accepted here is to collect paintings and support the Art Museum," says one woman. As an example of a couple who has done just that, in the face of what might seem insuperable odds, everyone points to Mr. and Mrs. Walter Annenberg. He is the wealthy publisher of the Philadelphia *Inquirer*. On the surface, Walter Annenberg might seem to have little to recommend him to membership in the highest of High Society in the nation's most socially conscious city. He was born elsewhere — in Milwaukee; though not a practicing Jew, his forebears were; and his father, as a result of a disagreement with the Internal Revenue Service, spent some time in jail. ("But nobody here talks about that.") Yet the Annenbergs, who live in Wynnewood, are now considered "one of the most popular couples on the Main Line. Nobody would turn down an invitation to their house. And they did it through their devotion to the community, and to Art."

Another excellent way to get into Main Line Society is to raise horses, or at least to ride and hunt. "An arty person can be horsey *too*," one woman explains. "But horsey people are a class unto themselves." In seating a dinner party," she adds, "if I have a girl who's horsey, I *have* to seat her next to a man who at least knows the front end of a horse from the rear. Otherwise the two would have absolutely nothing to talk about." In its own way, the horsey set is just as exclusive as the Arty Set. The limitations of horse language being what they are, it may be even more so.

The Main Line has always been strongly oriented toward athletics. There is a cricket set, a golfing set, a tennis set, a swimming set. There is also a beagling set, including such prominent Main Liners and beaglers as Mr. and Mrs. David Randolph. The Gardening Set on the Main Line is not exclusively a female preserve; many Main Line gentlemen are avid gardeners. The Pennsylvania Horticultural Society was founded by a group of men. The Gardeners, however, is a women's group, and a number of years ago a group called the Weeders was formed by a group of dissident Society girls who got tired of waiting to get into the Gardeners. At the time, the name "Weeders" was considered a great joke. Today when someone like Mrs. Samuel Eckert says, "My mother was a Weeder," you are not supposed to laugh. Recently a new Main Line group was informally organized — the Safari Set. Well-connected Main Line families who know each other have taken to shooting expeditions in Africa, and are apt to come home comparing notes on rhino, dik-dik, and white hunters. The stuffed carcasses and skins blend oddly with the chintz-covered chairs and cabriole-legged tables and highboys that characterize so many Main Line interiors.

Still, for all its diversity and contradictions, there is a uniformity of feeling on the Main Line, a consistency of tone. There are attitudes and aspects of the Main Line that seem indigenous to it, which can be encountered in any of its groups and throughout its length. There are traits which the Main Line owns, and which it clings to. "The most astonishing thing to me about the place," says one woman, "is how many people move out here from other parts of Philadelphia, and from other parts of the country, and begin acting exactly like 'old' Main Liners. They begin to dress Main Line and talk Main Line and think Main Line." This, of course, is due to the towering influence of the Old Guard Society upon the rest of the populace. There are always the Ins, and always the Outs, and the two groups eye each other cautiously all the time. One New York man whose Main Line friends are still Out, said recently, "There's a funny Main Line practice, have you noticed? The minute you arrive they pile you into a car and take you on a tour of the best neighborhoods, pointing out all the houses of all the people they don't know." Main Line Society, meanwhile, is aware that its behavior is being watched, that its style is being studied, and this gives Society a sense of purpose, duty, and responsibility; it must *set* the tone and *point* the way.

On the Main Line, Society does not fulfill the function it does in Chestnut Hill (where "nearly everybody" is in it anyway); here it feels it must truly guide, nobly lead. The inner and the outer Main Lines do more than complement and balance one another; the two groups actually support and nourish one another, each feeding the other's dreams.

"My God!" said one young woman the other day. "My daughter's started talking with that Main Line accent. She's picked it up at school. She's started using Main Line words — words like 'yummy.' The other day I asked her how a certain party had been, and she said, 'Oh, Mummy, it was such a giggle!' " Children attending the Main Line's private schools — Shipley, Agnes Irwin, or Baldwin for girls; Haverford or Episcopal for boys — seem to acquire the accent and language by osmosis, if they have not already acquired it from listening to their parents. The terminology is quaintly special, one might say precious. One is not startled on the Main Line to hear a businessman conclude a deal with a cheerful "All righty-roo!" Or to depart from a party with a bright "Nightie-noodles!" to his host and hostess. As for the accent, Barbara Best calls it "Philadelphia paralysis," or "Main Line lockjaw," pointing out that it is not unlike "Massachusetts malocclusion." Mrs. Best recalls that when she first moved to the area a native said to her, "My dear, you have the most beautiful speaking voice. I can understand every word you say!"

Some observers have noted a slight improvement in Main Line *couture* in recent years, and give the credit to such New York stores as Bonwit Teller and Lord & Taylor which have recently opened up Main Line branches. A young woman named Ann Pakradooni has opened a small, expensive boutique in Wynnewood where she designs dresses and where her stated aim is to "style up" the Main Line woman. The Main Line woman, meanwhile, considers Mrs. Pakradooni's clothes "amusing," but a bit *outré*. The rule is still, "Nothing flashy, nothing low-cut" when it comes to clothes, and the Main Line uniform remains Peck & Peckishly immutable: for spring, print cotton blouse, cotton skirt; for summer, print cotton blouse, Bermuda shorts; for fall, cardigan sweater, pearls, tweed skirt; for winter, good black suit, pearls, good junior-cut mink jacket, little hat.

"Most of us have gotten a little better," says one woman, "but there are, I'll admit, a lot of women here who think it's all right to go to a dinner party dressed for golf." As for the men, the Philadelphia banking community has always set the style and bankers have probably never, as a group, been known as fashion plates. "In dress we're very English here," one man says. "A lot of men have their suits made in London and — well, you know how kind of funny English tailoring fits." Philadelphia bankers are also respectably a little out of press, and the rest of the Philadelphia men follow their example. One man, who is particular about his clothes (and buys them in New York), is always being kidded by business associates for "trying to dress fancy, like a New Yorker."

But even more distinctive than the Main Line dress and speech is the Main Line manner. An out-of-towner who had attended a Main Line party honoring a gentleman of an old Main Line family, said afterward, "He seemed like a nice enough fellow, but the poor chap must have had a few too many drinks beforehand. He sat there all evening, absolutely rigid and glassy-eyed, and never said a word." "But he wasn't drunk," a friend explained. "That's just his *manner*. He didn't know who you were, you see." But there is more to the manner than immobility in the face of strangers. Not long ago, at a Main Line gathering, a young woman from out of town said, "How very *serene* all these people seem." Whether she intended this as praise, or whether she found Main Line serenity faintly unsettling, it is hard to say. Since she was from New York, however, one suspects the latter. New Yorkers enjoy their active, competitive pace. There are even those who insist that there is a palpable difference between the New Haven Railroad trains leaving for Westchester County, and those of the Pennsylvania Railroad, leaving for Bryn Mawr. The New Haven starts off with a jolt and a rattle; the Pennsylvania, they say, glides out of the station *serenely*.

A curious negativism floats in the Main Line air. "Oh, I don't think so" is apt to be the Main Line response to any suggestion. There is also a tendency to run everything down a bit — other people, other cities, even the Main Line itself. You may be invited to a restaurant where, you will be warned in advance, the food is not very good — hardly palatable, in fact. If you ask whether, perhaps, there is a better place, you will be told yes, there is one, but it is always so crowded that no one can ever get a table. You might be asked to come out to the Main Line for the weekend although, your hostess may explain, you will doubtless be bored stiff; there is nothing to do. Main Liners spend a great deal of time explaining what the Main Line isn't ("It isn't like Boston . . . it isn't like New York") and hardly ever get around to what the Main Line *is*.

The Main Liner usually turns out to be against most things — most developments, that is, or anything new. He is against high-rise apartments, against public housing, against newcomers — so contagiously against them that the newcomer who has just moved into a high-rise apartment quickly develops into an opponent of high-rise apartments and newcomers too. The Main Line is strongly Republican but, when it talks politics, it is more anti-Democrat than anything else. The Main Line remains loyal to Philadelphia, but when it talks about Philadelphia it is often in terms of what is wrong with New York.

Main Liners are masters and mistresses of the flat reply. Sometimes, this can leave the impression of startling, disarming honesty. At other times, it emerges as naïveté, or simple rudeness. Not long ago, a woman who had recently moved here was planning a party for some out-of-town friends. As a neighborly gesture, she invited the couple who lived next door — Main Liners of long, long standing. She mailed the invitation, and two weeks went by without a word. Finally, with the date of her party at hand, she telephoned the neighbor: Had the invitation been received? "Oh yes," said the neighbor, "we got it, but we didn't think we'd be interested in coming. There'd be nobody there we'd know." Later, the hostess said, "I was hurt beyond belief at the time, but now I'm beginning to understand how they felt. That's the way things are on the Main Line — settled. We moved too quickly. We put them off."

An even more pronounced characteristic of the Main Liner is his imperturbability. His composure is complete in the most crucial moments; almost nothing astonishes him or ruffles him. There are the many local tales of ladies who have lost their underpants while standing in receiving lines. If all the tales are true, there has hardly been an Assembly, wedding, or debutante ball without its underpants crisis, and the elastic in Philadelphia lingerie must be particularly unstable stuff. In every anecdote, the woman in question bears an ancient Philadelphia name, and the point is always the magnificent aplomb with which she carried the situation off. One woman bent over, picked up the collapsed bloomers, slipped them in her purse, and went on shaking hands. Another stepped out of them and continued down the aisle of Old St. David's Church (Episcopal) in Radnor, without missing a beat of the wedding march. Still another, pushed the garment aside with the toe of her slipper and gestured to her footman to pick it up. The Main Line chuckles endlessly over these alleged episodes. But each Main Line woman knows that there is only one way to behave when, at some glittering gathering, her own drawers descend.

The *nil admirari* attitude often means that the Main Line discovers the things that it is against long after it is too late to do anything about them. It is characteristically Main Line that the giant new Wynnewood shopping center, including a large branch of Wanamaker's and a larger traffic problem all around it, was finished and open for business before a group came forth to oppose its construction. One woman, who resents the prevailing apathy toward the spoliation of the landscape, says, "I swear most of these old Main Line people don't even *see* what's going on — or else they think it's beneath their dignity to notice such matters. One morning they'll wake up and see that it's happened — that there isn't any Main Line any more."

Two newspapers, the Main Line *Times* and the Main Line *Chronicle,* cover affairs in the area, and the two present wildly differing pictures of what life on the Main Line is really like. The *Times,* according to Ben Kramer, publisher of the rival *Chronicle,* "caters to the Main Line psychology," and the Main Line psychology is that all is well, or soon will be. To be sure, *Times* readers are regularly reassured that nothing much is happening, and that there is no threat of anything happening in the future. According to Mr. Kramer's *Chronicle,* however, things are in a dreadful state everywhere from Overbrook to Paoli. "Lewd teenagers" are being "fined as drunks"; child molesters prowl the playgrounds; exposure artists ply their trade from parked cars in broad daylight; a naked man "prances" through a popular bar at night. "Sluts," "thugs," and "teenage toughs" throng nightly to a local riverbank which the paper has labeled "Boozer's Beach," where they do goodness knows what-all. Call girls, meanwhile, do a brisk business from the lobby of a new motel. Petting parties, gambling, marijuana, LSD, murder, and suicide abound in the *Chronicle*'s Main Line. "Out-of-town sluts," "hoods," "thugs," "mugs," and "boozers" from alien places like South Philadelphia are often singled out as the chief troublemakers, but it is just as apt to be "a member of a fine Main Line family," and through it all the police are accused of laxity, and respected town officials are suspected of misdemeanors ranging from graft to sex offenses.

The truth about the local situation probably lies between the two papers' views. The *Chronicle*'s Kramer — who says, "I've spent thirty years studying the Pennsylvania libel laws" — is a soft-spoken, courtly man quite at odds with his newspaper's journalistic mien. He admits that he would like to "shake the Main Line up a little," and rattle it out of its traditional air of complacency. Some of the articles he publishes may be injected with a bit of artificial fervor. Still, his has been an uphill job. The elite of the Main Line euphemistically call the *Chronicle* "controversial," and therefore do not read it — not officially, at least. One woman, quoting something she had read in the *Chronicle,* hastily explained, "It was an item my cook pointed out to me." And Kramer insists he is making some headway against the wall of indifference; at least one Main Line dowager has begun to function as an unofficial tipster for him. Early in 1961, for example, the lady telephoned his office to say — in a husky whisper — "If you really want a hot scoop, Ben, I'd look into what's going on between Nelson Rockefeller and Happy Murphy." Ben looked into it, and scooped every newspaper in the country with a story that said Nelson Rockefeller's first marriage was in trouble.

But on the whole, the Main Line is secure in the belief that everything turns out for the best in this best of all possible places. Partly this is due to the Main Line notion of tact. It is not *polite* to get aroused over issues, or to behave otherwise than agreeably. This studied equanimity often affects Main Line attitudes toward human relationships, and even conventional morality. A Main Line matron confided recently that she was "really very annoyed" with a young bachelor friend who had been a guest at her home for a weekend. "I've put him on probation," she explained, "and told him that he will not be invited back for at least six months. After all," she added, "he raped my maid. After everybody was asleep he went into her room and raped her. You can imagine the commotion it created — absolutely ruined the whole weekend. All the next day she was in tears, and wouldn't come out of the kitchen to serve. And there I was, with a houseful of guests! She was a treasure of a maid, too." The lady and her husband had decided "simply not to mention" the affair to the offending gentleman but, as she put it, "The next afternoon, over cocktails, my husband couldn't resist kidding him a little about it."

Two Main Line ladies, lunching at the Barclay Hotel in Philadelphia — the Main Line's favorite in-town eating spot — were overheard in a conversation that was ritually punctuated with little cries of, "Oh, my dear, how ghastly!" And, "Oh, my dear, how divine!" Her precious poodle, the first woman was saying, had come down with Rocky

Mountain spotted fever, and had had to be "put to sleep." ("Oh, my dear, how ghastly!" her friend commented.) The disease, furthermore, could be communicated to humans, and so the poodle owner's doctor had insisted that everyone in the household receive inoculations against it. They had all, then, received their shots — except the family cook who, for religious reasons, had refused. Well, sure enough, the storyteller continued, the cook had come down with Rocky Mountain spotted fever, and had died. ("Oh, my dear, how ghastly!") "But," the first woman added, "she was really something of a trial — always singing hymns in the kitchen. I have a new girl now that I like much better." "Oh, my dear," said her friend, "how divine!"

Like Grosse Pointe, the Main Line insists that racial and religious prejudice do not exist there. Unlike Grosse Pointe, the Main Line believes that it is telling the truth, though it would be truer and more exact to say that the manifestations of prejudice are very few — since they would not be tactful. There are sizable Negro populations, for example, in Bryn Mawr and Ardmore, and a smaller one in Radnor, but there are few signs of racial strife. Everyone points out that "Woodmont," the huge turreted castle built by the late Alan Wood in Gladwyne, is now owned by Father Divine and his Angels, "and nobody minds their being there." A young Negro executive of the General Electric Corporation recently bought a house in a select section of Bryn Mawr and moved in without incident. The family has not precisely been clasped to the bosom of Main Line Society but, again, "nobody minded." As for Jews, one Main Liner says proudly, "Jews are more accepted here than in any other American city," and, in a sense, this is true. It depends on what sort of Jew one is. In the early days of Philadelphia, many prosperous Jewish families mingled freely with — and married — members of the Christian upper crust, with the result that many, if not most, "old" Philadelphia families today have a Jewish ancestor or two, and many non-Jews have "Jewish-sounding" names. Subsequent "waves" of Jewish immigrants from Europe have fared differently, however, and today an *apartheid* exists between the "old" Sephardic families, the somewhat newer Germans — both of which are socially acceptable — and Jews from Eastern Europe, notably Russia and Poland, who are not. Pockets of the Main Line remain restricted against Jews of any variety, and Mrs. Irving Fried, who is Jewish, speaks humorously of "the border patrol" around one area in

Wynnewood where Jews are unwelcome. "Still," says another woman, "they can do everything — except, of course, join the clubs."

That is, they cannot join certain clubs — the clubs of the inner Main Line. These — the Philadelphia Country Club, the Merion Cricket Club, the Merion Golf Club, the Gulph Mills Golf Club, and the Radnor Hunt Club — are strung out along the length of the Main Line, and, as they march westward from the Philadelphia Country Club (the least fashionable of the five), they become increasingly exclusive until one reaches the Gulph Mills where, as they say, "someone has to die" before a new member can be taken in, and the "dear old cozy" Radnor Hunt, a paddock, as the name implies, for the horsey set. (Good Americans, Oscar Wilde once observed, go to Paris when they die; good Philadelphians, it is locally believed, just go farther out on the Main Line.) Whether all these clubs, which are traditionally Gentile, actually and actively discriminate against Jews is a question many Jewish Main Liners have pondered. The clubs themselves, of course, politely say that they do not. But still the Jewish population remains wary. Jews have been entertained as guests of members at the Merion Golf Club, and Jewish children take tennis lessons at the Merion Cricket. But, when it comes to applying for membership, Jewish families have preferred not to risk embarrassment or rebuff. "My husband wants to try, but I just don't want to be snubbed," one woman says.

The one Main Line club "which no Jew would ever *dare* to try to join" is the quaintly named Philadelphia Skating Club and Humane Society. The Society was organized more than a century ago, when the Main Line passion for skating on the Schuylkill was at its height, and when the skating parties were punctuated by mass drownings as shelves of ice broke loose and skaters were carried over dams to the tune of the "Skater's Waltz." Members of the Humane Society skated with lengths of rope lashed to their shoulders for rescue operations. Today, however, humanity and humaneness are secondary concerns of the Skating Club. It remains the area's most socially important and exclusive club. Meanwhile, the answer to the anti-Semitism of many Main Line clubs has been the formation of Jewish clubs — such as the Radnor Valley Country Club — which are just as exclusive in their own way.

Early in life, Main Line children acquire the attitudes and values of their elders. Two small boys in the sixth grade were recently picked up at school by a local car pool, and were overheard in the following conversation:

"Where did your mother make her debut?"

"Well, she never did, actually."

"That's funny. My mother made her debut, and she's not even pretty."

When a Main Line ten-year-old was showing his collection of old automobile license plates to a visitor, he was asked how he had managed to come by plates from such remote states as Idaho and Wyoming. "My father suggested that I take the *Social Register* and look through it for people with out-of-state addresses," he explained. "I wrote to them, then, and asked for their old plates — and of course I told them who I was, and how I'd found their names." A Wynnewood mother, whose fourteen-year-old had been entertaining a classmate from Episcopal Academy with an afternoon of rather noisy horseplay, stormed into her son's room to say, "Now you two boys get this mess picked up!" Later her son said to her sternly, "Mother, do you realize that you were screaming at the Pretender to the royal throne of Portugal, Miguel de Bragança?" "Oh?" said the mother sarcastically. "And how is his father, the King?" "It's not his father," the boy explained, "it's his grandfather."

Because of its excellent school system, many wealthy Main Line families — particularly those with newer money — send their children to local public schools, rather than to the private academies, and this has had a somewhat disquieting effect on the public school population. The private schools have a more or less socially homogeneous enrollment, and opportunities for snobbery are few. The public schools, however, according to observers, have lately become the scene of "a great deal more social and money snobbery." Here the line between the Main Line rich and the Main Line poor is more sharply, and cruelly, drawn. A definite "rich kids" clique exists, and the poor — among them Negro children — are forced to join in bands of their own. Very little intercourse exists between the groups except as eruptions and something very close to gang fighting. But again, among the Old Guard, whose children do not go to public schools, there is little concern, or even awareness, of this situation.

The Old Guard of the Main Line have, as a result of their attitudes, been depicted as stuffy, stupid, and self-satisfied, obsessed with formality and ritual. But to those who compose the Old Guard, the situation is quite the opposite. Within Society's comfortable circle, a jolly air of good-fellowship prevails. It is all grand fun, and nobody bothers to dress up much or to fuss over expensive jewelry or furs or other "frills." Such social life as does not center on athletics revolves happily around entertaining, and Main Line parties are known for their number, their size, their supplies of good food, and their good wines. Terrapin and canvasback duck mark a hearty, and traditional, Main Line feast. The cocktail hour is firmly entrenched here, and often goes on for a good deal longer than an hour. Petal-scented evenings rock with bibulous laughter from drawing rooms, terraces, and poolsides. Some people say the Main Line does a bit too much tippling, and various clergymen have taken their congregations to task about it. Because most of it goes on in private homes and clubs, its effects are seldom publicly apparent.

Perhaps things were more stiff and formal here in the days when Mr. and Mrs. George W. Childs Drexel used to receive guests while seated on golden thrones. But nowadays it is not uncommon to sit down to dinner in a "great" Main Line house, with servants in attendance and with silver spread like xylophone keys on either side of your plate, and find the catsup bottle on the table. One eats amid cries of, "Pass the rolls!"

"I believe we were the first city in America," Mrs. George Roberts once said, "to omit the sherry with the soup course." Since then, Philadelphia Society has dispensed with many other amenities and formalities, and the result is an atmosphere that is warm, convivial, cozy, and just-plain-folksy. So unaccustomed to courtliness was one Main Line hostess that recently, when an attentive male guest from out of town pulled out her chair for her as she was about to sit down to dinner, she sat down hard on the floor. Being a Philadelphian, she rose perfectly to the occasion. She got up, went through with her dinner party, and then reported to her doctor with a fractured coccyx.

The Main Line also has the ability, which can be quite endearing, to laugh at itself. The true Main Liner thoroughly enjoys all the irreverent jokes about the Main Line, the parodies of it, even the broadsides hurled at it and the accusations that it is a dead and stultifying place. Tell a story that makes a Main Liner — particularly an old Main Liner — seem pompous, silly, or downright stupid, and the whole Main Line will laugh and slap its thighs. Such stories, perhaps, reconfirm the Main Liner's impression that his is a rare and special place to live. The Main Line loves its de-pantsed dowagers and it displays a very English affection for its local eccentrics. Anyone who is a little odd, and rich enough to get away with it — money is the only thing an eccentric needs — is a huge source of entertainment. For all the vitriol he hurled about him while he lived, the Main Line loved having the "terrible-tempered" Dr. Albert C. Barnes in its midst (the vast Barnes art collection, housed in his Merion mansion, can now be viewed by the public), and it enjoys recounting all the outrageous things he used to do and the naughty things he used to say. It tells with relish the story, apparently true, of the gently-bred lady art patron who came begging permission to see his paintings, and whom Barnes told, "The last woman I let in here gave me the clap!" One Main Line man says that he loves living there because, "I think it's the funniest place in the world," and, to be sure, it may be.

Along with sherry-with-the-soup have gone other Main Line rules. ("Never call on newcomers until you've seen their wash hanging out to dry; if they have ragged sheets or linen, you don't want to know them. . . ." "Never speak to anyone on shipboard until you're four days out . . ." were two that were handed out by a Main Line mother to her daughter thirty years ago.) It is still not easy to be accepted by Main Line Society. But it is certainly easier today than it was a generation ago — and for a reason involving one of the ways in which the Main Line really *is* changing. As the late great social secretary, Mrs. MacMullan, once put it, "Philadelphia Society has not stood up against the new money the way it might have" — and *ought* to have, she seems to have implied. Old money, in other words, should stand up against new money as a matter of principle. But instead, old money has let down some of its bars, and the new money has come in.

It used to be the rule that "It takes at least three generations to be accepted here." Now many people manage it handily in one, or even less. "Look at the young Liddon Pennocks," Mrs. MacMullan used to say, "one of the most popular couples in Philadelphia, even though it's first-generation money, and he's in trade." Pennock operates a flower shop.

Society here, as elsewhere, has been involved in the business of creating enduring *families* — families bound by blood and common interests — and in building from these families an enduring community of wealth. To fill its ranks, and replenish its coffers, Society has had to turn to the newcomers with the new money. "I'm really very anxious to meet some of these new people," said one Main Line mother of a debutante daughter. "Of course I want to meet the *attractive* new people." But with so many Main Line people working so hard at being attractive, attractive people are not hard to find. In addition to a blurring of old money with new, there has been a noticeable new mingling of the generations, who seem to be enjoying one anothers' company more wholeheartedly. The "sets" of Society still form small islands of special interests, but nowadays, at the best Main Line parties, silver heads are side by side with gold.

Though the complexion of Main Line Society may be slowly changing, something else is going on which in the long run may mean that Main Line attitudes and the Main Line manner will become even more thoroughly crystallized and localized in the string of towns. This has a lot to do with the new shopping centers and — as is the case in Grosse Pointe — the new self-sufficiency of suburban living. It has always been, first and foremost, the *Philadelphia* Main Line, with an iron cord, symbolized by the railroad, binding the suburbs to their mother city. Today, however, it is increasingly unnecessary for a Main Liner — a woman, particularly — to venture into the city at all. At the same time, as corporations build plants and research centers in the area, more and more men are to be found who both live and work on the Main Line.

The cultural life of Philadelphia, represented most strongly by the Art Museum and the Philadelphia Orchestra, still draws the suburbs to the metropolis. But there are already indications that the Main Line, by means of local art shows, local musical and theatre groups, may be developing a solid cultural life of its own — again, as in Grosse Pointe. Some Main Liners are already beginning to feel themselves somewhat cloistered. Not long ago, a group was formed which whimsically called itself the Society for the Preservation of Cultural Relations Between the East and West Banks of the Schuylkill, in an attempt to bring the Main Line and Chestnut Hill into communication through the medium of an annual dance. But whimsy sits oddly upon both the Main Line and Chestnut Hill. Also, when faced with the disruption of a tradition, the Philadelphian digs in his heels. Response to the S.P.C.R.B.E.W.B.S. has been only halfhearted.

If the present trend continues, with the Main Line growing more self-sustaining, more self-nourishing, the area may one day be completely self-sufficient, totally insular, socially and emotionally, and intellectually withdrawn from the great "city of four million" beyond it. Whether or not this will be a pleasant development, no one knows. But not long ago the Main Line was presented with an alarming statistic — some thirty per cent of its young people, according to a study at Villanova University, are moving to other parts of the United States; Society is losing manpower here. Actually, this percentage of deserters is not significantly different from that to be found in other prosperous suburbs, but this is no consolation to the Main Line — which always presumed it had *special* statistics. Now there is anxious talk to the effect that what is happening everywhere is now happening on the Main Line — the young are flying from the nest.

But the inner, Old Guard Main Line is not really alarmed. As Mrs. Wintersteen puts it, "In one form or another, there will *always* be a Main Line." To have its attitudes die, or be dissipated elsewhere, would, in the long run, never be permitted. Mrs. Wintersteen, to be sure, is of the older generation of the Establishment. What of the younger? Again, they seem to stand with her.

One member of this generation recently heard from was nineteen-year-old Alan McIlvain, Jr., heir to a fortune which the J. Gibson McIlvain Company, one of the largest wholesale lumber companies on the East Coast and one of the oldest family-owned businesses in America, has been building for Main Line McIlvains for nearly one hundred and seventy years, the equivalent of eight generations. From the wings of this imposing establishment, young McIlvain, the elder son of the company's president, says, "I plan to enter the business in the tradition of my forefathers."

In addition, he is interested in all the traditional activities of a proper Main Line gentleman. He lists hunting, fishing, skin-diving, soccer, tennis, squash, and swimming ("in their designated seasons") as his favorite athletic pastimes. Like young gentlemen everywhere, he is properly interested in young ladies in *their* designated seasons, and manages one or two dates a week except during the heavy winter social season, when the pace for debutantes and their escorts picks up. Like so many sons of wealthy parents, he is given a Spartan spending allowance — one dollar a week. Any other money he must earn "by doing jobs around the place" (it is a very large place, with much to do) and, of this, one half is banked for the future.

Alan McIlvain displays an aristocratic aloofness toward matters political. "Though I enjoy trying to analyze political strategy," he says, "I would never seriously consider entering politics." Looking ahead, he says, "Besides just inheriting the business, I want to improve and utilize it to its benefit. I hope to exploit [sic] new fields, and exercise the knowledge I will have spent so many years receiving. I would also like to have a happy social life by marrying and settling down in the Main Line."

13

The Company Town:
West Hartford, Conn. 06107

HARD by every major United States city it is possible to encounter at least one suburban stretch containing the styles and attitudes which have come to a kind of climax on the Main Line. There are the celebrated North Shores of both Chicago and Boston; Cleveland's Shaker Heights; Pittsburgh's Sewickley; the Clayton-Ladue towns west of St. Louis; San Francisco's Peninsula; and the Pasadena-San Marino complex outside Los Angeles. But the suburbs of smaller cities have somewhat special sets of problems.

Hartford, Connecticut, unlike most New England cities which have a tendency to sprawl smokily at river mouths, has a skyline of a certain drama. From whatever direction one approaches the city, the skyline signals with a single exclamation point: the tower of the Travelers Insurance Company, a pinnacle that has served as the city's symbol of success since 1918. Around the Travelers Tower cluster a number of much more modern structures, glittery with glass, including several other insurance companies. At night the Travelers's pale beacon floats above the city lights, and can be seen by airplane pilots from as far away as Providence. When the Prudential building was completed in Boston, the Travelers Tower became New England's second tallest building — a bitter pill for Hartford to swallow, but Hartford swallowed it with traditional dignity. An insurance city knows how to take disaster in stride.

The city sits beside a gentle curve in the Connecticut River with an air of complacency, ignoring its reflection in the water. The river means less to Hartford than it once did — much less than when the city's founders, led by Thomas Hooker, came down from what is now Cambridge, Massachusetts, in 1635 and settled on this western bank. Since then, the river has seen many changes. Steamers no longer ply between Hartford and New York. The river no longer freezes solidly from shore to shore, allowing skaters to waltz to Glastonbury and back again, as they did fifty years ago. Its waters, sullied by towns that have sprung up along its length from Long Island Sound to its headwaters in Canada, no longer lure great races of salmon as they once did. From the western slope of the city, there was once a Currier & Ives eye view of a New England river port. On these slopes, in the late eighteenth century, a group of intellectual artists known as "the Hartford wits" gathered in drawing rooms of Federalist houses. Here, in the nineteenth century, Charles Sigourney built a mansion where his wife, Lydia Huntley Sigourney, the most prolific lady author of her day (over two thousand articles, more than fifty books) held literary salons.

Today, the view of the river from these rises is blocked by banks of buildings, and the atmosphere in Hartford is somewhat less cerebral, somewhat more statistical. Hartford, since Mrs. Sigourney's day, has been largely based upon the law of averages which the fifty-odd insurance companies with home offices in the city have used to build businesses with total assets close to twenty billion dollars. For over a hundred years, the insurance business, and nothing else, has set Hartford's social tone.

Residentially, Hartford — as is the case in most cities — has always taken to the hills, and Hartford's hills range to the west and northwest. In Lydia Sigourney's day, the best people built their houses on the first rise of hills, an area which is now virtually a part of the city proper. Soon the fashionable residences moved westward to the next rise in the terrain, along Forest and Woodland streets, which were the city's finest streets until shortly after the First World War. As the city surged westward — the only way it had to go — so did fine houses, and mansions are hard to spot on Forest or Woodland now. The best people pushed higher, to the highest spot they could find and, in an ecstasy of extravagance, Prospect Avenue came to be.

For many years, Prospect Avenue was Hartford's ultimate street, climbing from south to north to a high hilltop studded with turrets. Beyond its shaded sidewalks, its manicured lawns, rhododendron-shrouded drives, and porte cocheres, Hartford's noblest and best secured themselves. Society stratified itself along the streets leading up to Prospect Avenue. In great houses on Prospect and nearby streets lived Battersons (insurance), Beaches (insurance), Cooleys (banking, but many insurance-company directorships), Bulkeleys (insurance), Brainards (insurance, but often considered newcomers, since the Brainards married into the older Bulkeley family as recently as the 1870's),* Goodwins (real estate, with numerous insurance connections via marriage to Beaches and Battersons, leading to the local observation that "the sons of Beaches always marry Battersons"), and other families who for years formed Hartford's Old Guard.

The view from Prospect Avenue was supremely satisfying as, from their tall, east-facing windows, the insurance families contemplated the city that had nourished them to greatness and, perhaps, considered greater days and statelier mansions to come. But today there is a strong body of opinion that Prospect Avenue may have been a mistake. In a way, it was a public statement that — despite the generous payments to widows and orphans, despite the care of the ailing and disabled— insurance was a very profitable business to those at the top. Viewed from below the hill, Prospect Avenue houses looked not only massive but aloof and disdainful as they poked their heads from among the trees. Prospect Avenue was not only the goal of the upstart, but a hated symbol of wealth and power to the left-behind. When Henry S. Beers was elected president of the Aetna Life Insurance Company in 1956, breaking the Bulkeley-Brainard family chain of leadership in that company, he was overheard to remark, "I guess this proves you don't have to come from Prospect Avenue to be president of an insurance company." Mr. Beers did not even come from Hartford, but from New Haven.

Prospect Avenue added to the insurance industry's public relations problem, for Hartford faces a sad fact: in most other cities, the insurance business lies somewhere near the bottom of the status ladder; the

---

* Curiously, many "first-cabin" Hartford families have names beginning with the letter B; to the above roster can be added such names as Brewster, Bushnell, Bunce and so on.

only person less welcome than an insurance salesman at a social gathering is an undertaker.

Now Prospect Avenue is feeling the relentless push of the city westward. One by one the great houses are going, or are being put to other uses. Shingles on Prospect Avenue announce beauty salons and apartment houses. The great brick fortress where, not so many years ago, Mrs. John C. Wilson, widow of the president of Colt's (firearms), liked to entertain visiting royalty, became the Seventh-day Adventist Church. A few Prospect Avenue houses still stand as they were, but the social goal of Hartford now lies in the next range of hills, in the suburb of West Hartford. The insurance executive may work in the city, buy his suits in Asylum Street, lunch at the sedate Hartford Club, but at day's end he more than likely heads homeward out Farmington Avenue to West Hartford. On weekends he plays golf at the Hartford Golf Club, also in West Hartford.

The suburb looks as if it had been built all at once. There is a shiny newness — new houses, new cars, new trees, new shrubbery — everywhere. Insurance men, no matter how successful, no longer believe in building massive houses, and modest, anonymous two-and-a-half-story frame Colonials are considered better for business. As a result, there is a considerable sameness to the landscape. Even on what are considered West Hartford's best streets, such as those which sprout from Mountain Road, the houses are surprisingly small. Few contain more than ten rooms, and most only eight. They sit primly and prettily at the end of walks lighted with coach lamps, beside 20 by 40 foot flagstone terraces, with shutters painted green, gray, or chocolate brown, looking like so many New England tollhouse cookies with raisin-eyes for windows.

Inside, the pattern of sameness continues — the cobbler's-bench coffee table, the wing chair with the ruffled skirt, the iron trivets on the wall, the copper planter-lamp with the chintz shade, the ship in the bottle on the mantel. West Hartford automobiles are generally models of the lower-priced three. Station wagons are favored. The atmosphere of simplicity does not mean, however, that money is lacking. West Hartford likes to say that it is one of the richest communities of its *size* in America. The wife of an insurance executive said, "Goodness, when anyone dies around here, they print the size of his estate in the newspaper. I said to my husband the other day, "Don't you *dare* die with less than a million dollars — I'd be so *embarrassed!*"

West Hartford, being to a large extent a one-industry town, subjects its residents to some curious social restrictions. If one is in the insurance business, it is less important who one is "on the outside" than how far up one is in his respective company. A mere office manager, in other words — even though independently wealthy — would be ill-advised to buy a house on a street where insurance company vice presidents live. A man whose position indicates that he drive a Chevrolet would be most unwise to buy an Oldsmobile. The social — to say nothing of the professional — consequences of such an act would be extreme. A New York girl who married a young insurance man and moved to West Hartford was given, by her adoring parents, a sumptuous mink coat. Sadly, her husband explained to her the facts of insuranceland: she would never be able to wear that coat in West Hartford — not, at least, until he had advanced considerably in his job. The same strictures apply to the wearing of jewels though, as one young woman explains, "They tend to forgive a large diamond if it's your engagement ring." A West Hartford junior executive who is a sports car buff secretly bought himself an Aston-Martin DB6 — he is not yet even in the category of Jaguar ownership. He is careful to drive his car only on lonely country roads, and at night. And when a West Hartford pair were entertaining out-of-town friends not long ago, they ushered their friends into a secret rumpus room created in a corner of the basement. "But don't tell any of our neighbors," the couple cautioned. "We're not supposed to have rumpus rooms yet." Needless to say, there is a great deal of "duty" entertaining; certain invitations must be accepted without question; and one climbs socially as one is promoted.

There is another attitude recognizable in West Hartford — and of which West Hartford is proud. That is Connecticut Yankeeism. A Connecticut Yankee, or so a Connecticut Yankee believes, is a special kind of Yankee. A Connecticut Yankee considers himself a little more successful than citizens of the other five New England states, a bit more socially conscious, a bit more sophisticated. His closest counterpart lives in Boston, but Connecticut Yankees believe that Bostonians have slipped a little, become a little lazy, while the Connecticut Yankee remains enterprising. A good example of the breed was Mr. Morgan Bulkeley Brainard. His son, Morgan, Jr., of the Aetna, recalls how vehemently his father insisted that he was "a Connecticut Yankee, a cut above the others." In his business, it was often necessary for the elder Mr. Brainard to travel to New York and other cities outside New England. He was usually driven, and he liked to doze in the back seat. But he inevitably woke up with a start whenever his car crossed the Connecticut state line. "There was something foreign in the air."

Mr. Brainard, a Yale man ('oo) like most proper Hartfordonians, was proud to have graduated from Hartford Public High School, and not from a New England prep school where, considering his family's wealth and position, he would most certainly have been admitted. Like many New England businesses, the Hartford insurance business starts early in the morning — at eight o'clock. As an example to all his employees, Mr. Brainard was always at his desk at precisely eight-fifteen and, to show he possessed the common touch, worked in his shirt-sleeves. (His son has followed Mr. Brainard's example, but has been known to arrive as late as eight-twenty-five.) Though Mr. Brainard had a car and chauffeur, his practice was to take the bus to work, and many of the Aetna's four thousand-plus home-office employees recall riding to work, seated, while their dignified president swung from a strap. For the homeward journey, Mr. Brainard preferred to walk, though the distance from his office to his home on Prospect Avenue was nearly three miles. On these walks, Mr. Brainard chose the left-hand side of the street so that his friends, driving by, would not feel obliged to stop and — even though they knew he did not want one — offer him a lift. Ritual and discipline, he used to insist, were vital ingredients of morality and good business. When Mr. Brainard was made president of Aetna Life, the company's assets were a scant two hundred million dollars. When he died, the figure was well over the three *billion* mark.

A Connecticut Yankee also was the late Mr. Brainard's uncle, Morgan Gardner Bulkeley, the company's third president and son of its founder. For eight years of his term as president, Mr. Bulkeley — mustachioed, spunky, and aristocratically outspoken — was also Hartford's mayor and, for four more years — from 1888 to 1892 — he was Governor of Connecticut. At the end of his first two-year term as Governor, he was not a candidate for reelection. Two candidates, Judge Luzon Morris, a Democrat and a political foe of Mr. Bulkeley's, and

General Samuel Merwin, a Republican, figured in a particularly close election. When the popular vote was counted, Judge Morris appeared to have won by exactly twenty-six votes, but the majority had occurred only because moderators in Bridgeport had thrown out one hundred and twenty-six Republican votes for Merwin. The Republicans, needless to say, insisted that those one hundred and twenty-six votes should *not* have been thrown out and, while controversy over the disputed votes mounted, Bulkeley was held over as Governor of the state. One morning, when the fight was at its fieriest, the state comptroller, a Democrat, ordered the lock changed on a door leading to an anteroom of the Governor's office. When Governor Bulkeley arrived and found this passage to his office locked and barred against him, his action was swift and decisive. He called for a crowbar and, with it, proceeded personally to batter down the door. There seemed to be little point, after that morning, in arguing about who should be Governor. Both Morris and Merwin withdrew, and Morgan G. Bulkeley held the office for two more years.

The Aetna's executive suite is contained in an elegant penthouse surrounded by an improbable roof garden. In 1932, long after Governor Bulkeley's death, the penthouse was filled with gloomy faces and gloomier predictions. The reason for this was the election of Franklin Delano Roosevelt to the Presidency of the United States. One of the gloomiest faces in the office belonged to Charlie, a venerable Negro who, for years, had served as Governor Bulkeley's office butler-valet. "I'm glad the Governor never lived to see this day," Charlie kept repeating. And then suddenly, more emphatically, he said, "Why, if the Governor was alive this wouldn't have happened. The Governor wouldn't have *allowed* that man to get into the White House!"

Another such Connecticut Yankee was James Goodwin Batterson, a stonecutter, some of whose stone is said to repose in the state capitol building. In the early 1860's, Mr. Batterson had an idea, and he took it up with a certain James Bolter, a Hartford postman. Batterson's notion was this: if Bolter would give Batterson two cents for each time he made his mail-carrying rounds, Batterson would guarantee that Bolter would not have an accident. If Bolter *did* have an accident, Batterson said, he would give Bolter a thousand dollars. Bolter liked the idea, and thus came the idea of accident insurance to America, and thus was

*Lawn bowls at Newport's "venerable Casino," an English tradition
faithfully carried on*

Mrs. Peter Beard, the former Minnie Cushing, tries surfing at Newport

*Cornelius Shields at the Larchmont Yacht Club has twice won
the coveted Seawanhaka Cup*

John D. Rockefeller III weekends in Westchester at his farm near Briarcliff Manor

born the multibillion-dollar Travelers Insurance Company which has enriched many succeeding generations of Battersons, if not Bolters.

A Connecticut Yankee, by assimilation if not by birth, is Mrs. Henry S. Beers. Mr. and Mrs. Beers live in a small, unshowy Cape Cod house in Glastonbury with a view of the river and Rattlesnake Mountain. Mr. Beers has served on the Town Finance Committee, and Mrs. Beers never misses a town meeting. In her bedroom is a cluttered desk from which she handles her various duties for the Smith Alumnae Association. Also in her bedroom is her sewing machine. The Beers's only servant is a part-time cleaning woman. For vacations, they usually hike in Maine, camping at night in a tent. When William Paynter, an executive of the Connecticut General Insurance Company, and his wife moved to Glastonbury, the first arrival at their door after the moving vans had left was Mrs. Beers, wife of the president of the competitive Aetna Life, bearing a neighborly cake she had baked herself.

Hartford has the reputation of giving newcomers a chilly reception. But, says Mrs. Millard Bartels, wife of a Travelers executive and a native of Chicago, "It's very easy to get 'in' in Hartford if you *do* things." Mrs. Bartels, an attractive woman who is a meticulous housekeeper and the mother of three, does several. She is on the board of Gray Lodge (a home for teenage girls "who might otherwise go astray"), and also plans garden tours for the benefit of the Hartford Art School. She is on the Women's Committee of the Wadsworth Athenaeum, on the Committee for the Children's Museum, is active in Church work, spends an evening a week rolling bandages and, somehow or other, finds time to bowl regularly at the Hartford Golf Club. Other causes for which she and other West Hartford wives toil — and are urged to toil by husbands who feel that community endeavor is good for business and for the insurance "image" — include the Community Chest, the Red Cross, the Boy Scouts, the P.T.A., the hospitals, convalescent homes, and museums, plus the Hartford Symphony and Opera Association, the Foreign Policy Association, the League of Women Voters and, of course, the Junior League. "With so many things to do," Mrs. Bartels says, "no new family should ever have any difficulty being taken into Society here."

There is, however, one circumstance which Mrs. Bartels and her friends may never have been in the position to notice. Insurance is a man's business, and Hartford is a man's town. Hartford men, no matter what their wives say — or how avidly their wives work for the community — make the social rules, one of the most implacable of which is the one which divides insurance company *management* people from the men who merely sell insurance. The Hartford Golf Club, for instance, is said not to want insurance salesman as members. An insurance salesman, of course — because he works on commission — may make a great deal more money than a vice president, who gets a salary. This makes no difference. The insurance salesman and his wife will not be invited to the houses of those whose names begin with B. The salesmen have tried many tactics — including calling themselves "agents" and referring to their customers as "clients" — but to no avail. One salesman speaks grimly of "the smiles and handshakes and first names and slaps on the back" that he receives from company officers at sales meetings. "But," he says, "when I meet these same men on the golf course, they look right through me." Some insurance salesmen, in order to cross this social barrier, have gone so far as to take office jobs, or transfer to executive training squads — at less money.

One change in insuranceland in the last twenty years is that fewer and fewer insurance company presidents come from "old Hartford" families. Nepotism, once so common, is rarer. Mr. Beers is not the only president who was born away from Prospect Avenue. Frazar B. Wilde of the Connecticut General is from Boston. J. Doyle DeWitt of the Travelers — a golfing companion of Dwight D. Eisenhower — was born in Sully, Iowa. But the newcomers adopt, with amazing ease, the prevailing Connecticut Yankee attitude. An example is Mrs. Charles Zimmerman, wife of the president of the Connecticut Mutual Life Insurance Company. Opal Marie Zimmerman, whose husband was born in New York City, hails from Oklahoma herself and, though her tanned, smooth-skinned face and superlative figure make her assertion hard to credit, she insists she remembers "walking in the parade, waving a flag" when Oklahoma was admitted to statehood in 1907. Before coming to Hartford, Opal Marie was a successful dress designer in New York, and she continues to dress with a flair not typical of Hartford women.

With her sense of color and texture, Opal Marie has decorated her West Hartford house vividly and lavishly — in a manner also most untypical of Hartford — and she has created one of the most spectacular private gardens in the city. But, despite these personal divergences from the norm — which, her friends admit, required a certain amount of courage to carry out and might easily have failed — she has become a Hartford woman through and through. She has devoted herself tirelessly to many civic enterprises, and is now thoroughly accepted by even the oldest of the Old Guard. "In fact," says one of them, "Opal Marie has added a little glamour to our lives."

Through Charlie, a Dartmouth man, the Zimmermans have a number of famous friends, including the Nelson Rockefellers — and this has helped Hartford take notice of the Zimmermans. In fact, Opal Marie Zimmerman is walking proof of the most successful way to climb socially — which is *never to appear to care* whether one is climbing or not. Now Opal Marie insists she would not trade Hartford for any other place. Not long ago she said, "Charlie asked me the other day where I wanted to live when he retires. I just looked at him. And then I said, '*Charlie!* In Hartford, Connecticut, of course!' "

For those who have lived in, and have learned to love, the world of life insurance, there is simply no place else.

14

The Power Elite: Society in the Capital

WHEN Mrs. George F. Baker gave her celebrated (locally, at least) dinner party for Senator Barry Goldwater at "Viking's Cove," her Oyster Bay estate, she was regarded very definitely as a pioneer. Great excitement preceded the event, and no one was at all sure what might happen. A number of "unusual" people had been invited. There were one or two journalists (to one of whom Mrs. Baker confided that her favorite author is Albert Payson Terhune, writer of dog stories). Mr. Roy M. Cohn, a New York lawyer and former member of Senator Joseph McCarthy's "team," was also there. Political figures included Senator John Tower of Texas. The late Styles Bridges, Senator from New Hampshire, had wired his regrets. Louise Gore, active in conservative politics in Maryland and, at that point, heavily involved in Senator Goldwater's campaign, had flown up from Washington with the Senator — or "Barry," as everyone was cheerfully calling him. In other words, a certain section of Society had decided to assert itself politically. "It's high time," Mrs. Baker announced, "that some of us who are in a position to do something *did* something — to get the kind of government we want."

Society's idea, it often seems, of a perfect political leader would be someone along the lines of Bing Crosby — affable, affluent, Republican, and fun. There are, in fact, a number of people around the country who feel that Crosby would make a better President than any we have had in recent years, and a similar small but ardent number favored the late Walt Disney. (Society often thinks of itself as in a kind of show business, and so its affinity for right-thinking actors — George Murphy, Ronald Reagan, Shirley Temple — is not surprising.) When North Shore Society turned out to meet Senator Goldwater, it discovered that he was a kind of super-Bing Crosby. Like Bing, Barry was a golfer. Like Bing, Barry had a Western breeziness and charm and, as the evening progressed, it turned out that Barry Goldwater could also sing. "He's the most attractive man I've met in ages!" one woman cooed.

There were a number of uncommon aspects to Mrs. Baker's party. For one thing, it was a party for a serious cause — to Save the Country. Society is accustomed to helping stamp out diseases by giving balls, but the matter at stake at "Viking's Cove" was of far greater moment. For another thing, this was a party in a private house where there would be speeches. Society people are notoriously poor public speakers, and the possibility that a number of Old New York names might be called upon to say a few words about Goldwater was the cause of considerable jittery apprehension. At the same time, Mrs. Baker's party illustrated — as well as anything — Society's own quaint approach to national politics and political issues.

Mr. Edmund C. Lynch, a New York broker (of Merrill Lynch, Pierce, Fenner and Smith), introduced Senator Goldwater as "a man with ideas we should all listen to," and everyone agreed that "Eddie did a wonderful job" with his speech. The Senator, however, was surprisingly glib and perfunctory, and his speech was over so quickly that no one was sure what he had said. He turned the podium over to Senator Tower, who proved to be quite a bit more articulate. In sonorous tones, he reminded the assembled members of Society who they were and what they represented — "the leaders of the great city of New York" — and he assured his audience that their traditional and happy "way of life" was seriously threatened. "I look at you beautiful women," the Senator said, "in your beautiful dresses and your beautiful jewels. Unless Barry Goldwater is elected President, all that will go — down the drain." The women of the group cast nervous looks at one another, and fingered the diamonds at their throats.

Senator Tower knew, it seemed, that the best way to arouse Society from its traditional political lethargy was to suggest that it faced a change in the status quo. He offered Barry Goldwater as the status quo's savior and preserver. Similarly persuasive as a North Shore politician is Steven B. Derounian, Congressman from the Second District of New York (which includes the North Shore). Though considerably less socially polished than either Senators Goldwater or Tower, Representative Derounian — an immigrant from Bulgaria, a graduate of N.Y.U. and Fordham Law — is, nonetheless, much in demand as a guest at the best Long Island parties in the largest estates. "He helps us get our long driveways plowed in winter," one man says, but there is more to Derounian's appeal than that. Also a conservative Republican, Derounian likes to hint that if conservative Republicans are not at the helm in Washington, the very fabric of Society is about to be torn apart. "Do you know what will happen if this man Kennedy gets into the White House?" he once predicted. "Clubs like your wonderful Piping Rock will be *forced* to take in at least fifty per cent Jews." Everyone shudders at thoughts like these.

After the political speeches, Mrs. Baker's black-tied and begowned guests turned to dancing and otherwise enjoying themselves, and an atmosphere of wealthy reassurance began to return. The country was surely soon going to be in good hands. At about eleven o'clock, Goldwater and his party were preparing to leave for the airport, and Mrs. Baker's guests gathered under the vast portico of her house to bid him good-bye. Waving and blowing kisses, the Senator stepped into his limousine, and the great car started down the drive. Suddenly the wheels spat to a stop in the gravel, and the Senator emerged from the car, ran back to the trunk, opened it, and withdrew a bottle of whiskey. He waved it cheerfully in the air, ran back to the car, climbed inside, and was off. Everyone cheered.

"Isn't he wonderful?" one woman said. "And what he says makes *so* much sense. I just know he's going to win."

"I just wish," said a friend, "that they'd passed the hat after the speeches. With all the money that's represented in this house tonight, he could have raised millions for his campaign."

"Oh, but you couldn't have people writing checks with all these servants running around," the first woman said. "I'm always afraid my servants will find out how much money I have. If they ever did, and there ever *was* a Communist take-over, I know they'd murder me in my bed."

"Still, I know he could have collected an awful lot of money."

"He should try calling some of the men here in their offices tomorrow," the first woman said.

"Oh, but he won't be able to get a *tenth* as much out of them tomorrow — when they've all sobered up — as he would have if he'd tried tonight," said her friend.

Meanwhile, in Washington, both Society *and* politics are somewhat differently regarded. "Oh, baloney! There isn't any *real* Society here! 'Society' is just a word made up by a lot of *boobs* on newspapers for a lot of other *boobs* to read about!" said Alice Roosevelt Longworth not long ago as she sipped tea in her wisteria-shaded Massachusetts Avenue house. "More tea?" she offered her guest. "Or would you like a snort of something serious?" "Mrs. L.," as she is affectionately called in Washington — "Auntie Sis" to members of the family — is still, at over eighty, slender, fair, and elegantly beautiful as when she was known as "Princess Alice," and when the color "Alice blue" was named after her. Her wit is quick and caustic. Even if she were not the daughter of one United States President (furry mementoes of her father's big-game hunts hang upon her walls), and the cousin of another, she would still be considered a member of the American aristocracy. At Truman Capote's celebrated *bal masque* in 1966, when women who considered themselves "of Society" spent hundreds of dollars on elaborate masks, Mrs. L. showed up in a thirty-nine-cent mask from Woolworth's and was the grandest woman there. And yet she insists that her own life has not been typical of what she calls "real" Society. "My life has been all publicity-publicity-publicity," she says. She feels, instead, that her life typifies *Washington* Society, which is a somewhat special thing. "I came out in the White House, for instance," Mrs. Longworth says with a little shrug of her shoulders. As is the case with many people who are in Society in the capital, Washington is only an adopted home for her. "Washington Society," she says, "is all come-and-go." It is all newcomers.

This is why, to Real Society, Washington Society seems incomprehensible — a contradiction in terms. It *can't* be real. It actually *welcomes* newcomers. Newcomers seem to be Washington Society's life-blood and, even more baffling, most of the newcomers are politicians.

Real Society has never favored politics as a career. By its very nature, politics involves a stepping-out from the enclosure of family and wealth, and an attempt to make all sorts of friends. When its members have occasionally gone into politics, Real Society families have always elaborately forgiven them, while treating the occasional political-minded Rockefeller, Roosevelt, or Lindsay as strays. "Heavens," says a Philadelphia lady, "I'd always be polite to a politician. They are our public servants." She would be equally polite, she implies, to any servant. After Senator Goldwater's rather decisive defeat at the polls, Mrs. Baker and her Long Island friends decided that they, too, had been unwisely dabbling in affairs best left to menials. That they themselves had been politically naïve was never considered, much less mentioned. "It was the machine," said one woman vaguely, "that brought Barry down." "Of course I'm not sorry I'm a Republican," said another. "This sort of thing merely proves that we should support the Republican party more and more. But as for the politicians — they're best left for other politicians to handle." The odd distinction that Society in America so often makes between *voting*, which is regarded as a sort of moral stance, and *politics*, which is simple skulduggery, was never more apparent. "It was one thing for Edith Baker to vote for Barry," says a friend, "but quite another to give a political dinner party for him. After all, the way to get a man elected is with money."

To Real Society, Washington Society seems all wrong. Real Society has always been based on a wish to maintain the standards and the balance of things. In its battle against change, Society must be admired for its spunk and pitied for its defeat. It has tried, again and again, to establish something that could be called a system, and it has seen, again and again, its systems collapse. So it is particularly painful to look at Washington where, regardless of who is in or out of Society, Society continues to function, and with a certain order and predictability. It has done so, furthermore, for more than a hundred and fifty years. People come and go in a steady stream, but the architecture of Washington Society stays. Socially, it is the most fluid and yet the most stable of American cities.

The concerns of other cities simply do not occur in Washington. The most successful social voice in town may belong to Polly Guggenheim Logan's bird, which says *"Hellew!"* in a powdered accent to visitors as they enter. ("It talks that way," its owner explains, "because it was trained by Mr. Guggenheim's valet.") Where one went to school, or where one's daughter came out, matters little. Nor does it matter much where one is from because nearly everyone is from somewhere else, and this is often a town no one has heard of.

"I feel sorry for people who come here from Oshkosh, get a taste of our Society, and then have to go back," is an observation frequently heard in Washington. In Washington, "Oshkosh" is shorthand for elsewhere; venture twenty-five miles from the Capitol steps in any direction and you enter, socially, Oshkosh. Because Washington Society is easier to get into than Oshkosh Society, and because the returnee to Oshkosh may find himself just as much out of Society as before he went away, he may elect to stay on in Washington long after his political job has ended.

Washington is populated with ex-Senators, ex-Representatives, ex-Cabinet members, and ex-diplomats who are now practicing in downtown Washington law offices. "Making the job tougher for those of us who were born here," says one local lawyer. Similarly, widows of Senators, Representatives, Cabinet members, and diplomats have shown a preference for staying on. But to a majority of those in politics and government, the escape from Oshkosh is only temporary, and for those who go home, Society in the capital remains a dressy memory and a scrapbook-ful of old invitations and yellowing newspaper clippings.

The way the transient quality of its people lends permanence to Washington Society's design is visible everywhere — most strikingly, perhaps, in peoples' houses. Political fortunes change, administrations arrive and depart, but the silken background against which Society moves remains as immutable as the Pyramids, or New York's Plaza Hotel. After attending a handful of Washington parties, you begin to get the sense, as you enter each new house, of having been there before. Decorative details repeat themselves. The furniture is in the stiff and gilded style of Louis XIV and XV, but — different from *real* Society furniture — it is usually not *véritable* French. Reproductions, Washington finds, are better at withstanding the traffic of the comers and goers. The curved love seat is everywhere.

Washingtonians decorate their houses in pale, beige-y shades and, of course, there is good reason for this. Neutral colors, no more personal than those in an average hotel suite, are more likely to satisfy a succession of different owners. When a new Senator buys a house in Washington, he must consider the possibility that he will not need it six years later. So he is cautious about making extensive structural changes. Personalizing a house too much can lessen its resale value. He is usually willing to buy, along with the house, the former owner's beige carpets, off-white draperies, and love seats — while the sellers of Washington houses usually have their own furniture waiting for them back in Oshkosh.

The monogrammed matchbook, considered middle class elsewhere, serves a triple function in Washington, which is why no house is without an abundant supply. A Washington woman may not be able to repaint her drawing room, but she can sprinkle every tabletop with her initials. Mrs. Lyndon Johnson who, as the Vice-President's wife, moved into Mrs. Perle Mesta's old house, accepted some of Mrs. Mesta's furniture, but lighted her cigarettes with "LBJ" matches. Now, of course, she is in somebody else's old house. Matchbooks are also a quicker means of identification than calling cards; a glance in the Steuben ashtray will remind you instantly where you are, and this is considered helpful to a politician in a busy season where he may drop in on as many as ten functions an evening. Also, matchbooks tell others where you have been; they are status conveying, nonverbal name-droppers. A gentleman lighting a lady's cigarette with White House matches will not fail to produce a flutter of respect. No one leaves an important Washington party these days without artfully pocketing a handful of matchbooks.

Washington has been called a "company town," the main industry being politics, but this is a quite superficial appraisal of the Washington situation. Washington is a city — one of a very few cities — where Society wields true power. It is the taste of power, more than the taste of wealth, that is addictive in Washington and that keeps the ex-Senators, the ex-diplomats, the ex-Cabinet members and their widows staying on in the city, the scene of their greatest triumphs. And Government power — which is merely the magnetic core of the power that is achievable in Washington — is not the only power of importance here. Around the government have gathered satellite powers, and the men who represent these satellites — the lobbyists, the representatives of industry, of agriculture, of trade unions, of banks and legal firms — are as important to politicians in the balance of power as politicians are to them. Socially, these too must be reckoned with. Then, among the most powerful of all, are the journalists, the representatives of the newspapers, magazines, and broadcast media. A Senator may wait for months for a personal chat with the President of the United States, but a journalist can set it up for tomorrow morning. Everyone is aware of the power of these men and women and, socially, they have probably the easiest time of it. They are on everyone's invitation list for they can make or destroy careers. Everyone, too, is concerned with "handling" the press, for politicians have learned how the press can handle them, how a reporter — by artfully disguising himself as "a spokesman close to the White House," or "a close observer of the Washington scene" — can slant a story any way he wishes. "Socially, the press corps here is more powerful than the diplomatic corps," one wife says. "At every party I give, I make damn sure that the press people are having a good time."

There is also the possibility of getting into Washington Society by making politics a hobby. The young Washington housewife, if she is willing to devote a few hours a week to the furtherance of the career of a favorite Senator, perhaps helping him organize a campaign or speaking tour, helping him solicit funds, will find herself — like her Scarsdale sister who spends an afternoon a week hemming sheets for the hospital — swept into the Washington social whirl. In fact, because of the nature of American government and politics, Washington is a town where everyone is given a fighting chance; in Washington, everyone is essentially nice to everyone else — even to total strangers who wander in. Those strangers could, if nothing else, be voters.

Unlike the visitor to New York, Philadelphia, or Boston, the visitor to Washington — who would like to go to Society parties — can simply telephone his Senator or Congressman. Immediately, a little snowfall of invitations will descend upon his mailbox. Or he can just crash. The noted hostess Mrs. Gwen Cafritz admits that all her parties contain crashers. If they behave themselves, they are allowed to stay. They may even be invited back. But it would be a mistake to think of Washington's determined hospitableness as true "friendliness." "Remember," warns the capital's leading social arbitress, Carolyn Hagner Shaw, "that personal friendships *do not count* in official Washington." They never have counted. Washington friendships are business friendships, instantly breakable, just as they were when Dolly Madison was giving the parties.

Perhaps it is because the pattern of Washington Society never really changes that everyone looks for change wherever possible. With each new administration, a new and vigorous search for change begins. Possible signs of it become the major topic of conversation. The New Frontier, under President Kennedy, was said to have "changed everything." But Scottie Lanahan, the blond daughter of F. Scott Fitzgerald who has lived in Washington during several administrations and was considered a full-fledged member of the "New Frontier Set," says, "The only change I remember is that when the Peter Lawfords came to town, the Sargent Shrivers had a party and had Lester Lanin's orchestra flown in from New York."

One reason why Washington Society changes little is that its tenets were established — albeit accidentally — by the United States Constitution. Another reason is Oshkosh. To the Oshkosh politician and his wife, Washington is the end of the rainbow. Arriving in Washington at last, they want exactly the kind of social life they have read about, with its cocktails, Gulf shrimp, black-tie dinners with five courses and three wines, and with — more than anything else — its traditional gaiety. "Boy, if the folks back home could see me now!" said the wife of a recently arrived young Senator as she turned, in her sequinned ball gown, admiring her image in a pier glass before leaving for a ball.

Washington has had somber periods, but they haven't lasted long. Gaiety comes bouncing back, and even national disasters can do little to dampen it. Betty Beale, a chatty columnist for the Washington *Star*, stated the situation accurately not long ago in a whole column devoted to gaiety. She observed that Washington was so gay one might think the town was caught up in "the excitement of a war." For anyone who is active in political life, or who "takes the town seriously" and enjoys feeling that he is close to the pulse of things, there is enough *required* gaiety to keep an engagement calendar solidly booked. An up-and-coming State Department man, for instance, who feels he ought to attend foreign embassy parties, finds that there are over a hundred foreign embassies in Washington, most of which have one important function a year — on their national days — if not two. This is already quite a lot of gaiety. Then there are the parties within his own department, the parties of other departments and agencies, the military parties, the press parties — and many more.

Also, as a matter of form, each newcomer is given a party. "It sometimes seems to me as though we could keep busy going to nothing but

Welcome-to-Washington parties, and farewell parties," sighs Mrs.
Archibald Roosevelt. Prominent out-of-towners also add to the load of
essential entertaining. "They come, they expect a party, and of course
they want to meet a lot of big shots," says Mrs. Longworth. "So people
here throw something together for them — a few dining-out Senators,
a Cabinet member, a couple of ambassadors — it's like putting
together a salad."

Not every newcomer to Washington finds the gaiety buoying. Mrs.
McGeorge Bundy, for example, a member of an old Boston family,
found the change from quiet New England to busy Washington initially "a little frightening." She says, "All those parties — I wasn't
used to it, you know. It took a lot out of me." "I'm afraid we shortened
his poor life at least ten years," says another woman sadly, referring to
a diplomat who, after an unusually heavy dose of farewell parties, collapsed on the gangplank of the ship that was to take him to his new
post. "It's not easy," a Washington man confessed, "to be perpetually
charming." And those who cannot be, or who simply do not wish to
be, have often had to resort to desperate solutions. One of the more
ingenious of these is offered by a Washington woman, the mother of
nine, who says wryly, "Washington Society is to blame for all my
children. I decided the only way I could avoid them was to be perpetually pregnant. Still, when I offer that as an excuse, people say to
me, 'But that doesn't stop Ethel Kennedy.'"

Another visitor, a Philadelphian, finds Washington's gaiety "all
rather mechanical and cold-blooded." He had been invited to a party at
the Francis Biddles' — "charming people, but I hardly had a chance to
say hello to them" — and found himself cornered by a young man
"who proceeded immediately to explain that he had seven parties to go
to between six and eight that evening, and he had them all *ranked*.
The Biddles' was going to get nineteen minutes of his time. The next
people would get only eleven minutes — and so on, down to the last
two parties which he would only pop in on."

One unfortunate aspect of Washington parties is that they tend,
like Washington social schedules, to become quite crowded. Often
there seem not only to be too many people but too many important
people, so that the effect of seeing so many dignitaries packed together
is dizzying rather than impressive. Only in Washington can one become numbed by the sight of famous faces, weary of shaking famous

hands. "At the Stewart Alsops' one night," a guest recalls, "I got caught in a jam between Hubert Humphrey, Walter Lippmann, and what's-his-name, the French ambassador. The Secretary of the Treasury was behind me, trying to push through, and in front of me were three people named Roosevelt. The only thing I could think of was how to get out." Later, this same man says, "A girl lost an earring, and when I stooped to look for it I saw that the Alsops' rug was covered with stamped out cigarette butts."

The best-known way of getting into Washington Society, if one is not elected or appointed to it, is to party-throw one's way in. The late Evalyn Walsh McLean did so. Peggy Eaton, the wife of Andrew Jackson's Secretary of War, did so. So did Kate Chase, the daughter of Lincoln's Secretary of the Treasury, and dozens of others. The only necessary ingredients for success are determination, energy, and a great deal of money. To these might be added a few secondary requirements such as a thick skin, a shrewd eye for the value of publicity, and a sympathetic — or preferably absent — spouse. Washington has long been a city where wealthy widows and divorcees and other maritally displaced persons, who have been left out of things in other cities, can come into their own. It has also been ideal for the woman (the game of "Washington hostess" has only rarely been played by a man) whose money, for one reason or another, would not buy her a place in Society elsewhere.

A smallish but very rich widow from Oklahoma named Perle Skirvin Mesta tried the party-tossing road to High Society first in Oklahoma, then in Pittsburgh and Newport, with minimal results. She then came to Washington, and the rest is musical comedy history. Washington provided a similar field day for a little girl from Budapest named Gwendolyn Detre de Surnay Cafritz. To others who envied her success, she once warned, "It is not enough to be Hungarian. One must also have talent." Yet also successful were Mrs. Marjorie Merriweather Post Close Hutton Davies May, from Chicago, and Mrs. Patricia Firestone Chatham, from Akron, and they were not even Hungarian.

The pattern is simple: a big new house on Foxhall Road, a refurbished Georgetown mansion, or a vast apartment in Foggy Bottom; a stack of engraved invitations, a copy of the Washington "Social List," the name of a caterer; and the hostess is ready to begin. It is not necessary, as in New York, that she first establish herself as a worker for worthy causes; politics is Washington's favorite charity. It is not even necessary, as it certainly is everywhere else, that she personally know any important people. When her late husband, a real estate man, started on his way toward considerable riches, Gwen Cafritz set her sights, and she set them high. "I started out having little attachés," she says. She then went on to bigger attachés. Then, "I worked my way up to the Supreme Court." The late Morris Cafritz, an unassuming little man, was content to stand on the sidelines of his wife's social career. At her parties, he often made himself helpful by holding open doors as the great and famous passed through, and one guest, thinking he had tipped a footman, realized he had pressed a five-dollar bill into the hand of Morris Cafritz. Typically, Mr. Cafritz did not remonstrate with the man, but merely smiled and thanked him.

There are a few tricks that Washington hostesses have learned over the years. "There's a way they have of inviting you," Scottie Lanahan says. "It's hard to put into words, but it's a tone of voice they use over the phone. They ask you to a party in such a way that you're terribly flattered. They make you think that you must have done something pretty important recently, or you wouldn't even be considered." A hoarier technique is that of giving a party "in honor of" someone. A call to the wife of the Attorney General, asking her to a party honoring the British ambassador, is almost certain to get an acceptance. Political necessity demands that such an invitation be accepted. Then, quickly, another call to the British ambassador's wife, inviting her to a party for the Attorney General, will complete the ruse. Similarly, other important guests can be played off against each other.

But guile is not really required of the Washington hostess because Washington uniquely *needs* its Mmes. Cafritz, Mesta, May, Howar, and all their spiritual sisters present and future. Washington has always looked for ways to make the running of the United States government more efficient but, as government agencies have multiplied, the job has become increasingly complicated. An official's day is bound up in regulations, protocol, red tape, clogged telephone wires. But protocol and tape and switchboard delays blur and dissolve at parties. Parties become a tool for doing business and, therefore, an implement of government — for which, miraculously, the taxpayer does not pay. Gwen Cafritz was amused not long ago to read in her newspaper that a certain Supreme Court decision would be reached on "October 8."

This was a Sunday, when the Court would not be in session and, of course, the Court traditionally decides on Mondays. But the eighth was the date of Mrs. Cafritz's annual Supreme Court party, the event Mrs. Cafritz likes to call "the real beginning" of the city's social season. Though the date was a typographical error, Mrs. Cafritz felt that it unknowingly stated the truth. "That decision will be made right here in my drawing room!" she announced. Here one can sense again the feeling of power that Washington Society enjoys — the thrill of knowing that events are taking place at one's dinner table that may, by morning, command the attention of the entire world, and that one may even have had a hand in helping to shape them.

It is possible that, in a social situation, an embattled Defense Department man can buttonhole a stubborn Congressman and perhaps, before the evening is over, the two may come to an agreement on an appropriation that it would otherwise have taken months to reach. Also, it is important for men in divergent branches of government simply to *meet* one another. Parties provide the meeting places. The belief that they are helping the ponderous wheels of national government move an inch or two forward adds to the Washington hostesses' sense of high calling.

Politics may be in the back of everyone's mind at a Washington party, but the political differences are almost never discussed, and, if they are discussed, they are almost never argued about. On the rare occasion that an argument does start, it is kept determinedly friendly — thanks to the hostesses. "No one ever fights at *my* parties!" Gwen Cafritz says grimly, and the others are with her to a girl. Political rivalries, they feel, should be subordinated to the greater cause of let's-all-pull-together-for-the-good-of-the-country. Trying to tame warring factions after five o'clock may not produce any permanent results, but the hostesses feel that compromise is the best way to end a stalemate, that negotiation is a path to peace, and that dinner music can soothe the savage breast when Dove sits next to Hawk. Like jungle missionaries, they feel that their first task is to get the headhunters into Mother Hubbards.

Parties are also an important news medium. A new crisis in the Middle East reaches the ears of Washington partygoers a full two hours before it reaches a network television screen, and twelve hours before it reaches the morning readers of the New York *Times*. Washington parties exist, among other things, for gossip and gossip in Washington is highly respected. Indeed, it has almost reached the level of an art form. Information, news, hard fact, rumor, hints, interpretations, analyses, innuendoes, and guesses pass from guest to guest with astonishing speed and with an even more astonishing degree of accuracy.

"Secretary Rusk said to me just now . . ." a Washington hostess begins, and all ears turn toward her. She then pauses, framing her quotation carefully so as to relay an exact transcription of the Secretary's words and tone and implication. Then, for minutes afterwards, the Secretary's meaning will be dissected; possibilities will be weighed, examined, reassembled with laboratory care. Often, of course, the Secretary's words may amount to a general observation of no importance or news value. But there is always the possibility that they will amount to something large and startling. A woman who is poor at passing along gossip properly will never become an important Washington hostess.

There is always, too, the more titillating possibility that someone, somewhere along the line, may be made indiscreet by Martinis and reveal a full-scale secret. But the unwritten rules of Washington Society carry a built-in protective clause: the worst social gaffe that can be committed in the capital is to have too much to drink at a party.

The power that Washington hostesses share with the officials of government is not always looked on kindly by the male population in the city. As they slump over their brandy and cigars in the library after dinner, Washington men often ask themselves: what is the psychology behind the "hostess drive"? Is it compensation for an ego bruised in childhood? Is it a sex substitute? Do these women really want to usurp the power of Washington men? The speculations bubble down to the general conclusion that, for a city in which social position is supposed to be determined by a man's position in government, Washington women have gone too far.

Women's admission to the sacred second floor of the Metropolitan Club was bad enough. So were Congresswoman Clare Boothe Luce's efforts to use the men's gymnasium in the House of Representatives. "But I'm sure you'd think I looked so pretty in my little bloomers!" she was quoted as having said at the time. "I sometimes wish the girls would stick *just* to parties," one man says sadly. But, on the whole, most Washington men are resigned to what Washington women do, and try to make the best of it.

Like other cities, Washington has loved to think of itself as being divided into sets but, always, the lines separating most of them are tenuous and indistinct. It is hard to tell, for instance, where the "Georgetown Set" leaves off and the "Foggy Bottom Set" begins. But there are a few sets which really *are* sets, and which have managed through the years to retain an identity of their own, largely by removing themselves from the mainstream of Washington's government Society.

To be a member of the "Cave Dweller Set," one must theoretically belong to a second- or third-generation Washington family. The cave dwellers, needless to say, choose to think of themselves as "the real backbone" of Washington Society, distinctly above the city's political and diplomatic comings and goings. Because of this attitude, the cave dwellers have been ignored by the Society of politicians and diplomats. As the latter's ranks have grown in size and importance and influence, it often appears that the cave dwellers have merely been passed by — and today have no real importance, social, cultural, or otherwise, at all.

Out in Virginia, in towns like McLean and Middleburg, there is a definite "Fox-Hunting Set," and several branches of a family named Lee who also hover on the fringes of Washington Society. And in suburban Maryland there are well-to-do Washingtonians who live apart from the gaiety of politics. Indeed, members of the "Chevy Chase Set" seem unaware that any sort of life goes on in the capital area other than their own. "There are girls I've grown up with in Washington," says Louise Gore, daughter of a family long prominent in politics, "I've gone to school and college with them, but when they marry and move to Chevy Chase, something happens to them. They gradually withdraw from things here, and then completely disappear." Another woman says, "I think those Chevy Chase people are *afraid* to enter the real social life of Washington. They're afraid that they don't have enough to offer, and that if they mixed with the rest of us they'd be boring." It is certainly true that when, on a rare occasion, a Chevy Chaser finds himself at a non-Chevy Chase party, curious things happen. Friends still tell the story of a young Chevy Chase matron who found herself at a party honoring Madame Hervé Alphand: she seemed unaware of who Madame Alphand was and, in fact, addressed her repeatedly as "Madame Elephant."

Getting into the Chevy Chase set is not at all as easy as getting into official Washington Society. The social center of the set is the exclusive Chevy Chase Club, considered "much more exclusive" than the Metropolitan Club — but not so exclusive as the 1925 F Street Club, which is called "the most exclusive club in the world," and "so exclusive that no member knows who the other members are." Members of the Metropolitan are a little bitter about the Chevy Chase because it was the Metropolitan that got the unfortunate publicity when a group of members, led by Senator Robert F. Kennedy, resigned in protest over the exclusion of diplomatic emissaries from new African nations. The Chevy Chase Club, Metropolitan men point out, is even *more* exclusive — and many of the men who resigned from the Metropolitan continued, quietly, to be members of the Chevy Chase.

If Washington's feeling about Negroes is not surprising, considering the city's geographic location, its anti-Semitic streak is more mysterious. The Washington Junior League, for instance, has a firm policy against Jewish members. During the Kennedy administration, the League was confronted with a ticklish problem. To its annual bazaar, it customarily invites all cabinet officers and their wives — but what was it to do in the cases of Secretaries Goldberg and Ribicoff? The ladies solved the dilemma ingeniously — by not issuing invitations to Secretaries Goldberg, Ribicoff, and Stewart Udall, a Mormon.

"Washington is just a country town," says Carolyn Shaw who compiles the Washington "social list." And Mrs. David Bruce, wife of the former American ambassador to the Court of St. James's says, "Why, Washington is like — like Cranford, New Jersey! Morgan's Drug Store, right here in Georgetown, is the clearinghouse for news about practically everybody." Mrs. Wilfried Platzer, wife of the Austrian ambassador, says, "Every year or so they say, 'Look how Washington has changed!' But I don't think new people coming in ever *change* Washington. To me, it seems the other way around. Washington is such a vivid, *live* place that it simply makes the new people conform to it."

All these observations come close to describing Washington. Washington has a bit of everything — Southern hospitality, Western openness, New England Puritanism (particularly in matters of dress),

New York sophistication, Cranford gossipiness, French cooking — all mixed together in a special concoction that is particularly American, and which Washington serves with a special gusto. Perhaps the rarest thing about Washington Society is that it approaches everything it does with joy. Unlike her social sister in New York, arranging yet another charity ball, the Washington hostess planning a party is not looking for an escape from boredom. She is looking forward with a kind of breathless excitement to the possibilities the evening may hold. "Of course I don't have any figures to prove it," one woman says, "but I'm sure there's a lower percentage of people going to psychiatrists here than in New York or Los Angeles."

Washington Society is based on love and duty. It *loves* the world's Oshkoshes, and wants their love in return. It is snobbish, but snobbish in recognizing achievement and hard work. Its particular sense of power lends it a sense of purpose, too. And through the whole fiber of Society runs an old-fashioned sort of Fourth of July patriotism, binding everyone together with red-white-and-blue bunting.

Those outside official Washington Society will always complain that it is "all come and go," and insist that it is the cave-dweller group of families that supply Washington with both standards and continuity. But, says one cave dweller, "It does sometimes seem as though the rest of them are having more fun than we are."

Part Three

HOW MONEY PLAYS:
A Selection of Pleasures and Playgrounds

15

"Society's Most Enduring Invention"

THE newest form of *en masse* fun to be devised by man, with the possible exception of the rumble, is undoubtedly the cocktail party. The first cocktail party was certainly held in 1920, shortly after the adoption of the Eighteenth Amendment; before that, social drinking was done almost exclusively in public saloons and was therefore an almost exclusively masculine pastime. But Prohibition forced America's drinking population underground. The safest place to drink became the living room where, of course, the ladies were. The ladies couldn't have liked it more.

Cocktail parties were a gesture of defiance against those who had inflicted Prohibition on the country. They were the bold, the daring, the naughty thing to do. There was an air of excitement about those primordial parties, the kind of excitement that is generated by jauntily breaking the law. Each cocktail was an adventure too. Depending upon the bootlegger, a few swallows might make one pleasantly tiddly or violently ill. Bathtub gin (which, incidentally, was hardly ever mixed in such quantities as required a bathtub) could be made with alcohol, glycerin, essence of juniper, and a few other odds and ends, and had a taste that cried to be covered up by some other substance — sugar, bitters, fruit juices, or syrups. The same was true of other bootleg liquor. And so came the invention of the hundreds of cocktails, slings, punches, toddies, and nogs that now fill the pages of *The Bar-*

tender's Guide. H. L. Mencken once estimated that 17,864,392,788 different drinks could be concocted from the available ingredients, and many of them were. There was rivalry, which added to the fun. Each cocktail party host tried to come up with better, or cleverer, cocktails. Recipes were invented, sampled, and quickly passed around. Into the shakers went whites of eggs, yolks of eggs, milk, honey, Worcestershire sauce, orange-flower water, wines, herbs, spices, and mixers of every and the most incompatible variety. Weirder grew the drinks, scarcer got the real stuff, and higher went its price. Still people cried, "Come for cocktails!" A Chicagoan recalls not being the least surprised at being invited to parties where he was charged for drinks. Instantly, the cocktail ritual — and the cocktail party — were taken up by Society. They have never been dropped. "Cocktails," the late Elsa Maxwell once said, with more than a bit of a sneer in her voice, "are Society's most enduring invention."

Miss Maxwell also said with her usual asperity, "Cocktail parties are ghastly businesses! I can not bear them. I don't give them, and I rarely go to them. There are a number of people in this world whom I don't care to meet, and whenever I go to them, there they all are! Cocktail parties! They're full of noisy chatter, wretched people, and horrible hors d'oeuvres made with rancid mayonnaise and tired tomatoes, poisonous little finger-sandwiches, warm drinks made with inferior liquor. *Cocktail* parties! They're boring, dull, and inefficient — the most miserable form of entertaining there is, and also the cheapest. Cocktail parties! I avoid them like the plague." Miss Maxwell added, "Fortunately, I was born drunk." Unfortunately, *real* Society never paid much heed to Miss Elsa Maxwell, nor was it lucky enough to be born in her state of intoxication. It has always needed a little drink. Cocktail parties have endured despite her.

In Westchester County, where cocktail parties on Sunday evening — a favored moment everywhere when one is in the "country" — create traffic jams on the parkways, most hostesses hire one or two servants from catering firms. Over the years, certain bartenders have grown to be much in demand. A visiting Englishman who had been entertained in Westchester turned to his hostess one evening and said, "You know, it's funny. That man of yours. I've a feeling I've bumped into him somewhere before." "Well," his hostess replied, "he serves at all the best parties in Bronxville." At a party in New York, meanwhile,

given by Mrs. Whitehouse Harjes, a particularly courtly and decorative antique passed the drinks. "Your man!" whispered a guest to Mrs.
Harjes. "I've got to have him for my next party. Where did you rent
him?" "He happens," said Mrs. Harjes icily, "to belong to the family."

Servants or no, "a cocktail" is certainly the civilized world's easiest
form of entertaining. This helps explain why cocktail parties survived
after their reason for being — Prohibition — had disappeared. When
the Eighteenth Amendment was repealed in 1933, ending the fun by
making it legal, cocktail parties should have gone into a long decline,
but they didn't. It has been said that cocktails had become a national
habit; it was too late to stop. It has also been said that cocktail parties
continued to be given out of nostalgia, as wistful, bibulous reminders
of the era of wonderful nonsense. All this may be true, but it is also
true that with repeal came the Depression. Though cocktail parties
were robbed of their old *raison d'être*, there now was a new one. Cocktail parties may not be the "cheapest" way to entertain, but they are
certainly among the most economical. Though the country's fiscal
picture is brighter than it was in 1933, cheapness and ease are qualities
appreciated by the rich as well as the poor.

"I can give a cocktail party for fifty or sixty people, and pay off
*every*body, and — if I want — handle it all by myself," a well-to-do
New York woman says. "Or, I can hire a bartender to fix the drinks
and a girl to pass the canapés. But I couldn't give a dinner party for
that many people without twice or three times that many servants."
Large dinner parties, she points out, are simply beyond the capacity of
most modern households. Gourmet food? "Climbers serve that," she
says, "you know, all those dreary little ladies who watch Julia Child on
television." Cocktails, once the daring way to entertain, have become
the practical way. And there is another modern advantage: they can be
tax deductible. "We always throw in a few business friends at a cocktail party," one woman says. "That way, we can write it off."

"They're so easy to give, it's insidious," says a bachelor. "What I do
is, I mix the first round of drinks, and after that I let every man take
care of himself. That way, I can sit and relax and enjoy my own party
just like a guest. I usually ask a date — to do the washing-up after." A
Chicago man gives cocktail parties by placing glasses, bottles, and
bucket of ice in a child's red express wagon and pulling the wagon
around the room. The William H. Vanderbilts are similarly casual

cocktail hosts and, after drinks, guests may retire to the kitchen of their large house while Mr. Vanderbilt cooks pancakes and the guests pitch in with the dishes. In artless Philadelphia, afternoon tea moves with no difficulty at all into the cocktail hour, particularly at the John Inger-solls'. Mr. Ingersoll pours a little inexpensive Vermouth into a bottle of medium-priced gin, shakes the mixture vigorously with his thumb over the bottle top, and then offers his guests room-temperature Martinis poured directly from the bottle.

It has become, in fact, a habit in Society to serve less expensive liquor. It is essential that the bar be well-stocked, but the appearance of a costly label is said to be the mark of the parvenu. Even more the mark of the parvenu is the trick — which one woman calls "utterly middle class" — of starting out with "good" liquor and then, after an hour or so, "when no one notices," bringing out the cheaper stuff. The American upper class starts right off with the mediocre — and never apologizes. Victor Bergeron, the "Trader" of Trader Vic's restaurants, has reported a cocktail party at which he became suspicious of what was being served him under the guise of "Scotch." He quietly explored the bar and found that the heavy and expensive crystal decanters — variously labeled "Gin," "Rum," "Vodka," "Brandy," "Rye," and "Scotch" on heavy and expensive silver necklaces — all were filled with an identical cheap blended whiskey, except for the decanter labeled "Rum," which actually contained, perhaps by accident, Scotch.

This was a party in New York. It would probably not have happened in San Francisco, as Mr. Bergeron was the first to point out. Cocktails are taken with considerably more seriousness in the Western United States than in the blasé East. The news that someone is about to give a cocktail party stirs up little excitement among New Yorkers, but, for some mysterious reason, it sends a flutter through the hearts of residents of Tulsa, Boise, Lincoln, and Bakersfield, and may actually make its way to the pages of the morning paper. Perhaps there is a "social time lag" between the East and West Coasts, as has been suggested. Certainly parties, moving westward, become more elaborate. Hostesses spend more time preparing for them, pay more attention to table decorations, flowers, and food; lady guests pay more attention to their clothes. A Western visitor in New York expressed surprise and shock at being served a paper napkin; an Eastern visitor in the West appeared at a party in a cut-out, peek-a-boo dress, and was told politely, "Not in Denver, dear."

In smaller cities, deprived by their size of such things as charity balls and debutante cotillions, cocktail parties become an adjunct to Society; they rate Society-page attention. In the Modesto, California, *Bee* not long ago a write-up of a cocktail party ran to two-and-a-half columns long, with photographs, describing the table decorations, listing the guests, telling who wore what — all with a fulsomeness that the New York *Times* would consider extreme, even to describe a Rockefeller wedding. To a certain extent this is true in Hollywood, too, a city that in many other ways resembles a commuter suburb of New York. Even the simplest Hollywood cocktail parties seem to have been produced in Cinemascope. In Washington, so mandatory is the cocktail to social ritual that elaborate measures must be taken to maintain sobriety — which is also mandatory. The most popular method is to sip tall glasses of champagne on ice — a practice that appalls wine fanciers. "They look like highballs, and you can drink a lot more of them," explains a Washingtonian.

Regional differences aside, as the cocktail party has become a social institution, the cocktail itself has become a fact of life. It cannot be avoided. It must be faced. In Society, one must serve drinks, and one must drink them. One must drink them not only often, but well. Dr. Ernest Dichter, the noted Motivational Research man, talks of "the vast swing to suburban living," and says, "The cocktail hour is changing from an exclusively party-associated interlude to a family-centered custom." In Society, there is more to it than that. Outsiders are frequently impressed — if not astonished — at the amount of liquor consumed throughout a perfectly average, unremarkable Society day. It is consumed steadily, slowly, in regulated amounts, throughout every waking hour. While it would be incorrect to say that Society is intoxicated all the time, it is certainly true that most of Society is never entirely sober most of the time.

One lady of the New York Old Guard, who would never, by her worst enemy, be called a drunkard, likes, and is always served, a whiskey sour by her butler on her breakfast tray. So the day begins. As it proceeds, through the rituals of morning — a glance at the papers, an inspection of the mail, the morning telephone calls, a note or two dictated or dashed off — such a lady may sip a glass of beer or a Bloody

Mary. Lunchtime is approaching, and if there are to be friends or family at the table, there will be pre-luncheon cocktails — Daiquiris, perhaps, or White Spiders, made with vodka and white *crème de menthe.* Then there is lunch, with wine or beer and, very probably, a little something afterward — a Starboard Light, say, which is the same as a White Spider but made with *green* mint liqueur. A Scotch or two is usually called for to carry one through the afternoon until, of course, one achieves the cocktail hour. "By drinking light, sweet drinks, drinking them slowly and spacing them with a certain care," says one observer of the social scene, "they manage never to appear drunk or even visibly tiddly. They hardly ever become boisterous or unmanageable. This helps convince these people that they are not in the least *addicted* to drink. Yet, when — as occasionally happens — they find themselves in a situation where liquor is unavailable, their displeasure becomes ferocious and their anxiety extreme."

After a particularly strenuous April in Paris Ball in New York not long ago, the ladies trooped into the Colony restaurant next day at lunchtime, enthusiastically comparing notes on the night before, effusively greeting and kissing Gene Cavallero, the restaurant's *maître d'hôtel,* and ordering their pre-luncheon cocktails. "Just think of it," said a wondering stranger to Cavallero. "These women were working on the Ball Committee all day yesterday. Last night, they danced until four and five o'clock in the morning. And here they all are today — raring to go. Where *do* you suppose they get their energy?"

Mr. Cavallero replied, "From alcohol."

"It was one of the great troubles with Mister F. Scott Fitzgerald, you know," an elderly New Yorker recalled recently. "He wanted so badly to be taken into Society, and to be accepted *as* Society, and he was certainly attractive and amusing enough to have made it easily. But he drank so *badly,* you see. He would get blind drunk, or he wouldn't show up — he was very unreliable, a very disorganized sort of man. No one minds a bit of drinking — social drinking — we all do that. But there must be *organization.* Without organization, Society simply cannot exist."

16

"July Was Always for the Shore"

THE theory behind the summer resort was that it allowed one to broaden one's range of acquaintance somewhat, that it permitted the upper class of one city to mingle a bit with the corresponding numbers of another. Allied with this was the upper-class belief that outdoor sport, particularly lawn tennis, was good for one, particularly for young people; it kept their minds from impure thoughts. One might drink and dance until the wee hours at a coming-out party, but one was expected to show up in one's whites on the court the next day, ready to be nimble and healthy. This is why, in wedding announcements, it is considered better when both partners to the union can produce two addresses, when each can say he is *from* somewhere, *and* somewhere else. This not only indicates money enough for the upkeep of two houses; it also advises that the couple have broader-than-usual backgrounds.

Where one is from *and* from is, naturally, of vast importance. An upstart, apparently trying to impress Alice Whitehouse Harjes, said to her, "I'm from New York and Massachusetts." Mrs. Harjes, whose debut at the family's summer home in Newport featured warships of the United States Navy which cruised offshore and bathed the party with their searchlights, replied coolly, "Well, those are both familiar states."

What counts in a summer resort, or in any other playground of Society, is not necessarily grandness. In fact, resorts generally have followed a curious law: the more elaborate the concept, the more rapid the decline. Take Tuxedo Park. Founded not so many years ago by Pierre Lorillard, the tobacco man, and built in the wooded hills of Rockland County, New York, near the village of Tuxedo,* the place was conceived on a magnificent scale. Not one but three lakes were installed between the hills — one for boating, one for bathing, one for fishing. Miles of bridle paths were threaded through the forest. A court for court tennis — still one of a mere handful in the country — was built and, since neither Mr. Lorillard nor any of his friends knew how to play the game, a court tennis instructor was imported from England. So seriously did Tuxedo Park take itself as a bastion of the best that Mrs. George B. St. George, who served as Congresswoman from the area, once addressed a gathering of her female constituents saying, "Ladies of the Park . . . and women of the Village . . ." Today, however, though Tuxedo Park continues to hold its annual Autumn Ball, which it insists is the "official" opening of the New York winter social season, the place has a decidedly seedy air. Many mansions, in need of paint and gutter work, stand empty; others have been turned into apartments. A new house has not been built in Tuxedo Park for years.

Or take Newport, often considered the queen of American resort cities. Newport became fashionable as early as the late eighteenth century. As John and Jessica Bridenbaugh wrote in *Rebels and Gentlemen:* "Over a hundred Philadelphians . . . voyaged to Newport for summer sojourns between 1767 and 1775, there to mingle not only with native New Englanders but also with wealthy South Carolinians, Georgians, and West Indians who were likewise investing the profits from commercial enterprise in a few months of expensive recreation in the refreshing northern climate." New York, seventy years later, was still not much of a city, but Philadelphia was, and Newport was well on its way to queendom. As Sidney Fisher wrote of Newport in 1844:

No other resort could exhibit a crowd so distinguished for refinement, wealth and fashion. The number of persons who were vulgar or underbred was so inconsiderable as to produce no appreciable effect. Far more recherché indeed

---

* The "informal" or "country" style of formal wear for men, the tailless dinner jacket, worn buttoned, without a vest, and with a black instead of a white tie, came into fashion at Tuxedo Park, and the tuxedo thereby earned its name.

than . . . our cities where society is rapidly losing its tone. Philadelphia was very well represented — Mrs. Ridgeway, the beauty of the season, Mrs. Jno. Butler, Mrs. Wilcocks, Miss Waln, Pierce Butler, etc. We had two balls each week, and two fancy balls. Among the novelties was a new dance, the Polka, just introduced in this country. It is somewhat like a waltz. Ten years ago everyone would have been shocked by it, but we are improving.

The only thing that Mr. Fisher complained about was that, in coming to Newport, the train was "crowded to excess with all sorts of people . . . The masses in this as in everything else have destroyed all decency. In coming from New York there were 5 Negroes in the same car with me. This I have never seen before."

Life in Newport in those days was decorous and seemly. For all the heavy schedule of balls, days were spent in sport, in eating large and healthy meals, and in ritual exposure — from verandas and under parasols — to the reputedly salubrious sea air. A certain rusticity was cultivated, and Newport's "cottages" were, though commodious, really cottages. It was not until after the Civil War that the age of the gilt-and-marble Newport palace began, and vulgarity was introduced by such "new" wealthy people as the Burdens and the Vanderbilts. The phenomenon that is today castle-lined Bellevue Avenue came to be, with the Vanderbilts contributing "The Breakers," certainly the most famous, if not technically the largest, of Newport's mansions. Once again, the concept of the place had become too grand. Newport was being spoiled by ostentation. Older people of "refinement, wealth, and fashion" took a horrified look at what was happening, and began moving quietly away.

A few families — the more "intellectual" ones, it was said at the time — removed themselves from Newport by crossing Narragansett Bay to Saunderstown, Rhode Island, where their houses stand today and appear to frown at the glitter of Newport across the water. But such folk as the Butlers, Walns, Wilcockses, and Mrs. Ridgeway retreated, for their summers away from the city, northward to Bar Harbor on Mount Desert Island in Maine. It was hoped that in Bar Harbor the elegance that had been Newport might be recaptured. Once more, everybody tried to be rustic and athletic. Lawn tennis was an essential activity, but so were hiking, blackberrying, and swimming in the island's icy waters. Everyone tried to climb as many of the island's hills as possible in the morning, and then sat down for picnic lunch where, according to one report, "the servant busied himself with the lunch, and put the wine to cool in the brook . . ."

But, once again, new money followed old, and mansions started to go up. It was Newport all over again. Along came Mrs. Edward Stotesbury who bought the A. J. Cassatt house, pronounced it "too small" — it had only fifteen servants' rooms — tore it down, and built another on its site with forty servants' rooms. When this house was finished, she visited it, walked through it, said, "No, it won't do," and had it torn down too. A third and larger house finally satisfied her expansive tastes, and the Stotesbury yacht was permitted to dock at the foot of the lawn. Once again, the "old" families, particularly the Philadelphia group, felt obliged to move on — this time to the other side of Mount Desert Island, to Northeast Harbor. New money continued to pour into Bar Harbor — from the Dorrances of Campbell's Soup, from the Atwater Kents, a radio fortune, who built a house with a fifteen-car garage. But soon it was clear that Bar Harbor, too, had got too big for its britches; hard Maine winters took an expensive toll on the Renaissance palaces which were not designed for New England weather. The marble portico of one house, which had filled a freighter's entire hold when it was carried from Italy, filled with frost and cracked apart during its first winter in Maine. Other mansions began going to seed. Mrs. Stotesbury's great house was presently being sold — for five thousand dollars — to a junk dealer who was interested only in salvaging the lead in Mrs. Stotesbury's plumbing. Her gold doorknobs left him unimpressed.

In 1947, for the ancient sin of *hubris,* Bar Harbor was punished by avenging gods. A great fire swept across the place, destroying nearly all the great houses remaining — many of which by that point stood untenanted and untended. At the time, families who had migrated to Northeast quietly congratulated each other on the wisdom of their move. *"That,"* murmured one woman, "will show those upstarts in Bar Harbor."

The few holdouts in Bar Harbor today occasionally find themselves in odd company. Mr. J. Howland Auchincloss, for instance, of the New York Old Guard, still keeps a Bar Harbor house. Not long ago, when a "new fellow" bought the house down the road, Mr. Auchincloss decided to do "the decent thing," and invited his new neighbor to lunch. The man accepted and, as the two were chatting before the

Editor and country gentleman Cass Canfield at his Westchester house

Philadelphia's Mrs. Nicholas Biddle and her dogs

Washington's ebullient Louise Gore, one of the first Society girls to open a restaurant as a profitable hobby, at her Jockey Club

Angier Biddle Duke alights on the White House lawn

The Cocktail Hour in a Palm Beach garden

Cushing "cottage" at Newport, hard by Bailey's Beach

Partying on Long Island's North Shore (left to right) Colonel Serge Obolensky,
"Shipwreck" Kelly, and Elizabeth Iglehart

Robert David Lion Gardiner, sixteenth Lord of the Manor (at Gardiner's Island),
entertains at his Fifth Avenue house

meal, the new neighbor said, "Excuse me, Auchincloss, but may I use your urinal?" Later Mr. Auchincloss — a silver-haired gentleman of great presence — asked, aghast, "Do you suppose he's installed one in that lovely old place?"

Northeast Harbor, Maine, proved a certain point. The proper upper-class summer resort, to be successful and enduring, should not look or act stridently rich; it should not proclaim itself with spires or minarets, nor with gates emblazoned with golden family crests. One can often say more with a wisteria-shaded veranda than with two hundred granite columns, and the weathered "shingle-style" can be both more appropriate and more meaningful than a portico of Carrara marble. Also, it seems to help if the resort can maintain a certain one-city cast.

Other miniature, or at least scaled-down, Newports have evolved throughout the country. New York has its North Shore of Long Island, the "Gold Coast" whose capitals are Locust Valley and the Piping Rock Club. It also has Southampton, on Long Island's South Shore. Though there is a certain amount of rivalry — and even more competition — between these two places, both are considered "merely extensions of New York city life," revolving around "parties, drinking, and dressing up in expensive clothes and jewels," according to one New Yorker. Other, quieter members of New York Society find much to favor in Watch Hill, Rhode Island, while still others prefer Edgartown, Massachusetts, on the island of Martha's Vineyard. Of these two places, one woman says, "Watch Hill is very stylish and gay while still being a very *family* place. Edgartown is more boat-y and Bermuda-short-y."

One can get the best of both these latter two worlds on Fishers Island, New York, a tiny principality of New York Society in the middle of Long Island Sound. Here, though a public ferry goes back and forth between the island and the mainland, the islanders are never troubled by tourists or other outsiders because, as one woman puts it, "There is simply nothing here at Fishers that anyone who doesn't belong here would want." Another woman says, "We're glad that Fishers Island isn't very pretty. This way, there's nothing to attract people here." On Fishers Island, everything is kept deliberately second-rate. The landscape is flat, barren, and rocky, and little more than poison ivy can be coaxed to grow in the island's acid soil. The beaches are mediocre, and the weather is quite often simply terrible. (No less

imposing an affair than a Vanderbilt wedding was once called off
because of an impending hurricane.) The two clubs — the Hay Harbor Club and the Fishers Island Yacht Club — are dowdy affairs.
Tennis courts are inferior, and the two golf courses on the island are
considered the world's least challenging. Yet this of course is just as
Fishers Island wishes it. Life here is barefoot and elaborately "un-
social," and one gets the strong impression of the rich playing at being
poor. (Actually, there are some practical reasons for this: servants are
hard to induce to Fishers and, once induced there, hardly ever want
to stay for there is no place for them to go and nothing for them to
do.) Fishers Island is Society's Petit Trianon, sort of, and the little
telephone directory — a page and a half long — reads like a conden-
sation of the New York and Philadelphia *Social Registers,* with Alsops,
Bakers, Blagdens, Canfields, Coles, du Ponts, Firestones, Peabodys,
Rutherfurds, Whitneys, and Wilmerdings predominating. No addresses are given in the phone book; why should such people need
street names, much less numbers? At the same time, when a surprising
name appears on the list, such as that of Mr. A. R. Grebe, the list
points out that he is an "electrical contractor." The Reverend Arthur
Lee Kinsolving, of St. James's in New York (and whose wife is a
Blagden), is there in the summer months to guide his little flock (who
are also his close friends) along the paths of Episcopalian righteousness
and, as one old resident says, "What else could we possibly want?"

Boston, too, is fragmented when it comes to ocean resorts. But each
resort that Boston favors is kept distinctly Bostonian in flavor. Much of
old Boston prefers the North Shore of Massachusetts Bay — such venerable resorts as Swampscott and Nahant (where lawn tennis was first
introduced to Americans). Others go farther north along the Bay, to
the towns of Prides Crossing, Beverly Farms, and Manchester. In Boston, certain family groups traditionally summer in certain towns.
Frothinghams and Cabots can be found at Beverly Farms. Chandlers
go to Small Point, Maine. Members of the venerable Fuller family,
and several nearly-as-venerable Bowditches, have claimed a tiny and
select stretch of New Hampshire's diminutive coastline called Little
Boar's Head. The Adamses, often considered the grandest family in
America, show their superiority to fad and fashion by summering on
the *South* Shore, in Minot and Scituate, Massachusetts.

Northeast Harbor, meanwhile, which might be considered the model for the above resorts, continues to be remarkable. Here, in splendid isolation, and in large but determinedly unflashy houses, *is* summer Philadelphia in its home away from home. Here, after the first week in July, is everybody one has seen a week before in Philadelphia, ready to pick up the threads of friendship once more. Everything that mattered to a Philadelphian has been brought, intact and in person, to Northeast. Here a group of men from Philadelphia's Rabbit Club established, in 1899, a summer version — the Pot and Kettle Club. Like its parent, its membership is strictly limited — to fifty — and, like the Rabbit, it is "a gentlemen's cooking club." At one time it was said that the Pot and Kettle's membership controlled eighty-five per cent of America's wealth — though where this imposing figure came from is not clear. It is possibly another example of the Philadelphian's tendency to inflate statistics pertaining to his city. But it is true that, at one of the Pot and Kettle's dinner meetings, as many as thirty-five yachts have been counted moored off the club's float.

For years, the headmasters of Philadelphia's two favorite schools, Groton and St. Paul's, summered at Northeast Harbor; the rectors Endicott Peabody and Samuel S. Drury mingled there with their students and alumni. Each summer Sunday Dr. Drury held Holy Communion and conducted his Bible class. Both men were fixtures of Northeast's social life, though Dr. Drury once wrote in his diary, " 'Sassiety' . . . this lunching & munching that knocks a whole day askew, this kid glove silliness . . . We come home exhausted, and hug our cottage fire." ("Concordia," the Drurys' Northeast "cottage," was hardly as primitive as the rector makes it sound.)

The Episcopal Church, too, was very much a part of the summer life at Northeast Harbor. In 1911, Dr. Drury wrote from "Concordia," "As I sit here I hear the clicking of another and rival typewriter. It is that of the Bishop of New York! Bishops! I should say so! They are as thick almost as the blueberries on yonder bush." Northeast Harbor still draws easily the largest bushload of Bishops in the East. The Reverend Matthew M. Warren, present headmaster of St. Paul's, may also spend a bit of summer time at Little Boar's Head, but he does not neglect his boys, old and new, at Northeast, helping provide a continuity of family, religion, and education — fibers that strengthen the fabric of the resort's life.

Continuity builds loyalty — blind, sentimental, absolute. "I simply cannot imagine a summer without Northeast," one woman says. In 1899, George Wharton Pepper spent the summer there with his fiancée and father-in-law-to-be. "Thereafter," he writes in his autobiography, "there have been only three summers in fifty-four years when we have failed to visit our beloved Mt. Desert." And when Mrs. J. Madison Taylor of Philadelphia died in 1952, it was noted in her obituary that she was preparing for her seventy-fifth consecutive summer at Northeast Harbor.

"Talk about continuity!" cries an old friend. "She *was* Northeast." She still is.

17

"August Was Always for the Mountains"

THE July-for-the-seashore-August-for-the-mountains rationale —
which has something to do with the scheduled appearance of biting
insects — has never had much basis in fact. The no-see-ums of Maine
and the black flies of the Adirondacks have never seemed to consult a
calendar before making their appearance in their respective places. Instead, there are definite "shore people" who see nothing to be gained
from the mountains, and there are "mountain people" who cringe at
the thought of salt spray. Which air was better for the health — mountain or sea — used to give Society something to argue about. Now it is
simply a matter of taste. Furthermore, whether one prefers shore or
mountains has nothing to do with status. It is not like the New England Shore as opposed to the New Jersey Shore, where one has cachet
and the other is second-rate. Mountain people and shore people know
that *both* are fashionable. But mountain people and shore people just
don't see much of one another during the summer. It is like the difference, in winter, between those who ski at Stowe and those who ski at
Vail.

Each locality has its favorite range of mountains — Philadelphia's is
the Poconos — but the mountains with the longest and most complicated special history in America are the Adirondacks of upper New
York state. An Indian legend is worth re-telling here.

So long ago that only the eldest of the tribe remembered it, the

Great Spirit had tried to imprison all the doers of evil in the hollow
trunks of trees that stood along the trail. Some had struggled to escape
through the encircling bark, and their agonized, uplifted arms and
clutching fingers could still be seen as gnarled and twisted branches.
A few had managed to free themselves altogether, and one of these
was Oquarah, a wicked sachem of the Saranacs.

For several years, so the legend goes, there had been friendly rivalry
between two young braves of the tribe — the Wolf and the Eagle.
Whenever the Saranacs raided the Tahawi, the two youths vied with
each other as to who would bring back the greater number of Tahawi
scalps. The contests between the two friends delighted everybody in
the tribe except Oquarah, who longed only for dissension. One day,
hunting together in the forest, the Wolf and the Eagle became separated. The Wolf spent hours searching and calling for his friend until,
at day's end, he returned sadly to the camp to announce that the Eagle
was lost. Old Oquarah saw his chance. "I hear a forked tongue," he
cried. "The Wolf was jealous of the Eagle, and his teeth have cut into
the Eagle's heart!" Stoutly the brave insisted that he did not lie. The
argument grew heated, and suddenly Oquarah leaped at the Wolf
with his hatchet raised. Seeing this, the Wolf's young wife threw herself in front of her husband and Oquarah's blade sank into her skull. A
moment later, Oquarah too was dead, with the Wolf's knife in his
heart, and immediately there was chaos in the camp. Two factions
formed. The Wolf — with half the tribe — fled down the Sounding
River to new hunting grounds; the rest remained behind. In the years
that followed, whenever the two halves of the divided Saranacs met,
the rivers ran red with blood.

The story, it turns out, has a belated happy ending. The Eagle returned, many years later, an old man. He had fallen in a rock chasm
the day of the hunt, had eventually been rescued by passing hunters
on their way to Canada, had followed them, had married a northern
squaw, had joined the British Army against the French, and had
finally made his way home. Learning their mistake, the warriors of
both branches called a council and swore a peace. But, with the exception of this last touch, the story of the split tribe might have set the
pattern of history in the Adirondacks. Because here, ironically, in one
of the most beautiful regions in Eastern America — in one of the largest stretches of unspoiled wilderness in the country — the human

story, both past and present, is underscored with conflict, argument, discord, and friction between factions; quarrels and schisms and confusions and misunderstandings and animosities that have managed to stop just short of bloodshed. Oquarah's spirit lives on, it sometimes seems, making trouble in paradise.

Wherever you stand in the Adirondacks, a great deal of what you see belongs to the public. In 1895, the state of New York added Section 7, Article VII to its constitution declaring that the Adirondack Forest Preserve could not "be leased, sold, or exchanged, nor shall the timber thereon be sold, removed, or destroyed," and that "the Forest Preserve shall be forever kept as wild forest lands." Using blue ink, the cartographers drew a line enclosing all the Adirondack region. Within this line fell not one but five distinct and parallel mountain ranges, with over a hundred peaks worthy of being called mountains, nearly half of which are over 4,000 feet high; the line enclosed some 9,425 square miles, roughly an eighth of the land in New York state, an area somewhat larger than the state of Massachusetts, next door, making Adirondack State Park by far the largest state park in the country, and nearly twice as large as our largest National Park (Yellowstone).

The amendment to the state constitution, and the existence of what is still referred to as "the blue line," was the start of all sorts of trouble, which is not to say that there hadn't been plenty of trouble before that. (In 1609, for instance, Samuel de Champlain came to the area and to the lake that now bears his name, and there was an immediate scuffle with the Indians; Champlain shot two Iroquois, and there was war for the next one hundred and seventy years.) The blue line encircled whole townships, many of them sizable, all or part of eleven counties, to say nothing of a number of privately owned lumber and mining companies, resort hotels, and private estates that antedated 1895. But all the land that was not privately owned became state owned and, as private lands became available, the state snapped them up. Today, the state owns over two million acres of land.

It became a battle, needless to say, between the conservationists and the developers, but this is reducing the argument to its barest skeleton. From this core have sprouted offshoots of controversy as multifarious as the branches of a pitch pine tree. The central battle has led, at times, to warfare between state and local governments, between Democrats and Republicans, lumbermen and hotelkeepers, hotelkeepers and *motel* keepers, between people who love to pitch tents in the woods and all the people who would just as dearly love to sell them rooms for the night, between highway departments and conservation departments, mountain climbers and motorists, sailboat fanciers and motorboat owners, canoeists and beaver-fanciers, wets and drys, summer people and winter people, Jews and Gentiles, property owners and tax collectors, and — most significantly — between the rich and the dirt-poor.

Even the various conservationist groups — composed, by and large, of the Adirondack rich — do not agree with one another, nor with the New York State Conservation Department in Albany. What do the words "forever" and "wild" mean, anyway? They are certainly strong and sweeping terms. In general, the department has followed the wording of the amendment quite literally, insisting that nothing on state land be touched. A fine is imposed for chopping down a state owned tree, and even dead trees are protected and must be allowed to topple of themselves and rot on the ground, since that is the way a "wild" forest is. But some conservationists feel that a wild forest is not necessarily a healthy one, and that woodlands should periodically be cleaned of old and dying trees. In general, all conservationists are opposed to the carving of new highways through the mountains, and when a highway threatens an area of large private estates the outcries become particularly loud. At the same time, men in the tourist business cry, "We've got all this beauty here and no way for people to get to it."

Adirondack lumbermen, who consider themselves the true aristocracy of the area — as opposed to the vacationing members of Society — are staunchly opposed to all conservationists, and for good reason. In his private journals, the late Ferris J. Meigs, who headed the Santa Clara Lumber Company near Tupper Lake, spoke derisively of "the so-called Society for the Prevention of Cruelty to the Adirondacks." Obviously, everything they wanted to see left standing in the woods he would have preferred to see rendered into toothpicks and ice cream spoons. Lumbermen like Meigs were traditionally anti-liquor, preferring to keep their workmen sober. After a lengthy struggle, Prohibition was enacted in the town and the Santa Clara Lumber Company jubilantly blew its whistle. From across the street a saloonkeeper came charging out and shot the whistle full of holes.

In the southern Adirondacks, Saratoga Springs was a resort contemporary to Newport, and by the mid-nineteenth century this "Queen of Spas," as it was called, was every bit as fashionable. The August races of the Saratoga Association for the Improvement of the Breed of Horses, organized in 1863, drew brilliant gatherings year after year. In August, Society flocked to Saratoga from as far off as Chicago, arranged itself on the extensive verandas of Saratoga's great hotels, drank and bathed in its chalky springs (heavily charged with carbonic acid gas that was said to "flush" the liver), and changed its clothes. It was the era of the private railroad car, and the capacious Saratoga trunk was designed to handle the wardrobe required for the Saratoga Season.* Soon, however, the resort became a battleground. For one thing, the "curative" waters of the springs were so heavily exploited — bottled and sold — that the springs themselves were going dry. Also, after the Civil War the resort was going through a Newport-like transition, with newer and more ostentatious money coming in. Saratoga was becoming "vulgar," and the older members of Society retreated to large and isolated "camps" along the northern lakes — Lakes George, Saranac, and Tupper.

Saratoga's resort hotels began losing business, and one of them — the largest — the Grand Union, decided to do something about it. In August of 1877, the hotel turned away the New York banker, Joseph Seligman, who had spent many Augusts there with his family, on the grounds that the hotel had a new policy and did not accept "Israelites." In the long run, however, this action lowered the resort's prestige among Gentiles as well as Jews, and Saratoga entered a long period of decline.

"Camp" life, meanwhile, was a return to studied rusticity. Well-tended by servants, Society roughed it — under beams and on furniture that had, at great expense, been chipped at with axes to look hand-hewn. Chandeliers were crafted out of antlers, and stuffed heads gazed down from every wall. (Conservationists who cared about trees were somewhat less thoughtful of the wildlife that grazed among them.) Mass-manufactured Indian blankets graced every bed whose head and

---

* John ("Bet-a-Million") Gates once bet Evander Berry Wall, a dude of the era, that he could not change his costume fifty times between breakfast and dinner at Saratoga. Gates won. Wall made it through only forty changes.

footboards were of logs still in their bark. Massive fireplaces brought heat to chilly mountain nights.

The next inevitable step for this sort of Society was to form a rustic mountain club; the great resort hotels of Saratoga were languishing, and a new sort of center for social life was needed. To fill this need there came, in 1891, a strange, brilliant, neurotic man named Melville Louis Kossuth Dewey. Dewey had always wanted to create monuments to himself. While a student at Amherst he had invented the Dewey Decimal System for classifying books which has been adopted by libraries all over the world, making Dewey the father of modern library science. He was also a proponent of simplified spelling, and dutifully simplified the spelling of his own first name to "Melvil," though he was reluctant to drop any letters from his last. Waggish friends used to say that if it made sense — as Dewey said it did — to drop the "ue" from words like "tongue," and "rogue," then why not do the same with words like "true," and "argue"? Dewey's spelling influence is noticeable in the mountains today, where "Adirondack" is variously spelled "Adirondak," or "Adirondac," and where the main lodge of the Adirondack Mountain Club is called "Adirondak Loj."

Though Dewey himself was not a member of the Four Hundred and, as far as is known, had no particular social ambitions, when he arrived at Lake Placid he had a vision of a place where "congenial people . . . the country's best" could meet in an atmosphere of culture and refinement. He named his vision the Lake Placid Club.

This was an important moment in the Adirondacks. The Mauve Decade was under way, post-Civil War fortunes were firmly established. At the midsummer peak of mountain-bound traffic, the tracks of the New York Central Railroad leading to Lake Placid were strung with private railway cars bearing Harrimans, Vanderbilts, Whitneys, Goulds, and Goelets to what was becoming the "heart" of the Adirondacks. It was becoming popular for camp owners to build rail spurs of their own from the main line of the Central directly to the camps themselves. At Nehasane, deep in the woods, Dr. Seward Webb, son-in-law of William H. Vanderbilt, built an entire private railroad station to serve his 112,000-acre camp. (According to an agreement with the Central, it is still technically impossible to buy a ticket to Nehasane, New York, unless one can produce a written invitation from the Webbs.) In this perfumed atmosphere, Dewey's notion for a club was immediately well received, and founding members — each with ready cash to invest — made themselves available.

Dewey had specific ideas about who "the country's best" were. Perhaps he was influenced by the Grand Union Hotel's action a few years earlier; perhaps not. In any case, according to T. Morris Longstreth, one of Dewey's chroniclers, Lake Placid Club guests were classified as follows — rather like library books: "Class C — common client, welcome, neither specially advantageous or disadvantageous; Class B — some talent, some distinguishing traits that make him desirable; Class A — those admirably suited to further the ideals of the club; Class D — doubtful or deficient characters; Class E — unsuitables who, if already in, must be eliminated; if still out, must be excluded for the protection of the rest." Lake Placid Club literature went on to add these bluntly worded provisos:

No one will be received as member or guest against whom there is physical, moral, social, or race objection, or who would be unwelcome to even a small minority. This excludes absolutely all consumptives, or rather invalids, whose presence might injure health or modify others' freedom or enjoyment. [Dewey himself came to the mountains for his hay fever, and his wife suffered from "rose cold" but their sneezing was evidently considered acceptable.] This invariable rule is rigidly enforced; it is found impracticable to make exceptions to Jews or others excluded, even when of unusual personal qualifications.

Mr. Dewey's Lake Placid Club was such a success that other builders of clubs and resorts in the area quickly took it as their model. The Ausable Club, near Keene, was built, and is considered "like the Lake Placid Club, but smaller and more exclusive." The anti-Semitism of Adirondack resorts became blatant. One hotel advertised, "Hebrews need not apply." Another said, "Hebrews will knock vainly for admission." Discriminatory statements in advertising are now against the law in New York, but various hotels have found clever ways of getting their point across. One may say, "Guests will enjoy our Christian religious library." Another, in a reservation coupon, asks, "Please state your Christian name."

"You must never underestimate the influence of the Lake Placid Club," one nearby property owner says. "Over the years, the club's influence has been absolutely tremendous. The club has influenced the entire Adirondack region." This is true. But whether that influence has in the long run been malignant or benign is another matter. Oquarah's cranky, restless shade may pace the mountains overhead, setting man against his fellow man. But in this enterprise he has had efficient human helpers, and many of these have been members of the Lake Placid Club. Today, the main clubhouse is a vast, rambling affair, part brick, part timber, and it broods at the edge of Mirror Lake where, on sunny days, it can see itself imposingly reflected. It is surrounded by numerous outbuildings and houses available for summer and winter rental. It has golf courses, a theatre and lecture hall, its own dairy and poultry farms, its own shops and laundry and dry cleaner, its own symphony orchestra, called a "Symphonette," its own ski and toboggan runs, its own tennis courts, miles of roads, and over seven thousand acres of farm and forest land. The club today has a membership in the thousands. Oddly, it is cheap as clubs go. Nonresident members pay a hundred dollars a year.

At the same time, Mr. Dewey and the men who followed him had succeeded in splitting the Adirondacks along religious lines, and the division persists today. For Jews who wished to visit the mountains, the answer was to build Jewish resorts and clubs. Rumor has it, — as it always does in discriminatory clubs — that one or two "secret Jews" have been sneaked into the Lake Placid Club, but if the club has any Jewish members they are keeping very quiet about it. For many years the Lake Placid Club operated its own boys' prep school. This was a posh affair indeed. "Every playboy you've ever heard of went there at one time or another," says a local woman. The school was a unique adaptation of academic life to resort life; fall and spring terms were conducted on the schoolgrounds at Placid but, for the winter term, school and students packed up and entrained for Palm Beach. Today, the school — renamed Northwood — occupies grounds hard by the club, but is separately chartered. The school will accept Jewish boys, but it uses club facilities for many of its activities. And any parent who is aware of the club's long reputation, and who reads in the school's catalogue that Northwood "maintains a close relationship with the Lake Placid Club" may wonder whether Northwood is the place to send his son.

The widely publicized membership policy of the club has created certain social drawbacks for "the country's best" who belong to it. In 1965, R. Peter Straus, president of radio station WMCA, publicly criticized Senator Robert F. Kennedy's brother-in-law, Stephen E. Smith, who had taken his family for a skiing holiday at the club, calling it "incredible" that Mr. Smith would stay at "a place that is known to discriminate against Jewish people." "Of course we were *never* like Newport," one member explains. "We were not competitive. We were more club-centered, more family-centered. We never went in for Newport's splash and show. We come up here to rest and be by ourselves." Still, Lake Placid likes to think of itself in the same breath with Newport. But, because of its policies, it has long been snubbed by Society editors of important Eastern newspapers — particularly by the New York *Times*, whose owners and publishers are related by marriage to Mr. Straus.

So the Lake Placid Club functions in a kind of social limbo, reduced to talking to and about itself. Through the years the club has had its financial ups and downs, but all seemed well until 1947, when the club entertained a record number of guests. Then a sudden decline began, and the club is now trying to find its way out of a mare's nest of financial woes. Members vary in their opinions of it. One woman calls life at the club "terribly gay, terribly fun," and defends its membership restrictions by saying, "After all, it *is* a private club. It has a right to choose those it wants as members." Others, particularly younger members, say it's "full of old fogeys," and describe the giant dining room as "a sea of white heads eating mediocre food." The Symphonette plays "constant Tchaikovsky," adding to the torpor of the mood. One member says, "The club is simply going to have to change its policy if it's going to stay alive." No early change in policy seems likely, though. And the club's future poses a dilemma to the entire community. It is virtually a year-round operation, and employs many local people. It is also an important taxpayer. Its death would be a severe economic blow to the entire area. Meanwhile, as the *éminence grise* of the Adirondacks, the Lake Placid Club's anti-Semitism may have done more than anything else to cause the Adirondacks's descent from ultra-fashionability. For the plain fact is that if mountains have lost chic generally, the Adirondack Mountains have lost more chic than other mountains. "We are now paying," says a local real estate man, "for the mistakes of past generations." And, around the Lake Placid shore, vacated and decaying private camps and lodges — one with its own little rusted railroad track running from the boat dock to the house, once used to trans-port guests and groceries — stand as testimony to what is happening.

It is astonishing to see how deeply entrenched the religious *apart-heid* in the Adirondacks has become. Another area that has changed greatly in recent years is the western shore of Lake George, where a once-famed "Millionaires' Row" stretching from Lake George Village to Bolton Landing has become a giddy string of motels, bowling alleys, and pizza palaces. "Jewish builders" are blamed by the old people who still summer here for the desecration of the landscape, but the cupidity of the estate owners, who sold their places to the highest bidders with-out caring what became of the property, is more to blame. The answer to the situation at this end of the lake, one wild-eyed woman explains, "is to keep Jews out of the Lake George Club. *That* will show them!" She adds, "I can't walk down the sidewalk any more. The Jews come along and push me right into the street!" The house next door, she explains, was sold to Jews. "And do you know what they've done? They've put up a *flagpole* on the front lawn!" Though her neighbors flew the American flag, she added, "Most of them are Communists."

Meanwhile, the old rich and the solid rich have moved elsewhere in the mountains. The rich have not abandoned the Adirondacks, not by a long shot, but if life around Lake Placid was "never like Newport" then it is even less like Newport in the lonely lostness of the south-western quarter of the park. Here, the Lake Placid Club is hardly ever thought of because, in a sense, each family has built a comfortable club of its own. William A. Rockefeller has large land holdings in this area. So do the William A. and Bayard W. Reads. Cornelius Vander-bilt Whitney — the famous "Sonny" — has a hundred thousand acre tract, and J. Watson Webb has a smaller tract of forty-five thousand acres. New York's McAlpin family also holds onto a sizable piece. Harold K. Hochschild, a wealthy copper miner, owns a great deal of land around Blue Mountain Lake, and the Hochschild family gave Blue Mountain its colorful Adirondack Museum. (Harold Hochschild is credited with being the first person to take an automobile into the Adirondack Mountains; the trip, in a 1905 Winton, took two days from Saratoga Springs, involved broken springs and five flat tires, but may have signaled the end of the private railroad car and the dawn of the motel business.) Many of these large properties are worked for lumber, but they are lumbered selectively, with strict re-planting schedules, so the effects of lumbering are only occasionally visible. Nearly all contain game preserves, and several have Christmas tree farms. Conservation and moneymaking have made an acceptable compromise.

Though not technically the largest, easily the most extraordinary of these big lumber estates is the Litchfield Park Corporation near Tupper Lake. Litchfield Park today is run by Edward S. Litchfield, a grandson of the man who built it. Mr. Litchfield, a brisk-moving man in his fifties with a peppery wit, sits in an office in New York's financial district where he manages his family's holdings, which range from lumber, maple sugar, and Christmas trees in the Adirondacks to New York real estate, a chemical company in New Jersey, and farm lands in Iowa. "Of course I'm peanuts compared with some of my neighbors," he remarked cheerfully not long ago, pointing out that Litchfield Park consists of only fourteen thousand acres all told, compared with nearby estates ranging from forty thousand to vastly more. Still, the Park is large enough to contain three lakes, two ponds, fifteen miles of paved roads, three wardens' cottages, many outbuildings, and a Main House that has become a legend.

"Hard to say," Mr. Litchfield replies when asked how many rooms the house has — a question he is asked often. One source gives the house ninety-four; another count has come up with a hundred and sixteen. "Oh, I don't think it's *that* big, do you?" said Mr. Litchfield to a visitor. "They must be counting the walk-in closets. My grandfather, you see, traveled quite a bit in Europe. He became interested in castles and things." The house was finished in 1913 and is in the French château style with two stout towers. Its stone was quarried on the property, and the walls range from three to six feet thick. There is a large art gallery reported to contain a "priceless" collection of paintings and sculpture. "Nonsense," says Mr. Litchfield. "It's all terribly bad stuff — everything my grandmother didn't want in her New York house. She was never as fond of the place as Grandfather was. There's some good armor, though." There is a two-story, five-thousand-volume library of sporting and general interest books, "plus all the Henty books, Rider Haggard, Tom Swift, the Rover Boys — things nobody reads any more." In the Great Hall, which is sixty-five feet long, thirty-five feet wide, and thirty feet high, there is, in addition to a marble fireplace from Stanford White's New York house, a collection of one hundred and ninety-three mounted heads, including elephant, rhinoceros, giraffe, dik-dik, bear, and buffalo (Mr. Litchfield has added to his grandfather's collection with some heads of his own) and, scattered about the house, "three or four hundred sets" of antlers. "What the place really *is*," says Mr. Litchfield crisply, "is an anachronism of the first order.

"You have to understand this place as part of the era," Mr. Litchfield says. "It was a magnificent Edwardian dream. Grandfather even *looked* Edwardian. There he is, over there," pointing to a portrait of the late Edward Hubbard Litchfield, lawyer, financier, sportsman, with clear, coolly appraising eyes and a neatly pointed Van Dyke beard.

Like so many other Adirondack dreams, the elder Litchfield's fell somewhat short of realization. Old Oquarah had to make his presence felt. Mr. Litchfield had placed some seventy-five hundred acres of his land behind an eight-foot wire fence, and released within the area many elk, boar, and moose imported from Wyoming. But falling trees crashed through his fences and poachers climbed them; animals escaped or were shot. Neighbors, overrun by wild boar, registered angry complaints. "On the whole," says Litchfield, "the experiment was a failure."

The older Litchfield also reintroduced beaver to the region and, says his grandson, "*That* experiment was almost *too* successful! But at least one of my neighbors seems to like them." (Others objected to having their streams and lakes clogged with beaver dams.)

Mr. Litchfield smiles dryly whenever he is asked how much it costs to keep the old place up, and says, "Yes, I have a *very* good idea." He prefers not to be reminded of the maintenance figure, which is a personal expense — not, in other words, drawn from lumber or Christmas tree profits. The house must be kept heated throughout the winter in order to preserve the paneling, furnishings, and marbles, and it has a coal-burning heating plant. "It's an enormous problem getting supplies into the place," he says. He smiles the same dry smile and adds, "And let us say that 'some additional help' is required to staff the house when it's in use. But everybody in the family makes his own bed. Guests are expected to make their beds too."

One reason why the Litchfield house has become such a legend is that few people in the vicinity have ever seen it. It stands five miles back from the main road at the end of its own fern-lined avenue and, though it is mentioned in local guide books, it is not open to the public. "We did open it to the public once, back in the twenties," Litchfield says. "It was open every Thursday afternoon. But do you know what people did? There were two big stone dogs on either side of the front steps, and people chipped off the dogs' *toes* for souvenirs!" Then antlers and small heads began to be missed, and the place was closed.

Why does Litchfield hold on to the bulky and hugely costly anachronism? He loves it. And he loves the mountains. "I also believe," he says, "that people who inherit property have a duty, an obligation, to maintain it, and to maintain it properly, as it was intended to be maintained, for as long as they possibly can."

18

The Palmy Beaches
(And the "Other" Miami)

MOUNTAIN lovers, loyal though they remain, face a discouraging fact: mountains have been steadily going out of fashion. Furthermore, for at least thirty years, summer resorts of all varieties have been declining. The summer vacation has become an increasingly middle-class preoccupation. Perhaps, just as the first Mrs. August Belmont made Thursday ("maid's night out") the fashionable night for the opera — "to show her superiority to household cares" — the rich now prefer to vacation in winter, thereby showing their superiority to the normal, seasonal cares of business. Practically coincidental with the languishing "Edwardian dream" of the Adirondacks began the ascendancy of an equally romantic dream: Florida.

The social history of Florida was largely the invention of a post-Civil War tycoon named Henry Morrison Flagler, whose fortune sprang — as did so many others of the era — from his profitable association with John D. Rockefeller and the Standard Oil Company. Flagler's special enthusiasm, however, was building railroads and vast hotels. Just as the Main Line was a railroad-real estate venture, so was the somewhat larger state of Florida — a four-hundred-and-forty-seven-mile-long peninsula seldom more than two hundred miles wide and rarely more than six feet high, which extends as though a giant rolling pin had been applied to the southeast corner of the country, and Florida had been artfully pressed out from the continental pie.

Mr. Flagler was a man of few words, or rather of briefly worded commands. He started, in the 1880's, pushing his Florida East Coast Railroad southward; from Jacksonville, Flagler's order was "Go to Saint Augustine," and there, in 1889, his railroad landed and, with it, the gigantic Ponce de Leon Hotel, the first of his chain. Overnight St. Augustine became a fashionable winter resort — the first, really, of its kind and, to many, the most fashionable of them all. The Ponce de Leon (locally pronounced Ponsi*dee*lion") is a vaguely Moorish confection of minarets, domes, spires, and vaulting archways, filled with rococo sculpture, tapestries, carpets, chandeliers, stained glass, frescoed ceilings, marble fountains, staircases, and embossments, which sprawls over six acres of downtown St. Augustine, a grandiose reminder of a more naïve time. How it continues to stay in business is a mystery, for St. Augustine has long since lost any shred of its former chic. Each year, though, a small but diminishing band of the ancient faithful returns to the hotel and gathers to sit, in drafty elegance, in the huge public rooms.

Flagler continued to extend his railroad southward, establishing resorts and building towns as he went. He built an equally imposing caravansary at Ormond Beach, now equally passé — his Ormond hotel has become a retired folks' residence — then on to Daytona where, aided by the influx of such Flagler friends as William K. Vanderbilt and John Jacob Astor, Daytona seemed about to outshine St. Augustine. From Daytona, he moved on to Titusville. Then, in 1890, at the age of sixty, Henry Flagler made a trip to a narrow sandspit consisting mostly of swampy jungle, known as Palm Beach. (A Spanish vessel, bound for Barcelona with a load of coconuts, had been wrecked offshore a dozen years earlier; its cargo had washed ashore and coconut palms had sprouted prettily from the sand.) Here Flagler had what must have amounted to a religious experience; he had a vision of his Ultimate Hotel.

Prior to Flagler's arrival, the area around Palm Beach had gained a certain local reputation as a social resort. A narrow-gauge railroad made an eight-mile trip from the town of Jupiter, stopping at the towns of Mars, Venus, and Juno — just north of Palm Beach Shores — and was known, not surprisingly, as "The Celestial." It was a gay little train in a Scarlett O'Hara mood, filled with ladies in flounces and crinolines on "dance days," and it made impromptu stops along the line so that gentlemen could leave the train for hunting forays in the woods. Arriving in Juno, the engineer tooted out "Dixie" on his whistle and sometimes, when the spirit moved, little groups took off for picnics on the "Palm Beach," while "The Celestial" waited for the spirit to move them to return.

Charming though all this might seem, it was the consensus in 1890 that Flagler had suffered a severe loss of business judgment when he announced plans to develop Palm Beach. But when word got around that Flagler was buying land at Palm Beach, the first Florida land boom was on. Jungle acreage which had been selling for a hundred dollars an acre skyrocketed to over a thousand. (Today, in defense of the boom, Palm Beachers point out that this same land now goes for as much as a hundred thousand dollars an acre.) In 1893, Flagler broke ground for the Royal Poinciana Hotel. When it was finished, nine months later, it had cost a million 1893 dollars, and was the largest hotel in the world. It had two eighteen-hole golf courses, tennis courts, motor boats, wheelchair carriages pedaled by Negroes (called "Afro-mobiles," and invented by Flagler himself), bicycles, afternoon tea dances, and evening cake walks. At the opening of the hotel, it was remarked that Flagler would be remembered by Florida the way the entire world remembered Noah. The place had rooms for eight hundred guests at the beginning, but in the wake of its immediate success it was enlarged to house four hundred more; sixteen hundred people could be seated at a time in the dining room. From the air (which few could get to in those days) the acres of the hotel were arranged in the shape of a giant letter F, not for Florida but for you-know-whom.

Vanderbilts, Whitneys, and all sorts of foreign royalty abandoned the northern Florida resorts and descended upon Palm Beach. Mrs. Edward Stotesbury — teaching her husband "how to play," as she put it, in Society — arrived to be the colony's social leader. Today, though the Royal Poinciana is no more, Flagler's second Palm Beach hotel, The Breakers (smaller than the Royal Poinciana but enormous by any other standard, and originally called, more modestly, the Palm Beach Inn) still stands, maintaining an exclusive guest policy, and is still very much a center of the resort's life, though there are now such clubs as the Everglades which count, socially, for more. And Palm Beach itself remains the most durable of all Henry Flagler's notions. Primly, at certain street corners, there stand receptacles for the deposit of old clothes. Periodically, the old-clothes collectors find ball gowns, tuxedos, and outworn suits of tails, deposited there as offerings for the deserving poor.

Flagler had no sooner planted his large initial on Palm Beach, where everyone thought he would surely stop, when a severe frost blighted the area. From balmier Miami, a lady friend named Julia Tuttle coyly sent Flagler a bouquet of orange blossoms, by way of showing him how much better Miami had fared during the cold snap. This prompted another of Flagler's terse orders: "Go to Miami."

Once in Miami, Flagler said, "Go to Key West." He built, at great expense, an elevated roadbed on pilings from Key to Key across the water. He had originally planned to build a solid causeway, but was stopped by a curious threat. The waters of the Gulf Stream move clockwise around the Gulf, gathering speed as they near the Florida Peninsula, and are forced rapidly between the Keys. There this water meets the northward-moving Antilles Current, and the Gulf Stream swings northward, then westward across the Atlantic. If, it was argued, Flagler dammed the Keys for his railroad, the Gulf Stream might be diverted southward, thereby considerably altering the climate of northern Europe. A European engineer was, in fact, dispatched to try to persuade Flagler to reconsider his plan and, faced with the awesome possible consequences, Flagler settled for his pilings. This project took seven years, and cost him fifty million dollars. In 1912, at eighty-two, Henry M. Flagler rode his train to Key West where, with characteristic simplicity, he said, "Now I can die happy. My dream is fulfilled." Shortly thereafter, characteristically true to his word, he did die. The Miami-Key West Railroad operated until 1935 when the great Labor Day hurricane swept it away, and a whole train with it, and along the Keys more than four hundred lives were lost.*

Meanwhile, another millionaire railroad man, Henry Plant, (who once asked Henry Flagler, "Where is this place you call Palm Beach?") was laying tracks and building hotels along Florida's *West* Coast. Plant was a less flamboyant personality, and his resorts — such as Clearwater — were less spectacular — cozy, homey, family-centered places. One exception was his Tampa Bay Hotel, headquarters of

---

* Sections of the present Key West Highway still stand on Flagler's original concrete pilings, and so that much of his dream remains.

Teddy Roosevelt's Rough Riders during the Spanish-American War, and currently the chief eyesore on the campus of the University of Tampa. While Flagler concentrated on luring celebrities and international Society to the Atlantic shores of Florida, Plant was satisfied with attracting quieter money to the Gulf. The difference between the two men's visions is responsible for the most striking difference in atmosphere between the East Coast and the West. The East Coast is glossy and gay, while the West Coast remains relaxed and easygoing. The East Coast goes in for polo, squash racquets, and a bit of discreet gambling; the West Coast prefers fishing, golf, badminton, and bridge. Such glittering figures as Mrs. Marjorie Merriweather Post Close Hutton Davies May are polarized around Palm Beach, while less publicized Society women, such as Mrs. Joseph R. Swan, co-founder of the Junior League, have traditionally wintered at Boca Grande, on the West. As one West Coast woman, with an eastward wave of her hand, puts it, "We enjoy ourselves here without trying to be snazzy." Palm Beach, says the West Coast, is for climbers, and "always was." The West Coast also hints that in Palm Beach the alcohol consumption is particularly high, that marijuana, LSD, and other drugs have become commonplaces of Society life, and that such traditions as marital fidelity are now utterly ignored.

The two railroad men succeeded, in other words, in defining a familiar line of battle — which place was nicer, the Gold Coast or the Gulf Coast. The Gold Coast used to begin at Jupiter Island, and extend south to Miami. Now, the first signs of fashionability are encountered somewhat north of Jupiter, at the sleek little community of Vero Beach. Vero Beach likes to call itself "the *little* Palm Beach," and to hint that its smallness is to its distinct advantage. On the opposite coast, however, the little town of Naples scoffs at Vero Beach's claims. True, much of Naples's winter money comes from fortunes made in such Middle Western cities as Cleveland and Louisville, but a number of Easterners — who always help things socially — have built houses there too. Along Gordon Drive is "Millionaires' Row," proudly pointed out to all visitors. "Very few people know about Naples," says a Connecticut woman who spends her winters there. She echoes a popular, and increasingly erroneous, Naples belief. Many, many people know about Naples now, and motels are springing up all around it, and the town is becoming increasingly tourist-oriented as, indeed, the whole

Gulf Coast from Cedar Key south is becoming. Still, Naples considers itself exclusive in the strictest sense (no Jews, please) and, though Naples needs Negroes for house servants, up until quite recently Negroes were not permitted to own houses in the town. "They had to *rent* their houses," one woman explains. "That way, we could control the class of colored people in Naples. Anyone who caused trouble could be evicted, you see."

Back on the Gold Coast, meanwhile, roughly halfway between Palm Beach and Fort Lauderdale, glitters Boca Raton. Boca Raton was the brainchild of another spectacular Florida personality, Addison Mizner. Before going broke — as so many Florida developers before and after him have had a habit of doing — Mizner built the gigantic Boca Raton Hotel and Club which, like the town itself, has had a varied social history. It was first a hotel, then a private club, then a hotel again. Now its chief target is the convention trade. Several years ago the late Arthur Vining Davis — who came to Florida as recently as 1948, and whose Arvida Corporation became one of the most powerful forces in South Florida real estate — bought the hotel. Soon it was pulling out of its slump. Davis built the Royal Palm Yacht and Country Club, now one of the most expensive residential clubs in the country. With additional financial infusions from men like J. Meyer Schine and his son, G. David Schine, the former McCarthy lieutenant who operates Schine hotels in Miami Beach, Boca Raton's fortunes are definitely on the upswing. Schine interests are building high-priced houses in the area and, though Old Guard Society tends to think of Boca Raton as "ruined" — and with Miami Beach money, of all things — those who are building and moving into costly houses there are laughing fondly at *this* attitude.

Fort Lauderdale for years was considered Florida's nicest, quietest, most comfortably family-centered upper-class resort — *"really* better than Palm Beach," as one old Lauderdale resident explains. "We *all* knew each other, and our children all knew each other — from the same schools, and from Edgartown in the summers. Oh, it was heaven in Fort Lauderdale." Fort Lauderdale was a yachtsman's place, and the Bahia-Mar Marina is said to be able to accommodate enough yachts to jam New York harbor, shore to shore. Fishing, cruising, boat-buying, and boat talk remain Fort Lauderdale's most popular pastimes. Though a number of large, tall, pastel-hued luxury hotels have arisen along Lauderdale's ocean front — hotels of a style that becomes increasingly familiar the nearer one gets to Miami — their presence was tolerated by property owners, since the hotels did not obtrude on the expensive residential districts along the canals, inlets, and island shores.

In fact, though the city was growing, Fort Lauderdale might have gone on its leisurely, boat-loving way had it not been for a curious and sudden annual event: Easter Week. How it happened to spring up there no one knows. In the thirties and forties, Easter Week — or College Week, or Rugby Week — took place in Bermuda, which was the favorite spring retreat for well-off college boys and girls. Then, shortly after World War II, it moved to Fort Lauderdale. As used to be the case in Bermuda, college students from all over the East suddenly descended on Fort Lauderdale — camping six-to-a-room in hotels, sleeping in parked cars or on the beaches. In the beginning the city was amused. As the lemming-like migrations grew larger, it became dismayed. Bermuda (the British having long been better at dealing with colonials than we Americans) used to manage to keep College Week under some semblance of control. But when Fort Lauderdale tried to crack down on, or at least, organize, the event, it sometimes disintegrated into riots and bloodshed and trips to the lockup. Police toughness did not discourage the youthful invaders; if anything, it added an element of excitement to the whole thing. But the teens are a fickle age, and other Florida resorts — Daytona, Pompano Beach, Hollywood-by-the-Sea — have begun to attract College Week crowds, and recently an impressive number have been making their way to Puerto Rico. Fort Lauderdale is relieved and, during its season — traditionally the months of February and March — is trying to regain its old composure.

As one approaches the vicinity of Palm Beach, one nears the storm center of more controversy. Palm Beach is at war with Hobe Sound, a fashionable upstart to the north. There is also a Palm Beach versus Delray Beach argument and, of course, one between Palm Beach and Fort Lauderdale. (The Palm Beach versus Pompano Beach feud is considered a side issue.) The Palm Beach versus Miami Beach battle has been going on for years, and a cease-fire no longer seems possible.

The chief (if perhaps not the most able-bodied) contender in all this strife, Palm Beach, has the advantage of age; she is now the *grande dame* of all Florida's still-fashionable resorts. Despite the aspersions cast at her through the years, she has kept her jeweled head high. And, it must be admitted, she wears her age surprisingly well. Whether one drives past the miles of trimmed lawns and pruned shrubbery in front of the mansions on Ocean Boulevard, or strolls in and out of the dainty, expensive, and "fun" shops and restaurants along Worth Avenue, the same sense of unity and control is apparent. It is as though Palm Beach were the creation of a single set designer.

Actually, there have been several. Following Henry Flagler, the extraordinary Addison Mizner — artist, miner, prizefighter and self-schooled architect — did as much as anyone else to crystallize the personality of Palm Beach. Along with Paris Singer, son of I. M. Singer, the sewing machine manufacturer, and famous as the traveling companion of Isadora Duncan, Mizner took Flagler's creation, face-lifted what was there and added a great deal more. Mizner's taste is responsible for Palm Beach's Mediterranean style of architecture which has been called "Walt Disney Castilian."

In the early 1900's, prior to Mizner's arrival, Palm Beach exhibited a strong tendency to gingerbread; Mizner got rid of all that and replaced it with the grandeur of fountains, pebbled walks, and topiary. He would certainly have approved of the presence of so many French poodles today, which look as though they had been clipped to match the place. Later architects have followed the Mizner pattern, though they have added a bit of the white-roofed Bermuda Colonial style, with which Mizner-Mediterranean blends more or less comfortably. "We are not fond of so-called 'modern' architecture in Palm Beach," one woman explains. Some of that has got in, apparently by mistake, but most of it is on the side streets and out of sight.

The things that are most impressive about Palm Beach — its manicured perfection and air of well-being — are the things which, after a while, become most oppressive about it to many people. Palm Beach has been accused of being full of *nouveaux riches* — those who, traditionally, are said to find a stiff and formal attitude more reassuring — and it is true that some of the older wealth has forsaken Palm Beach and gone to the much smaller community of Hobe Sound, where the atmosphere has become more relaxed and old-clothesy, and where tourists are given a chilly, if not openly hostile, reception. Palm Beach, meanwhile, counters by pointing out that *it* is not fond of tourists, either; it is proud of its police force which is credited with knowing, at any given time, just who belongs in Palm Beach and who does not. "We," says one loyal winter resident, Mrs. Edmund Lynch, "say that it's Hobe Sound that's become *nouveau.*" So there you are.

The composition of Palm Beach's winter population has changed considerably in the last thirty years. Palm Beach used to feel that it more or less belonged to New York, or at least to Eastern United States, Society. But lately there have been invasions from Middle Western cities, and from the oil lands of Oklahoma and Texas. Delray Beach used to be a Detroit community, like many other Florida communities which were originally settled by people from a particular city in the North. Now, Detroit money is represented in Palm Beach also, and millionaires like Charles B. Wrightsman, the Oklahoma oil man, have come to Palm Beach. There is no longer just one Palm Beach "set" but several — including the Old Guard, the Jet Set, and what is known as The Kennedys and Their Friends.

There are at least two other Palm Beach phenomena that are worth comment, and in certain ways the two are connected. One is the resort's recent sudden and avid interest in art, artists, and art galleries. Galleries have sprung up all along Worth Avenue, and young painters have discovered that they can often sell their paintings faster, and for higher prices, in Palm Beach than in New York. The market here is for paintings that are strictly contemporary — the more advanced and daring, the better they sell. At the same time, according to one artist, Palm Beach people don't really seem to *care* about art; they just want to buy it, which makes a Palm Beach gallery opening somewhat less satisfying to the artist than one in Manhattan. "These Society dames buy pictures the way they buy diamonds," he says. "For status."

The other phenomenon — not unique to Palm Beach, certainly, but explicitly apparent there — is the emergence of what might be called the Kept Man as a fixture of Society. The Kept Woman has certainly undergone a great decline — how many men have one of her kind today? — and the Kept Man has risen to fill her place. He performs, of course, a somewhat different function. One sees him all over Palm Beach at parties — never alone, always in a group, always impeccably tailored, yet always in some elusive way looking rather "extra." Usually homosexual (one assumes), he is usually handsome. He is usually young, or at least not specifically old, or even middle-aged. A middle-aged dowager may have several — a little retinue who follow her and flatter her and amuse her, wherever she goes. Each has a room in her Palm Beach house and, as a rule, in all her houses elsewhere. But the Kept Man is not exclusively an adjunct of women without husbands. Many married couples have one, even several, of their own. The Kept Man's function is to be decorative, attentive, and — most important — amusing. If he belongs to a couple, he is the wife's particular pet and toy — and is merely tolerated by the husband who recognizes that this man, while not a sexual threat, supplies his wife with something that he cannot. "He makes her laugh," one man says. "And they do things together — go shopping for antiques or clothes — that I've never really enjoyed doing with her."

France, Italy, Spain, and Greece seem to supply the greatest share of Kept Men to American women — who prefer men with a "Mediterranean look" — though England, too, has sent a number to these shores. Many Kept Men have titles — some bona fide, others not. Often the Kept Man will have some occupation or other, vague or specific, such as interior decorator, or he may be a hairdresser, a clothes designer, or a painter or sculptor or photographer needing sponsorship. But often as not his profession is uncertain, his antecedents dim, his source of income hard to find. He must be available for parties and be able to travel; few men can do all this and work, too. Sometimes, the Kept Man will actually be on his protectress's payroll, in which case he may be called a private secretary, though his duties extend far beyond the secretarial and his working day does not end at five o'clock. In several cases, the Kept Man has become an actual, permanent, "live-in" member of the household.* As far as can be discovered, the wages paid to such an individual are astonishingly small. One young man reveals that his employer — he calls her by her first name, of course — pays him only two hundred dollars a month. "Isn't that a bitch?" he asks with a wry grin. But of course, there are other compensations — fringe benefits such as meeting and being entertained by the rich, famous, and beautiful wherever he goes; having, when in Paris one autumn, his lady surprise him with a brown velvet suit — a fabric he had

---

* When the Kept Man does not live in, he usually returns, in the small hours, to shadowy lodgings on the other side of town.

helped her choose for a sofa — run up by Christian Dior. When in Madrid one spring, he was presented with a matador's full "suit of lights."

In many ways, the phenomenon of the Kept Man makes a certain amount of sense and, as an institution, he should have far less trouble surviving than the Kept Woman. The Kept Woman, to begin with, was often shrouded in a certain veil of sin and secrecy whereas, with the Kept Man, no threat or possibility of scandal exists. To the woman whose husband is often at the office, or whose business takes him on trips to boring places, the Kept Man is a pleasant, non-sexual male companion. He is nearly always lunchable and otherwise available to hurry over and cheer her up with witty talk and a bit of flattery. He is someone to have a cocktail with. If the woman's husband cannot — or will not — fly off to Paris for the Spring Collections, there is the Kept Man, waiting and ready with his passport up-to-date. In nearly every capital of Europe, it is considered inappropriate for a woman to appear on a street unescorted, and so the Kept Man fulfills this function too. And what woman — anywhere — enjoys going into a restaurant, or to the theatre, or to a party, except on a man's arm?

There are other kinds of husbands, too, than busy ones whose wives Kept Men serve. In New York, one Society husband is an arrested alcoholic and is uncomfortable in the liquid atmosphere of New York social life. He is delighted that his wife has found an elegant and attentive man to take her everywhere he cannot go; without such a man, she would have had to withdraw from social life completely. There is also the husband whose wealth is so substantial and whose ambitions are so modest that he does no work at all. The cruel fact that those in Society seldom admit is that between the parties and the lunches and the committee meetings and the travels stretch long, dull hours. With servants to care for them, how is a couple like this to occupy themselves in the still and stony fastness of their house? For the husband, television may provide sufficient entertainment. For the wife, the Kept Man helps fill the yawning hours with gin rummy and conversation.

If a woman is rich enough, she will have her own Kept Man; if not, she will share him with a friend or two. In most cases, the relationship between each woman and her man is kept carefully superficial but,

from time to time, strange things have happened and deep attach-
ments have developed. There have even been cases of widows or divorcees marrying their young men. A more common problem, if a
woman shares her man with others, is jealousy. In Paris not long ago,
an American Society woman had begun accusing her young man of
devoting an unfair share of his time to other women, of refusing to
answer the telephone when she called, of making shallow excuses, and
of other such hostile acts. The two began to quarrel bitterly. Walking
along the banks of the Seine, the woman and her young man accused
each other of the most terrible treacheries and, following a particularly
pointed insult from the young man, the woman reached into her purse,
took out a gold Cartier cigarette case he had given her, and hurled it
into the river. "That case cost me two thousand dollars!" the young
man cried. The woman hurried off. When the young man returned to
his room, he found his floor littered with one-dollar bills. When he had
picked them up, and counted them, there were two thousand exactly.

There are two other facts that make the Kept Man's place in Society
seem secure. The first is that except in extreme instances a Kept Man
can be counted upon to treat a woman far better than most husbands
treat their wives. Among the Kept Man's greatest appeals is his flatter-
ing interest in feminine matters — the style of his lady's hair, her
clothes, her furniture — and his gossipy interest in the doings of her
friends. Second is the fact that a Kept Man will usually take a good
deal more abuse from a woman than a husband will willingly take
from his wife. The Kept Man is also the woman's whipping-boy — the
target of all her fits of temper, her weepy moods, all her *angst*. The
Kept Man will put up, from time to time, with flying crockery, and
the husband is therefore spared. And, according to one such husband,
"Since G—— became a part of our household, she's been a hell of a
better wife."

One young man not long ago smiled faintly and said, "It's probably
the only way in the world to get into Society without having money.
But of course there are drawbacks. They have their ways of letting you
know where you stand. A trip is planned, and they'll say to you, 'Of
course you'll need a ticket, darling, won't you?' The ticket comes — it's
delivered to you. It's always First Class, of course. But it's just a single
ticket, charged to their Air Travel card. You travel with them, but you

travel alone at the same time like a kind of — well, like a kind of . . . luggage."

"Oh, what a shame you have to go to Miami," says a Palm Beach lady. "You'll hate it. It's *the* most ghastly place, completely different from here." Miami has become an international symbol of everything that is vulgar, meretricious, ostentatious and overpriced in the United States; Miami is Florida's painted lady. What many believers in international symbols don't realize, however, is that what they think of as "Miami" is actually Miami *Beach*. A series of long causeways joins the two places, to be sure, but it is still a considerable journey between them and, traffic conditions being what they are, a formidable one. Guests at the spectacular hotels along Collins Avenue in Miami Beach seldom suspect that there is another Miami on the other side. And those who belong to the "other" Miami often confess that they have never laid eyes on, much less been inside, the Americana, the Fontainebleau, or the Eden Roc. The "other" Miami has remained sedate, unpublicized — exactly as it has seemed to prefer it.

This was not always so, of course, for the genesis of all Florida resorts is similar, heavily dosed with press-agentry and avarice. Miami, in fact, was the child of the Great Florida Land Boom, born around 1920, and the boom was the child of a man named George E. Merrick. Merrick had been a poor boy, the son of a clergyman, who inherited one hundred and sixty acres of South Florida land for which his father had paid about a thousand dollars. Young George had a dream which seemed to verge on lunacy, or at least obsession — a dream of a beautiful city of beautiful homes, a city that would dwarf the then insignificant town of Miami, a city more magnificent than the world had ever seen, filled with the world's most magnificent people. It was a dream on a larger scale than William Van Duzer Lawrence's dream, which he brought to reality in Bronxville. Somehow Merrick managed to buy up some three thousand more acres, and to have some promotional brochures printed. Armed with these, he headed for New York, the money capital. Money turned out to be plentiful.

"He was an absolute spellbinder," says Alfred Browning Parker, whose father became Merrick's sales manager. "He had the kind of *charisma* and magnetism that the mad often have. He could sell anything." Like Flagler, Merrick wanted a luxury hotel — and soon there was one, the Miami Biltmore, costing $10,000,000. He wanted a championship golf course and a country club, and these materialized. According to Parker, Merrick was fascinated by — without really understanding — the great cities of the Mediterranean and Adriatic. Naples, Venice, and Barcelona, which he had never visited, became his models, with a touch of the South Pacific thrown in for good measure. (When he opened a swimming place called Tahiti Beach, "real Tahitians" — so Merrick said — were imported for decoration.)

He built streets and he built canals — forty miles of them — patterned after those of Venice, and he imported Venetian gondolas and gondoliers. The gondoliers were supposed to do nothing but pole their craft up and down the canals, singing, but whether anyone heard them above the din of moneymaking is doubtful. The American rich — always eager to be first in any place that is expensive, different, and new — began buying lots and ordering palaces in Coral Gables (as Merrick named it) as fast as they were able.

In the first few months of his boom, Merrick sold $150,000,000 worth of lots; sales then tapered off to about $100,000,000 a year. All the houses built in Coral Gables naturally had to have gabled roofs, and all had to be in the Italian or Spanish style, with archways, courtyards, and bell towers. The minute there was the slightest sign of a slackening in business, Merrick came up with a new promotional gimmick. He built a pool with underwater caves, through which Johnny Weissmuller was hired to swim. Paul Whiteman and his orchestra were hired to play Merrick's written-to-order theme song, "When the Moon Shines on Coral Gables," standing waist-deep in moonlit water. William Jennings Bryan, then getting on and in need of money, was hired at $100,000 a year to sell Coral Gables real estate with his famous "silver tongue," and Rex Beach, a popular writer of the era, was paid $25,000 to write a promotional brochure disguised as a "novel" called *The Miracle of Coral Gables*.

Meanwhile, faced with the miraculous example of George Merrick, other builders and promoters were rapidly "discovering" new areas and building new "cities" — Fort Pierce Farms, Key Largo City, Indrio, Moore Haven — on the swampy banks of Lake Okeechobee. Floridale was to be John Ringling's city. Soon the speculators had taken over. It was the era of the "binder boy," a colorful and popular boom figure in white knickerbockers who scurried around selling and buying "binders," or down payments to bind deals. As the binders changed hands, sometimes hourly, their prices doubled, trebled, quadrupled. Everybody chuckled at the binder boys. If some of their methods didn't seem quite on the up and up, it didn't matter since everything else was going up.

In many cases, the binders represented actual building sites; in others, it turned out, they did not. There was the case of Poinciana, advertised as "The Miami of the Gulf Coast." Poinciana, put on the Florida map by its developers, had to be taken off when it was discovered that it really wasn't there. Thousands of unsuspecting souls had bought thousands of uninspected acres for a thousand dollars each, and most of the "lots" were under water.

"It was a glorious, kind of nutty period," Alfred Parker recalls. Money literally seemed to grow on palmettoes, and everybody was making so much of it — and not only in building and real estate — that few bothered to notice what all the building looked like. If they had, they would have noticed that much of it was extremely ugly, haphazard, and that, with a very few exceptions (such as Mr. Merrick's Coral Gables castles) most of the new construction was so makeshift that it looked as though a puff of wind would blow it all away.

In 1925, there was a sudden, sharp recession. Furiously, developers pumped more money into Florida land, attempting to shore up the economy and, when a few Miami banks quietly closed their doors, and a few others began calling loans, and a few Northern investors made nervous noises, Florida developers shouted, "Don't sell Florida short!" The doubters were called worrywarts and killjoys. Glowing press releases, telling how a typical investor had paid ten dollars an acre for his land, and was now selling it at twenty-five hundred dollars an acre — were mailed northward to influential newspapers. Then, in the fall of 1926, the puff of wind came, at one hundred and thirty miles an hour.

One witness of the 1926 hurricane recalls seeing "sheets of steel flying through the air." Afterward, such phenomena were recorded as that of a broomstraw driven through the trunk of a tree. Estimates of the hurricane's damage ran as high as $105,000,000, and yet, in view of the financial disasters that followed, that figure is modest. Thousands of homes were destroyed completely and thousands more were damaged. Hundreds of lives were lost, and when Florida struggled out

Mrs. Leverett Saltonstall Shaw, who owns a plantation in New Iberia, Louisiana, in the garden of H. Loy Anderson's Palm Beach house

Wendy Vanderbilt in Palm Beach

Palm Beach socialite painter Channing Haire, whose subjects have ranged from Miss Beatrice Lillie to the "hamburger boy" at the resort's Bath and Tennis Club

One of Palm Beach's more stately mansions

Southern California's beautiful Mrs. George Cameron, richly surrounded

The Darryl Zanucks at home in Palm Springs

CHARLES C. AUCHINCLOSS
SEPTEMBER 13, 1956.

PHOTO BY
FREUDY N.

In the autumn of 1956, some 117 Auchinclosses — only a fraction of the membership of the clan — gathered in the ballroom of New York's redoubtable Colony Club to honor patriarch Charles C. Auchincloss, now deceased. Novelist Louis Auchincloss smiles at camera from lower right; Janet Lee Bouvier Auchincloss, Jacqueline Kennedy's mother, is the fourth lady down from the upper right-hand corner of the U-shaped table; her husband, Hugh D. Auchincloss, is seated on the far side of the opposite wing, the second gentleman down from the head of the table; Wilmarth S. Lewis, historian and Horace Walpole scholar, whose wife was the late Annie Burr Auchincloss, is the second gentleman to the left of the guest of honor who stands at the center of the head table (Photograph courtesy of Louis Auchincloss)

to see what the storm had done, it found that the boom was over, the glorious bubble had burst. Even the Wall Street crash that followed three years later came to Florida as a meaningless anticlimax.

With the vanishing bubble went George Merrick's career as a millionaire entrepreneur and city builder. For years afterward, he was a sad and familiar figure around Miami — a dazed and shopworn man with an echo of what was once his winning smile, always willing to buttonhole anyone who would listen (and few would) and tell his story of the dream of Coral Gables.

But Merrick's story has a belated happy ending. The tens of thousands of trees and shrubs he planted have grown to shade and embower the winding streets he so romantically named — Avenue Sistina, Avenue Paradiso, Avenue Jeronimo — and the fine solid houses that he built have mellowed and grown serene and queenly; with their handsome gabled roofs of Spanish tile, they smile from behind romantic gates and walls cascading with bougainvillea. With its parks and plazas and canals and splashing fountains in courtyards, with three golf courses and the campus of the University of Miami at its heart, Coral Gables is now considered not only a marvel of city planning, but one of the most beautiful residential sections in the United States. Since Merrick wisely placed Coral Gables a few miles inland, away from the ocean's edge, the area has been spared by Florida's hurricanes.

Compare Coral Gables with, say, John Ringling's Floridale. Nothing exists of Floridale today except streets — paved streets, but with no houses or other buildings lining them — running off in an orderly pattern into nowhere. In retrospect, George Merrick emerges a genius after all.

In Coral Gables live the best of Miami's year-round Society, whose lives are led with quiet elegance, whose sons go north to New England prep schools, whose daughters come out at the Debutante Ball at the Surf Club, and who speak with the "social voice," priding themselves that they do *not* — as Society does in Savannah and New Orleans — speak with Southern accents. Ever. Here, in other words, is Society organized much as it is in Northern cities, or in the smaller "social" cities of the West, such as Denver, San Francisco, and Portland.

Also to Coral Gables and nearby Indian Creek come a select group of winter visitors from New York, Philadelphia, and Boston. "The other Miami" is the term they use, affectionately and humorously, knowing that outsiders have absolutely no idea what it means.

One New York woman who winters in a huge, cool house in Indian Creek, says, "A lot of people think that we have to try to *live down* the fact that we spend our winters in Miami. They think that we must have to be constantly explaining that we go to *this* Miami, not *that* Miami, that we must always be having to apologize for it being, after all, Miami, which is a word which conjures up a certain image. Some people say to me, 'Why do you admit to it being Miami?' Why don't you say Indian Creek, or Coral Gables?' Well, all I can say is that only a climber or a very silly person would try to use a pretty label or disguise like that. *We* consider that sort of thing quite unnecessary. After all, those of us who *know* Miami know what we have here. We make no effort to cover up the fact that we winter in *Miami,* and always have."

19

The Palmy Springs
(All That Money Can Buy)

IF the "only way in the world" to get into Society is with money, then why is it that so many very, very rich people are not in Society? It is a question worth pondering. Is it because they lack some mysterious ingredient of "leadership"? Not really; many of these "outsider" men and women are people of great influence and power. Is it that they lack some qualities of polish or good manners? No, for many people solidly in Society are far less mannerly than they. Is it that they don't care? Not at all; they care greatly. Or is it that they think they *are* in Society? For one answer we might turn to a gold-plated desert mirage known as Palm Springs, California. For here is gathered a random selection of the richest people in America, strenuously enjoying all that money can buy.

The discrepancies between Palm Springs and Palm Beach are more than geographic, and rest upon more serious matters than differences in climate and the quality of the citrus crop. Palm Springs insists that it has *better people* than can be found anywhere else, Palm Beach included, and has the statistics to prove it. Palm Springs has, among other things, "More swimming pools per capita than any other city in the world"; to accommodate a winter population of 18,300, there are over 3,500 pools — or roughly one pool for every five residents. In summer, when the population drops to around 10,000, there is an even higher per capita gallonage of swimming space, and the proportion of pools to people may explain why most Palm Springs pools seem empty of swimmers at all seasons of the year.

Palm Springs also boasts more Cadillacs (locally called Caddies, or Cads), more Lincoln Continentals (Connies), more Rolls Royces (Rollses), and more Thunderbirds (T-Birds or Teebs) than can be found assembled on any other 41.6-square-mile area on this planet. During a recent nose count of Cads, Connies, and Rollses, the census taker was asked why he did not tally Bentleys. "We're interested in prestige cars," he replied. Palm Springs is also the home of "the world's most luxurious thermal baths," "the world's largest and longest single-span, passenger-carrying aerial tramway," "the world's most sumptuous Mobile Home Park," "the world's only flying great-grandmother," and "the world's wealthiest tribe of Indians."

No Palm Springs resident can escape for long his own personal, identifying superlative. A Seattle retailer is pointed out, in local promotional literature, as "the owner of one of the largest department stores in the West." A Milwaukee restaurant owner is referred to as "the head of one of America's biggest chains of steak houses." Clearly bigness is what counts in Palm Springs. A Pebble Beach lady named Laurena Heple is identified as "the world's largest manufacturer of remote-controlled gates." In the meantime, when one is not rubbing tail fins with Paul Hoffman, Benjamin Fairless, Conrad Hilton, Jack Warner, Leonard Firestone, Floyd Odlum, William Ford, or George Schmidt — "owner of one of the biggest amusement parks in the country" — a visitor may be grabbed by the shoulder with, "Hey, there goes Billie Dove! No need to tell you who *she* is. Hiya, Billie!"

If a superlative statistic can be attached to a slogan, so much the better — as far as Palm Springs is concerned. Palm Springs is advertised as "the Winter Movie Capital of the World," and as the place "Where the Sun Shines on the Stars." The Palm Springs Chamber of Commerce publishes a two-page list of "Hollywood Personalities with Homes in Palm Springs," with names arranged alphabetically from John Arcesi to Myron Zobel. Similarly, a list of "prominent business people" is available, ranging from George Allen, "friend of several U.S. Presidents," to Farny Wurlitzer, "Wurlitzer Music Corporation." Clearly, Society in Palm Springs is the Society of the self-made. The town is also touted as "The World's Friendliest Place," and proof of this, according to one resident, is that "Most of these stars and millionaires don't even bother to have unlisted telephone numbers out here. You'll find Allan Jones right in the book — go ahead, look him up! That's what I call *friendly*."

In Palm Springs, Society and public relations have merged, or at least have come to a working arrangement. Everyone is a booster. Conducting a tour of "Society mansions" in the low hills around Palm Springs, a resident delivered the following monologue: "Now here is the house where Debbie Reynolds and Eddie Fisher spent their honeymoon. Over there is the house where Eddie Fisher and Liz Taylor spent *their* honeymoon. I forget which house Liz Taylor and Mike Wilding spent their honeymoon in, but the house where Liz Taylor and Mike Todd spent their honeymoon is back over in that direction. Up ahead, that's the house where Debbie and Harry, her present husband, live now — some layout, huh? That other house belongs to the biggest parking meter manufacturer in Chicago — boy, what I wouldn't give to have his millions! He also manufactures the Yo-Yo — I guess you've heard of Duncan Yo-Yos. Hey! There goes Alice Faye behind the wheel of that white Connie! Hiya, Alice! No, sir, you can't tell *me* that this isn't the richest town in the U.S.A. We've got more than *three hundred* millionaires living here in Palm Springs! See that home up there on the hill? That's where Joan Crawford and Alfred Steele spent their honeymoon — they were a swell couple, Joan and Al. Yes, I guess you could say that the best in America is here in Palm Springs. Now over there — that's Alan Ladd's hardware store. He was a great guy, Alan. But there's one thing that burns me up, and that's folks who come out here and get the impression that Palm Springs is nothing but movie stars and millionaires. Why, we've got *much* more here than that. . . ."

Palm Springs is "The Winter Golf Capital of the World." Golf, which may have become a middle-class sport elsewhere, is the required Society sport here. Few who cared about advancing socially would admit to disliking golf. There are eighteen golf courses in full operation — most of them private clubs — and there are more abuilding. "And this," the booster reminds one, "doesn't count all the pitch-and-putt courses." Palm Springs is either "The Birthplace of the Golf Cart," or "The Site of the Development of the Golf Cart," depending on which handout you read, but in any case it undoubtedly has more golf carts per capita than it has golf courses, and can go so far as to make this dizzying claim: "More homes with specially built, semi-attached golf-cart garages than any other resort area." Because they speed the game, and allow the fairways to accommodate more players, golf carts are now required on nearly all Palm Springs courses. Though this may decrease the amount of exercise to be gained from a game of golf, one golfer comments, "You'd be surprised how much exercise you can get climbing in and out of a golf cart."

Recently, too, Palm Springs has become "The Playground of the Presidents," where, as one Palm Springer put it, "Three reigning U.S. Presidents have visited." The "reigning" Presidents have been Dwight D. Eisenhower (who continues to spend a portion of each winter here in a cottage on the grounds of the Eldorado Country Club); the late John F. Kennedy; and Lyndon B. Johnson. Harry Truman and the late Herbert Hoover visited Palm Springs as nonreigning Presidents. On the occasion of President Kennedy's last visit, barely two months before his death, a local Palm Springs magazine took it upon itself to state, rather loftily: "Desert residents are getting so used to Presidential visits that many, this past month, regarded the Kennedy sojourn as a prerogative of this unique resort area rather than as a compliment that would dazzle any other small community in the nation except, of course, Hyannis Port. So the excitement was confined to Democrats, traditionally a desert minority group, and visitors."

On the other hand, this blasé attitude was not at all in evidence during President Johnson's first visit in the spring of 1964. The town decked itself with hectic bunting, thousands of residents mobbed the airport, and the mayor declared, "We've got to get some kind of gimmick to welcome guys like this — something that will be symbolic of Palm Springs. You know, the way Honolulu greets folks with hula dancers? Is there anything we could do with a bunch of golfers in golf carts?"

The center of all this fanfare is a tiny corner of the crescent-shaped Coachella Valley in the great Southwestern desert of the United States, some one hundred miles east of Los Angeles — a flat, arid, windswept stretch of landscape, where less than three inches of rain fall yearly, where irrigated patches show surprising green (a million gallons of water a day are required to water the average Palm Springs course), but where even the city's promoters admit, "The predominating color is beige." Here, on this outwardly unpromising terrain, surrounded by implacable beige mountains, one of the most extraordinary real estate booms in the country has been in progress, dwarfing anything that ever happened in Florida. Since 1940, Palm Springs's permanent population has doubled itself every ten years; in the next ten years, it is almost certain to double again. The winter, or "in season," population climbs at an even more alarming rate, and during winter weekends as many as fifty thousand extra people a day crowd into the city. These figures, which would certainly dismay members of a traditional Society, delight the wealthy who have made Palm Springs their winter home; the popularity of the place assures them of the wisdom of their original investment.

Admittedly, the surrounding landscape has a certain drama. In early spring, acres of wild verbena outside the town come violently into bloom, turning the desert floor an intense purple, and casting lavender shadows in the air. A little farther on, the vineyards and the citrus groves are in blossom, and in the vast date gardens, rows of palms form deep cathedral arches. In rocky canyons, the century plant sends up its tall, improbable flower, and the bearded Washingtonia palms gather in conspiratorial clusters. As the sun moves across the valley, the deep ridges and arroyos which articulate the mountain slopes come vividly into focus, making slow, snaky patterns of light and shade, while the color of the mountains gently edges from beige to yellow to pink to mauve.

Great clouds of fog and rain often drift eastward from the coast and pause at the tops of the western ranges where, from the valley below, they can be watched doing battle with the hot desert air that rises from the valley; almost inevitably, the clouds lose the contest, dump their rain or snow on the mountaintops, and disappear. In fact, a true Palm Springs enthusiast keeps his eyes tilted loyally upward toward the hills — toward San Jacinto Peak to the west, or San Gorgonio to the north, or the soft sand mountains to the east — admiring their shifting shapes and hues.

Over what goes on at eye level he manages to draw a little curtain. He does not see Palm Springs the real estate phenomenon: the speeding, honking traffic, the gaudy motels, the trailer parks, the used-car lots, the pennant-flapping service stations, the pancake parlors, the giddily decorated shops and bars and real estate offices. These become, in a sense, invisible. When a new development of "exclusive, luxury

homes" called Southridge Estates began advertising "the most spectacular view in Palm Springs," it was not talking about what Southridge
overlooked at the time — a forlorn trailer park. It was talking about its
view of the mountains, several hundred feet above the level of the
chrome.

The invasion of civilization here has been, in many ways, reckless
and haphazard. Downtown Palm Springs, with its drugstores, dress
shops, and pastel-painted banks is indistinguishable from any of the
"strips" of Los Angeles or, indeed, from any other bright suburban
shopping area. The town is proud of a zoning law which prohibits
buildings over thirty feet in height, and of the absence of overhead
power lines; but these measures have merely emphasized the flatness
of the valley floor. Palm Springs is also proud of its main street, Palm
Canyon Drive, with its row of "exclusive shops" — so exclusive that
one woman complains, "You can find plenty of mink-trimmed sweaters
in Palm Springs, but you have to go to Los Angeles to buy a pillowcase." Yet just a short distance behind the exclusive shops lies an area
called Section Fourteen, which visitors are seldom taken to see. Much
of it remains a slum of appalling squalor, with rutted streets leading
past sagging shanties of tin and matchwood, where the rusting hulks of
derelict automobiles lie overturned in the weeds. Here is where many
of Palm Springs's Negroes and Mexicans live.

Most Palm Springs dwellers like their night views best. At night,
thousands of palm trees are dressed out with amber floodlights which
make the trees look like fiery torches; lighted swimming pools provide
sapphire dots across the valley floor;* and everything ugly that man-
kind has done to the valley becomes swallowed in a pretty sea of twin-
kling electric stars.

The mystique of "desert living," which has drawn so many fanatics
to Palm Springs, consists of many things. One of them, certainly, is
what Palm Springs calls "the world's most healthful climate."
Whether or not there is any basis in medical fact for this assertion is
debatable, but Palm Springs insists there is. Arthritis is what brought
such people as financier Floyd Odlum to the area; he conducts his
business while immersed in a pool heated to ninety degress, where jets

* Whenever an important visitor — a President, say — is scheduled to make a
nighttime arrival, Palm Springs pool owners are alerted to turn on their underwater
lights "for the best possible impression."

of water circulate around him as he sits aboard a floating chair, behind a floating desk, with a floating telephone. But it might be disputed that a climate in which the daily extremes of temperature may vary by as much as forty degrees — from eighty in the daytime to forty at night — is actually "salubrious," the word Bing Crosby uses to describe the weather. One Palm Springs housewife describes the following routine for keeping a house at a livable temperature throughout the day: "I get up in the morning and turn on the heat. Then, after an hour or so, I turn off the heat and open the windows. Then, around noon, I close all the windows and turn on the air-conditioning. Then, toward evening, I turn off the air-conditioning and open the windows, to let in the last of the warmth of the day. Soon it's time to turn on the heat again, and light the fires." Because of the chilly desert nights, nearly all Palm Springs swimming pools are gas-heated. And it must be admitted that Palm Springs people seem to suffer from colds and ague no more and no less than do those in Bangor, Maine, and that during the winter months the flu circulates as efficiently here as it does in New York. Still, when you ask a Palm Springer what he likes best about the place his first reply will certainly be "the climate." And the local health joke is, "Visitors come here and leave us their germs."

"You either love the desert and the Palm Springs way of life, or you hate it," one woman admitted recently. "There are desert people, and non-desert people, that's all there is to it. People who don't like it here should just get out!" This reaction is curiously common. Faced with a critic, the Palm Springs fan grows testy; he is not in the least defensive about the place; he is merely angry. When an Eastern visitor remarked, at a cocktail party, that she was "disappointed" in Palm Springs and "had thought it would be prettier," her hostess said, "Oh, go soak your head!" and left the room. The assumption here is that since Palm Springs was created by man's ability to spend money it has *got* to be pretty.

Non-desert-oriented souls object to the place for a variety of reasons. A Philadelphia gentleman recently found it "a concentration of everything that is vulgar, meretricious, and *nouveau riche* in America," and added, with a little smile, "and aren't we fortunate that it's all concentrated out *there*."

Others find the celebrated desert climate oddly debilitating. There is something about the crisp morning air and the brightness of the morning sun that makes one want to rise early; by 7 A.M. the pancake houses are doing a brisk business, and by eight the golf courses are crawling with golf carts. But as the day progresses and the mercury climbs, a curious lassitude creeps over one, a feeling of deep — though not unpleasant — physical exhaustion. The golf carts are now filled with dozing passengers. This is not the oppressive torpor of the Tropics, but a passivity of the senses and a spiritual languor. One longs merely to find the nearest unoccupied contour chaise and to stretch out upon it, content to gaze at the distant mountains, thinking of nothing.

Deserts traditionally provide havens for hermits, Foreign Legionnaires, and other escapees, and in this atmosphere one succumbs to solitude and lives with the minimum of effort. Perhaps this inertia accounts for the many mechanical devices developed in Palm Springs to make physical activity, or motion, unnecessary: for example, the "sun disk," a huge padded backyard lazy Susan on which a number of sunbathers can lie while an electric motor rotates them slowly in the sun; and the poolside telephone which one can answer without picking up the receiver.

The mental lethargy induced by the desert may also account for the fact that there is very little "cultural life" in Palm Springs, and even less political life. "People just don't get whipped up about politics out here," says Frank Bogert, the Mayor, who was elected on a nonpartisan ticket, "the only way I could be elected." He adds, "People don't come here to get whipped up about things. They come to relax." Another says, "We forget about international problems and national issues here — it's wonderful." And still another man says, "Fortunately, because of the time change, the brokerage offices open very early in the morning, to coincide with the opening of the New York Stock Exchange. So we all go down early, see how our stocks are doing, and then spend the rest of the day relaxing." Palm Springs is not a late-staying-up town, either. Nightclubs are few, and by 9 P.M. at parties most of the guests are yawning.

Other sensitive souls who find the desert a vaguely dispiriting place blame the otiose tenor of desert life not so much on the heat as on the ever present encircling influence of the mountains. "I feel hemmed in when I am there," one woman says, "and after a while it gets absolutely claustrophobic. I keep looking up at the hills, thinking: there must be some way to get over them, to get out." And not long ago a visitor who had ridden to the top of the Palm Springs Aerial Tramway, and had refused a specialty of the summit restaurant, a "tramburger," stood shivering in the thin, sub-freezing air at 8,516 feet above sea level, and asked absently, "What am I *doing* up here?" Then he said, "I guess it's because I *was* down there."

Among permanent residents in the valley, a good deal of controversy goes on as to whether Palm Springs is or isn't a good place to bring up children. One mother of a teenager says, "Well, the thing is that most of the people who move to Palm Springs are very rich. And, before a person gets very rich, he's usually pretty old. This is a community of wealthy retired people, mostly, and the young people feel pretty much out of things. Most kids who've grown up here can't wait to leave."

But another young woman, the wife of an up-and-coming business-man and the mother of a teenage daughter, feels that "It's good for children of medium-income families to grow up in a community like this, where they can mingle with the sons and daughters of million-aires. They learn that millionaires are no different than you or I, and it may even make them ambitious to become millionaires themselves!" She praises such local institutions as the Palm Springs Boys' Club, "where millionaires' sons and the sons of the less well-off can meet," and adds, "Even the high school has started teaching things like tennis and golf, the things that will really be important here, in later life." In fact, climate and leisure aside, the real inducement to live in Palm Springs is the coziness, even the joy, of being able to rub shoulders with movie stars and millionaires, in being able to speak with truth of having run into Benjamin Fairless or John J. McCloy at the supermar-ket, and in being able to talk about, and see at firsthand, all the glit-tery, improbable things that lots and lots of money can buy.

Take piano bars. Piano bars are so popular in Palm Springs that they are a commonplace; to enter a Palm Springs living or rumpus room and find stools around the concert grand is tantamount to find-ing a sofa and chairs in a Scarsdale parlor. A more imaginative piece of furniture is Bing Crosby's specially designed combination piano stool, tea-server, and bed tray. Equally unsurprising have become the various shapes into which swimming pools have been twisted, from the simple hourglass and kidney to the "monogram," built to match the owner's initial. In fact, plain heated swimming pools are becoming old hat. Nowadays they are being installed with whirlpools.

When it comes to building costs, Palm Springers do not believe in cutting corners, but occasionally one is forced to. One man reluctantly gave up plans to have an indoor swimming pool in his fallout shelter ("It would have been beautiful — it was going to be surrounded with tropical plants") because it was "just too impractical." Even so, the finished shelter, larger and more luxurious than most Fifth Avenue apartments, cost $75,000 and should provide a comfortable hideout come doomsday.

"No, many people here do not have good taste," admits Howard Lapham, the Palm Springs designer who has designed some of the town's most spectacular houses, including thirty-eight of the houses along the fairways of the Thunderbird Country Club. (The "cheapest" Lapham house, a three-bedroom, three-bathroom affair, runs $100,000.) "But we try to educate them toward good taste," he says. Lapham confesses to having mixed feelings about some of the residential fillips his clients have directed him to make. Somewhat ruefully he refers to the house he designed for Debbie Reynolds as "the flying boxcar." Cantilevered on steel beams, high on a hill — "It's so *heavy*-looking up there," he says.

One of Mr. Lapham's recent clients is Mr. S. A. Healy, "a big subway and tunnel man" from Chicago. In his shoot-the-works, damn-the-expense house, Mr. Healy — a man in his seventies — has a basement play area with two bowling alleys and automatic pinsetters; an electronic golf range with shifting photomurals projected on a wall to simulate progress from hole to hole; a Swedish sauna bath; and a whirlpool swimming pool. One nice thing about Palm Springs home builders, Lapham says, is that "Most of these guys okay a sketch, say, 'Let me know when it's finished,' and take off." They don't hang over an architect's drawing board, in other words, offering penny-pinching suggestions or otherwise making nuisances of themselves.

Home builders place similar faith in their interior decorators. People who don't want to be bothered with such details as upholstery and paint samples simply depart for several months in Europe, leaving their decorators with *carte blanche*. One woman, whose decorator chased her to the airport with living room fabric swatches, said airily, "Oh, just surprise me, darling," and climbed aboard her plane. When *My Fair Lady* composer Frederick Loewe left actor-turned-decorator Gar Moore ("I was once married to Nancy Walker") in charge of refurbishing his house and garden, he gave Moore only one instruction: "Don't move my mountain." But Moore, who had ideas of his own, got to work "rearranging" the mountain — actually a large hill behind the house — moving giant boulders by the ton, and in the end decided to build a whole new mountain somewhat closer to the house "for privacy."

As the time approached for Loewe's return, Moore grew apprehensive. "I decided to let him walk through the house and out into the garden alone, while I waited in the living room," Moore says. "Pretty soon, I heard him shouting, 'Gar! Gar!' I came running out. He was standing there, on one of the seven terraces I'd designed, looking at my new mountain with tears in his eyes, and he said, 'I don't deserve such a beautiful place!' " One of the subtleties of the garden, Moore explained, is that the boulders in it have been artfully arranged to suggest erotic objects, or rather certain parts of the human anatomy. This proves a great source of fun to Loewe's friends. Inside the house, in addition to such routine features as a sunken bathtub, curtains that open and draw on electric motors, and a television set that can be lowered electrically from the ceiling, there is Loewe's enormous glass-walled bedroom with a bed that can be power-swiveled about the floor so that its occupant can face whatever prospect pleases the recumbent. As the bed turns, its attendant bedside tables and lamps turn with it. "He can lie in bed and never get tired of the view," Moore says.

In his bar — surprisingly not the piano variety — Loewe likes to point out an arrangement of four framed pictures on the wall: an etching of two clasped hands "of friendship"; a depiction of a female nude; the photostat of a check; and a piece of sheet music. "These symbolize the things in life I value most, in that order," he explains. He has vowed that he will never write another line of music, and will not even tolerate a piano in the house. The check, symbol of his third most valued commodity, is payable to Loewe from Columbia Records in the amount of $1,840,000, representing a year's *My Fair Lady* royalties. The reverse side of the check has also been photostated. It is endorsed "For deposit only," and has been negotiated.

The rich and powerful of Palm Springs may have more fun with money than the rich of any other rich city in the world. Innocent jokes are always being played with checks, currency, or other tokens of exchange. Outside an elaborately done-up trailer in Sahara Park, the owner has installed a parking meter and "for a gag" has placed behind the glass of the meter's face a crisp new $1000 bill, to indicate that he lives in a trailer by choice and not out of necessity. The parking meter is one of the sights, along with the house where Joan Crawford and Alfred Steele spent part of their honeymoon, which visitors are taken to see. Palm Springs takes civic pride in such affluent, imaginative gestures.

Even the banks join in the financial whimsey. When the Palm Springs National Bank opened its doors not long ago, its directors decided to publicize the event by having their first depositor, the Eldorado Country Club, present a large check to the Desert Crippled Children's League. The check was four feet wide, nine feet long, and weighed one hundred and twenty pounds. The check was legal tender but, of course, would not fit in the bank's canceling machines. So the directors appeared merrily with electric drills and punched the proper holes in it. How the crippled children felt about the joke is not recorded. "Palm Springs is Free Enterprise at play," says one businessman with a good deal of accuracy. An Easterner, reacting with horror, says, "Palm Springs Society is a *perversion* of Society."

> *I sing of Palm Springs, and its joys multifarious,*
> *Be one hermit inclined, or a type most gregarious,*
> *All rustle and bustle, making bucks in a hustle;*
> *Or sunning, or funning, or resting, or nesting;*
> *Where you wear what you please,*
> *Where Eastern goes Western,*
> *Where the fair-skinned get tan-skinned*
> *And an eyeful of bareskin — and I don't mean a rug!*
> *Where great-grandmothers fly and visitors vie*
> *With characters local and whimsical*
> *Who wear zany hats, painted*
> *Cravats and costumes cut briefly, and lyrical!*
> *Where a President visits, and you and I hope*
> *It's a yearly occurrence —*
> *Rumor is that it will be.*
> *So stop in and see me at the fine*
> *Potter Realty*
> *In the heart of this glamorous town.*

So sings Mildred Southwick Potter, Palm Springs's poetess realtor, putting things in a nutshell, in her local ads, and proving, while she is at it, that Palm Springs, California, is a place where real estate and the arts have blissfully joined hands. It is a place where motion picture actresses have poolside conferences not about their careers but about their subdivisions; where silent screen stars sit under hair dryers in beauty salons discussing not their old loves but their new liens. It is a place where such as Desi Arnaz, Charles Boyer, Bonita Granville, and Gene Autry became hotelkeepers. It is where Bing Crosby — together with such stockholders as Jack Benny, Claudette Colbert, William Goetz, Phil Harris, Danny Kaye, and William Perlberg — has developed what must stand at the moment as the mobile-home park to end all mobile-home parks: Blue Skies Village.

The mobile-home, or trailer, park as an adjunct to the Social Establishment is worth pausing to consider, for that it is an offshoot — albeit a wild one — of Society there is no doubt. It is also a creation of the American Southwest. At Dana Point, on the Pacific coast, such established figures from Los Angeles Society as Mrs. Norman Chandler, wife of the publisher, retire to live in opulently outfitted trailers. So it is at Blue Skies Village in Palm Springs. In partnership with Crosby in this venture is a bubbly, roly-poly gentleman named Rex Thompson, who says, "We got a hundred and sixty-two families living here in Blue Skies, and twenty-one of 'em is bank directors! Fifty-two drive Cadillacs! Almost all of 'em is corporation presidents! We got three Rolls-Royces, eleven Thunderbirds, forty Lincoln Connies! We had a guy move here named Pierre Sicard, said he was a painter. Heck, I thought he painted 'Men' and 'Women' on doors, but it turns out he's got a $800,000 home in Bel Air! That guy's a great *artist!*"

To live in Blue Skies, one must lease trailer space in the park at rates from $750 to $1,200 a year. To this space one must add a trailer — agreeing, at the same time, to spend at least $7,500 "improving" or, one might say, immobilizing one's mobile home, because the surest thing that can be said about the trailers that have been brought to Blue Skies Village is that they will trail no more. The improvements proviso does not faze the residents of America's richest mobile-home community. On the contrary, it spurs them on to greater, more competitive, spending. In a recent eight-month period, Blue Skies trailer owners spent an aggregate total of $750,000 on terraces, porches, gazebos, cupolas, cabanas, and ramadas (a ramada is a super-structure covering an entire trailer). Several Blue Skies residents have gone off, unaccountably, on Oriental flights of fancy, and have enclosed their trailers in strange pagodas. One man, in an Egyptian mood, has surmounted his trailer with a replica of the Great Portal of the Temple of Karnak, complete with exterior friezes and frescoes.

Mr. Richard E. Bishop, retired president of the A. C. Horn Chemical Company, says he has spent "about $50,000" turning his 55 by 18 foot trailer into a facsimile of Mount Vernon. "I'm not quite sure how we got started on Mount Vernon," he says, "but we put on the big porch across the front with the white columns, and one thing sort of led to another." The Bishops' maid has a separate, smaller trailer of her own, also in the Mount Vernon style. Mount Vernon is topped by an enormous flagpole from which Old Glory can be seen from miles around, and upon which Mrs. Bishop occasionally hoists a flag emblazoned with a coffeepot, signifying that she would welcome other ladies for a *Kaffeeklatsch*. The Bishops also frequently fly the cocktail flag by way of asking neighbors over "for a little drinkie."

"People in other trailer parks around here call us 'the Blue Skies snobs,' " one trailer owner says, "and frankly we're proud of that label. We're a more international group than you'll find in other parks, and we're more social too. I mean Bing drops around for songfests, we hire professional entertainers for our shindigs, we have twenty-dollar-a-plate dinners — things like that. We're the only park that has cocktail parties. And sure we're exclusive." Blue Skies operates, he explains, as a private club. "No Tom, Dick or Harry can move into this place. We want *nice* people living here. We check on everybody. We even find out if they snore."

Meanwhile, the eyes of Blue Skies's manager Rex Thompson grow misty as he dreams of an America covered with mobile-home parks, based on the success of the Blue Skies venture. "I'm responsible for Dana Point, too," he explains. "I'm starting a whole chain of deluxe parks across the West! I'm building one right now in Vegas — it'll have everything this place has, plus slot machines! Most people in the East don't understand trailer living. Easterners look down their noses at trailer people, but tell 'em to come out to Blue Skies and see the aristocratic types *we've* got. Captains of industry! Why, these folks here hobnob with the cream of Palm Springs Society!"

Exactly what the cream of Palm Springs Society consists of is worth considering. It is a Society based — as elsewhere — on money and, in most cases, newly made money: first-generation fortunes that still have a bright, fresh taste in the fortune makers' mouths. It is a Society, moreover, that makes no attempt to disguise the fact that money is the whole point. As one man says, "Out here we say we're living on our heirs' money. So what? My son comes to me and says, 'Pop, you're dipping into capital!' I ask him, 'Who made it?' Why should I leave him ten million bucks? Let him go out and make it like I did."

There is a great deal of talk about exclusiveness, and which golf or country club is more exclusive than another. But there is a simple rule: the most exclusive clubs are the most expensive. Thunderbird, Eldorado, and Tamarisk are, therefore, three very exclusive golf clubs. Originally, Thunderbird was built as a Gentile club which specifically excluded Jews, and Tamarisk was its Jewish and equally exclusive answer (though it was happy to accept the non-Jewish Frank Sinatra). In recent years, however, the memberships of both clubs have blurred considerably, religious lines are no longer drawn and, as one Thunderbird member says, "All you need to get in here is the scratch." Eldorado, meanwhile, has the cachet of Eisenhower. Perhaps an even more exclusive club than these is Smoke Tree Ranch, which does not encourage golfers. Smoke Tree is not a country club but a private community of homes with a main guest building and cottages surrounding it, where life is determinedly ranchy. There are cookouts, riding picnics, chuck wagon breakfasts. For riding up into the chilly morning hills, members carry saddle flasks of vodka. The Bermuda Dunes Country Club, meanwhile, has the distinction of possessing the largest golf layout in the Palm Springs area. *Its* golf cars have refrigerated compartments for drinks. Bermuda Dunes is also the only local club with its own airport, its own hangar for private planes, its own fire department, and — for a reason that has never been quite clear — its own resident dentist. All these clubs are in the real estate business, and offer lots for sale, apartments for lease, or condominiums along the fairways for purchase.

For years the traditional club for movie stars was the Racquet Club, with its *éminence grise*, the retired actor Charles Farrell. Here, at various times, such movie people as Charles Butterworth, Warner Baxter, Carole Lombard, Gilbert Roland, Ginger Rogers, Mervyn LeRoy,

Mary Pickford, Frank Morgan, Marlene Dietrich, and "Big Boy" Williams could be seen playing tennis. Indeed, it was the arrival of Farrell and the club's co-founder, Ralph Bellamy, in Palm Springs in the mid-1930's that turned the first big spotlight of publicity on the area. The Tennis Club, on the other side of town, was created as the answer to the Racquet Club; it did not welcome movie stars or Jews. But here again, as Palm Springs has mushroomed, with all clubs furiously competing for members and in the selling of lots, membership restrictions have been dropped in both places, and movie stars and rich people of all faiths can be found in both.

Another very expensive and exclusive club is the Palette Club. Its membership, predominantly female, is composed of people who paint — the wives of millionaires and movie stars who clubbed together a few years ago to prove, as one member said, "that there is *so* some culture in Palm Springs!" The Palette Club occupies a comfortable old Spanish house which has been fixed up with antiques, mirrors, chandeliers, and a bar. Here, under the guidance of an affable bachelor named John Morris, the ladies gather for a painting lesson or a cocktail, or a painting lesson *and* a cocktail, draping their furs over their easels. Here one can see "Mousey" (Mrs. William) Powell working industriously on a still life, or the pretty young wife of an aging Texas oil man ("She's not *that* young," whispers Morris, "she's just had her face lifted") doing something "which expresses me." The club has frequent invitation-only shows of Western painters, and of its own members' work. The latter are particularly successful because, as one woman says, "We're very loyal about buying each other's paintings." During the summer months, John Morris, a genial Pied Piper, guides his little band of lady painters on an artists' tour of France, where his name becomes Jean Maurice.

But for all the talk about Society the plain fact is that Palm Springs isn't very social in the ordinary American sense. For all the vast sums of money Palm Springs people spend building and decorating their houses, the amount of entertaining done is relatively modest. So is its scale. Large parties are infrequent, the average get-together consisting of as many people as will fit around the piano bar. Hostesses keep things simple in terms of menus, party decor, and flowers. The never fading plastic blossom has been found to be intensely practical. The lavish wedding, the debutante ball, and so many other events that stamp Society in other resorts from Newport to Santa Barbara, do not take place in Palm Springs. There is only an occasional charity ball. Life in the desert becomes introverted, and the "type most gregarious" of Mrs. Potter's poem has a poorer time of it than those who are "hermit inclined." Palm Springs houses are built to hole up in, and some of the costliest places have never been known to entertain a guest. People who move here from other cities, expecting to find the advertised friendliness, are often disappointed. A new acquaintance promises to telephone, but never does. People are invited to dinner, and forget to come. "There's something about the climate here," one woman says, "that makes you fail to remember things."

Then there are those wealthy Indians who, in a sense, have had a bad time of it. The tribe was initially given thirty thousand acres of land; they were given "every other section," which divided the area in a checkerboard pattern. This grid design is quite apparent from the air as the pattern of Palm Springs's development because, unfortunately, clear title to Indian land for years could not be got for outright sale, and Federal law prohibited the land's lease for longer than a five-year period, which did not appeal to developers. So, while alternate sections have sprouted motels and golf courses, Indian lands lay bare. Recently, Congress declared that Indian lands could be leased for ninety-nine years, and so their development is under way. Also, under the Equalization Act, each individual member of the tribe was given land valued at $335,000. At today's soaring Palm Springs prices, each Indian — man, woman, and child — is worth easily a million dollars. The tribe, however, has dwindled. There are presently barely a hundred Indians left, and the number judged to be "competent adult Indians" is about forty. The wealth of the others is in the custodianship of banks. By the rest of Palm Springs's population, the Indians are simply ignored.

The real Old Guard of Palm Springs consists of exactly one woman, Mrs. Austin McManus, and even she is not a native. Still, Mrs. Mc-Manus, known throughout the valley as Auntie Pearl, is easily the First Lady of Palm Springs. She is a cheerful-faced woman in her eighties who looks considerably younger, and she says, "My heart is bound up in the desert!" So, it might be added, is her considerable fortune. Her father, Judge John Guthrie McCallum, arrived in 1884, having sought out the desert air for the sake of a tubercular son. Palm

Springs was a sleepy Indian settlement called Agua Caliente.* He became the area's first white settler. Judge McCallum bought up between
five and six thousand acres of land, built an aqueduct to carry water
down from the mountains, nineteen miles of irrigation canals, and began growing citrus, fig, and other fruit trees. He never lived to see his
investment become a success. At the time of his death an eleven-year
drought had dried up his canals and aqueduct — this was before Palm
Springs was discovered to rest on a series of underground lakes which
made water plentiful and cheap — and his fruit orchards had withered
and died. "Father died of a broken heart," Mrs. McManus says sadly.

But his considerable land passed on to his daughter who has managed her properties with a shrewdness that has won her the admiration
of every real estate man in town. She has also exercised a good deal of
taste, and the buildings for which she is responsible show a style and
dignity unusual in the town. It was she who built the handsome Tennis Club — which has been called, with customary Palm Springs excess, "the most beautiful two acres in America," but is nonetheless a
lovely place — as well as a number of the better-looking commercial
buildings downtown.

Because she is widowed and childless, without direct heirs, Mrs.
McManus has begun to think in terms of foundations and other bene-
ficiaries of her money and properties. She recently became interested
in the newly founded College of the Desert, a junior college outside
Palm Springs, only to discover that this institution, too, seemed to have
become afflicted with the curious logy-mindedness of the desert.

Not long ago she sent the college a check for $7,000. The president
called to thank her for the gift, and suggested that the money might be
spent to purchase new robes for the college choir. "Now wouldn't you
think," said Mrs. McManus indignantly to a friend, "that the
college — any college — could find something better to spend that
money on than choir robes? Why not *books,* for example? *Choir
robes!*"

It is real estate fever, Mrs. McManus admits, that has kept her
young. Standing on the wide veranda of her comfortable but unpretentious pink-stucco house overlooking Palm Springs and the acreage

* Named for the warm mineral spring which bubbled up through the sand, now
the site of the Palm Springs Spa and "The world's most beautiful bath house,"
which also belongs to the Indians.

her father bought, she talked not long ago of "whole new cities, whole new communities" being carved out of the far-off mountains and hidden canyons beyond. She had been taken on a private helicopter ride over some of those wild, lost ridges, and became excited about their development. "You see," she said with a smile, "I own some of those mountains."

"You see, son, this is *real* Society out here," said one of the many local boosters recently. "The real thing. Not your flibberty-gibbet fly-by-nights with fancy manners and their pinky in the air. This is *money*, son, and the men that make America run. The men that make Palm Springs are bigger than any *city* — why, they're international men, men that Presidents listen to, that can call up the heads of the biggest banks and give 'em hell. I'm talking about Ben Fairless, Len Firestone, Paul Hoffman, Monty Moncrief, Conrad Hilton, Greg Bautzer, Ernie Breech, Dan Thornton, Ray Ryan — *that* caliber. These men are the movers and the shakers and the doers, son — captains of finance, leaders of industry! That's what *I* call Society, son — the big wheels. As far as the other kind of Society goes, son, that's dead!"

Part Four

BUT IS IT REALLY DEAD?

20

"Obedience to the Unenforceable"

IT is one of the drawbacks of being rich and reasonably celebrated.
It happens occasionally to Astors, and with dreary regularity to
Fords and Rockefellers. They are always getting letters from people
bearing the same name, but of whom they have never heard, claiming
kinship. The letters come from strange way stations around the world,
and sometimes the would-be cousins live near at hand. The Manhattan telephone directory lists several "unreal" Rockefellers along with
the real ones. And, as often as not, the claimants can offer legitimate
and documented proof that they are relatives. But, whenever a new
member of a prominent family shows up, with or without credentials,
it is a distressing event. Because, in nearly every case, the "relative"
comes with an outstretched arm and an upturned palm. "Dear
Uncle . . ." began a letter received by one of the Vanderbilts not long
ago and, after a few amenities, continued:

. . . My Mother who was your Own Mothers cousin (in cradle with her when
they was two) always tell me when things turn bad for me you will lend a
hand. Last fall when I broke my back . . .

And so it familiarly went.
Fortunately for the American clan of Auchincloss, this cannot happen to them. It is one of several singular facts about this singular tribe.

Every one of the hundred-odd Auchinclosses now living in the United States is a member of the family, and they are all accounted for. There *are* no unreal Auchinclosses. And yet, a number of years ago, Mr. Hugh D. Auchincloss — or "Hughdie" as he is pet-named in the family — received a curious communication from an undertaker calling himself Auchincloss. The man was planning, or so he said, to do some advertising along the lines of "Let Auchincloss give you a classy funeral," or "Be Buried Like An Aristocrat Would — By Auchincloss." What, the undertaker wanted to know, did Mr. Hugh D. Auchincloss think of that proposal? Hughdie Auchincloss was, quite naturally, alarmed. Was the man attempting a kind of blackmail? Such advertising would be embarrassing, to say the least.

Hughdie Auchincloss weighed the matter carefully for several days. Then he remembered something his father had once said to him: "You are *not* responsible for your relatives. You are only responsible for your friends." Hughdie Auchincloss ignored the communication. The man was not heard from again.

If it is true that Society in the United States is based on *nothing* but money, then the Auchinclosses, again, are something of an exception. Though Auchinclosses have been prominent in Society for generations (a good seven, in fact), and though most of them have been, as Louis Auchincloss puts it, "respectably affluent," there has never been an Auchincloss family fortune as such. Indeed, if there ever had been, it would — unless strictest rules of primogeniture had been adhered to — have long ago been dissipated by division and taxation. It is rather like the Auchinclosses to have made assets out of these facts which, in other families, would have been considered distinct disadvantages. When John Winthrop Auchincloss (an uncle of Hugh D.) built his Newport house, "Hammersmith Farm," in 1892, he did not build it on Bellevue Avenue, Newport's fashionable "ocean side" where all the greatest mansions are, but on the Narragansett Bay side, or "wrong side" of Newport. And "Hammersmith Farm" itself — though a very large house and a handsome example of the shingle style, surrounded by seventy-five acres of land — is a dollhouse compared with the gilt and marble palaces for which Newport is famous. And yet, since John Winthrop Auchincloss was who he was, he made a number of Vanderbilts, Astors, and Goelets who had houses on Bellevue Avenue feel, uncomfortably, that they had done it all wrong. Perhaps John Winthrop had hoped they would feel this way; perhaps not. But such, by the end of the last century, had become the mystical power of the Auchincloss name in Society.

It all started in 1803, when the first Auchincloss, also named Hugh, set foot on these shores, having sailed from Greenock, Scotland, aboard the ship *Factor*. He was twenty-three years old, and enterprising. Within a short time he operated his own dry-goods store in downtown Manhattan. In 1806, he married a Philadelphia girl of Scottish descent named Ann Anthony Stuart whose father, though not wealthy, was a man of property. His will shows that he was able to bequeath his heirs such items as a "gold watch," "gold jacket-buttons," and a "Negro wench" to each of his children.

Hugh and Ann Auchincloss's was the first of many auspicious Auchincloss weddings. Hugh, meanwhile, was parsimonious, persevering, Presbyterian. Obituaries of him describe him in ominous negatives. He was *not* tightfisted, they insist. He was *not* disagreeable and mean. That was just his *appearance*. "The fiber of his nature was strong rather than delicate," stated his funeral orator, "hence some misapprehended him as blunt and harsh. The deceased was not a man of smooth words or disguised flatteries. . . ." It would seem that the Auchinclosses, at that point, had a long way to go. In a tintype of the first Hugh, he certainly looks sour, his mouth turned down in a perfectly inverted crescent. In *her* tintype, Ann Anthony Stuart Auchincloss merely looks glum. Because her maiden name was Stuart, her grandson, John Winthrop, had the crest of the Royal House of Stuart emblazoned on his silverware. His claim to the crest is particularly fuzzy. Ann Anthony Stuart Auchincloss was a tiny woman, so diminutive that she crawled into the family cradle to nurse each of her thirteen children. She was also, alas, no beauty. The prominent "Auchincloss nose" appears to have descended from her, and therefore should properly be called a Stuart nose.

Of Ann and Hugh Auchincloss's thirteen children, only one — the first John — had the proper dynastic talent to produce male heirs bearing the family name. Of his twelve brothers and sisters there are no descendants whatever today. Yet John is responsible for a remarkable circumstance. From him descend all the Auchinclosses in America — dozens upon dozens of them — with the exception of those in the embalming business. An Auchincloss family tree, prepared in 1957, lists the names of some three hundred and thirty descendants of John and, of these, fifty-seven have been males named Auchincloss. Genetically, this is an uncommonly high proportion. The family tree lists ten Hugh Auchinclosses, fifteen Jameses, eight Stuarts, seven Anns, twenty Elizabeths, and quite a few Johns, Williams, and Douglases. Included are ten sets of twins. More of each have been born, of course, since the tree was compiled. As happens in large families, cousins have married cousins, but this has not seemed to affect the rate of production. The first John had nine children, seven of them boys. In the second and third generations, multiple marriages begin to take place, giving Auchinclosses complicated step- and half-relationships.

Two marriages per Auchincloss today are commonplace, and three are no surprise. One pair of Auchincloss sisters married the same man, one Benjamin Betner, though not, naturally, at the same time. (The family tree delicately overlooks this somewhat unusual circumstance.) Hugh D. Auchincloss himself was married, first, to Maya Chrapovitsky, the daughter of a Russian naval officer, and their son, another Hugh, is called "Yusha," a rough Russian equivalent of his name. Hughdie was married, second, to Mrs. Nina Gore Vidal, the ex-wife of an aircraft executive, by whom he had two children, Thomas Gore and Nina Gore Auchincloss (and, for the duration of the marriage, had a stepson named Gore Vidal). Third, he was married to Mrs. Janet Lee Bouvier, mother of two Bouvier girls, Caroline Lee and Jacqueline Lee. By the former Mrs. Bouvier, he had two more children, Janet Jennings and James Lee Auchincloss. Mrs. Vidal was the daughter of T. P. Gore, the famous blind Senator from Oklahoma. "Thus," says Hughdie Auchincloss, "I was on two occasions connected with the United States Senate."

More striking than the Auchincloss divorce record is the family record for marrying well. Auchinclosses themselves don't like to be reminded of this fact — which delights their in-laws — but it is true: in each Auchincloss generation, there has been at least one brilliant marriage to carry the family upward onto new plateaux of prestige and privilege. No sooner had the first Hugh married Ann Anthony Stuart than the advantages of the union began to appear. What little Ann lacked in looks, she made up for in Scotch doughtiness and spirit. When war was declared between England and the United States in 1812, it found Hugh Auchincloss, still a British subject, an enemy alien. All aliens were ordered removed "at least forty miles from tide water so that they might not be able to render aid or give comfort to the enemy," and Hugh Auchincloss was promptly interned up the Hudson River in Poughkeepsie, far from his dry-goods store. His wife then took matters into her own hands. She boarded a stage for Washington — a three-and-a-half days' trip — determined to take her husband's case to the top, to the President of the United States himself, if need be. Once in Washington, she hired a hack to take her to the White House. On the way, her driver pointed to a pedestrian and said, "There goes Mr. Monroe, the Secretary of State." "Stop the hack!" cried Mrs. Auchincloss. She bounded out, confronted Monroe on the street, and demanded to see President Madison. Somewhat startled, no doubt, the Secretary agreed that she could come to the White House the following morning.

When she told her story to Madison he was at first unimpressed. But, according to her great-grandson John Auchincloss, "She stayed in Washington about a week, making such a nuisance of herself that the President and the Secretary of State, to get rid of her, for the country *was* at war, issued an executive order allowing her husband to return to New York and resume his occupation." Ever since, Auchinclosses have been unafraid of storming the halls of the mighty.

The exception that had been made in the single case of Hugh Auchincloss did not endear him to the other Britishers interned in Poughkeepsie. They kicked up a mighty fuss and, before long, the pressure was such that the President was forced to rescind his order. But this time, at least, Hugh Auchincloss was prepared. He had fitted himself out with a mule team and wagon and, instead of making for Poughkeepsie, he headed west, as a traveling dry-goods store. By the war's end, he had peddled his way as far as Louisville, Kentucky, and was a rich man.

From that point on, Auchinclosses have been rubbing elbows steadily with the highly placed in Society and government. The eldest son of Hugh and Ann (the first John) made what can only be described as an imposingly advantageous marriage. Though his bride wore the unprepossessing name of Elizabeth Buck, her pedigree virtually bristled with great Colonial names — Winthrop, Dudley, Wainright, Mainwaring, and Saltonstall. Her great-great-great-great-great-grandfather was John Winthrop, called "The Great Immigrant," Governor of Massachusetts and one of the founders of Harvard. Two other many-times great-grandfathers, Thomas Dudley and Joseph Dudley, were Massachusetts Governors; another John Winthrop was the first Governor of Connecticut, and still another was Chief Justice of the Massachusetts Supreme Court. One could go on and on citing the distinguished ancestors of Elizabeth Buck and, when one is talking Auchincloss family history, one does. One of her ancestors was Sir Richard Saltonstall of Huntwicke, and his wife — we are in the sixteenth century now — was said to have descended directly from William the Conqueror.

The late Charles C. Auchincloss, who took up genealogy as a hobby late in life, worked out an elaborate chart showing how William the Conqueror fitted into the family, and even Uncle Charlie's greatest admirers admit that he had to use both ingenuity and a certain amount of imagination to come up with that relationship. His chart shows how today's Auchinclosses are also directly described from the royal lines of England, Scotland and, for good measure, France, through King Philip II. Not one, but three of Elizabeth Buck Auchincloss's ancestors — Sir Richard Saltonstall, Governor Winthrop, and Governor Dudley — arrived in Salem aboard the vessel *Arabella* in 1630. Charles Auchincloss liked to point out that families who arrived on the *Mayflower* really had not accomplished much until the passengers from the *Arabella*, "named after the daughter of a duke," arrived to show the others what to do. Charles Auchincloss also used to somewhat infuriate his wife — who was the former Rosamond Saltonstall — by explaining, genealogically, how he, with his heavy dosage of Saltonstall stock, was really more of a Saltonstall than she was.

It is generally unwise, particularly with the older generation, to poke fun at the Auchinclosses' ancient and regal family claims, but one person who has done so, albeit affectionately, has been Wilmarth Lewis, the author and Horace Walpole scholar, whose late wife was Annie Burr Auchincloss, a collateral descendant of, among others, Aaron Burr. Speaking at a family reunion in the ballroom of New York's Colony Club (which Louis Auchincloss describes as "a tremendous feat, but more like a stockholders' meeting than a family gathering), Mr. Lewis took the Auchincloss family tree lightly to task. Speaking to the hostess of the huge affair, the late Emma Jennings Auchincloss (mother of the present Hugh D.), he asked Aunt Emma if she recalled "dear cousin Charlemagne Auchincloss," and "old

Uncle Henry the Eighth." Glancing at the Auchincloss charts, he noted that one of the Auchinclosses had married a Smedberg — "obviously of an old New York family" — and wondered if, therefore, there wouldn't be a good family reason to speak of "Cousin Noah," and, perhaps, "dear Uncle Adam," and "Aunt Eve."

Nonetheless, with Elizabeth Buck's entrance into the family, the Auchincloss name assumed a place in New York Society which it has never vacated. The couple built a spacious summer home in Newport, in then fashionable Washington Street, on the water's edge. They had nine children, seven of them boys, but it was their eldest daughter, Sarah Ann, who made the first brilliant marriage in *that* generation. She wed James Coats of the Scottish thread-manufacturing family and, in rather short order, a number of the Auchincloss boys became American agents for Coats Thread, a profitable endeavor. Next, Edgar Stirling Auchincloss married Maria Sloan, daughter of the president of the Delaware and Lackawanna Railroad. John Winthrop Auchincloss married a Russell, another family prominent in New York and Newport, and — from a money standpoint, the best marriage of all — Hugh Dudley Auchincloss married Emma Brewster Jennings, whose father, Oliver B. Jennings, was a founder of the Standard Oil Company. Jennings and the first William Rockefeller married sisters named Goodsell and, therefore, Auchinclosses of the Hugh Dudley branch are first and second cousins of the William-branched Rockefellers.*

Talk about a social power structure! The Hugh Dudley, Edgar Stirling, and Sarah Auchincloss Coats branches of the family are the three rich branches, but the others have not done at all badly. A daughter of the John Winthrop branch married another Jennings, a cousin of the first — and a daughter of the Henry Buck line married a Colgate, of the toothpaste family. Today, the Auchinclosses are "the most marvelously connected family in New York," according to a friend, occupying nearly two full pages of the New York *Social Register,* some forty-

---

* Often called the "Other Rockefellers," the "Greenwich Rockefellers," and the "Best Rockefellers." The descendants of William Rockefeller have generally tried to keep out of the spotlight which falls on the families of William's brother, John D. While the Rockefellers of Pocantico Hills, in Westchester, have been known for wealth, piety, vast philanthropy, and a certain humorlessness, the Greenwich Rockefellers are known for their wit, good nature, and charm. They are the "Fun Rockefellers."

seven separate listings, compared with forty-two for Rockefellers, eight for Vanderbilts, and a mere two for Astors. This, of course, does not include Auchinclosses who have migrated to such far-flung cities as Honolulu. Through marriage, the Auchinclosses are now kin, in addition to Rockefellers, Sloans, Winthrops, Jenningses, Saltonstalls, and Smedbergs, to such other redoubtable families as the Frelinghuysens, the Van Rensselaers, the Cuttings, the Reids, the du Ponts, the Grosvenors, the Truslows, the Tiffanys, the Bundys, the Adamses, the Ingrahams, the Burdens, the Vanderbilts and, of course, the Kennedys.

One might call them the definitive family of American Society. They describe its limits, and its design. The lacy branches of the Auchincloss family tree spread across its entire landscape. The Auchinclosses have never married Roosevelts. On the other hand, when young Lewis Rutherfurd married Janet Auchincloss at Hammersmith Farm in 1966, it was realized that Rutherfurd's step-grandmother, Lucy Rutherfurd, had for many years been F.D.R.'s mistress, making the Roosevelts seem somehow part of the family, or at least close.

It should not be inferred, because so many Auchincloss men married well-placed and wealthy ladies, that the men were fortune hunters. For the most part, Auchincloss men have been sober and industrious — whether as thread merchants, lawyers, bankers, or stockbrokers — and dutiful pillars of the Fifth Avenue Presbyterian Church. The Auchinclosses have produced a distinguished doctor, the late Hugh — a cousin of the present Hugh D. — who was Chief of Surgery at Presbyterian Hospital in New York, and Professor of Surgery at the Columbia College of Physicians and Surgeons. Even Auchincloss women have gone into business. Mrs. Maria Auchincloss Look, for example, was for several years the American packager and distributor of a product called "I-Snips," an ice-cracking tool. Auchinclosses dislike being idle, and no one has demonstrated this better than Louis Auchincloss, who works full-time as a Wall Street lawyer and has turned out an imposing array of novels and short stories in his spare time.

"The Auchinclosses have always been a very *nice* family," says one friend. As a member of the family puts it, "There have been several stupid Auchinclosses, but no *cruel* ones." There have been but few playboys or scapegraces in the family, and a gentle air of good behavior surrounds them all. This reputation for piety and rectitude has added to their legend and their stature, and is an important ingredient in the Auchincloss style. "One was always a little in awe of them," says a New York woman. "At least I was brought up to believe that if you saw an Auchincloss doing it it was *right.*"

In Bar Harbor, Maine, where the J. Howland Auchinclosses have long owned a summer place — grandly ignoring Bar Harbor's fall from fashion — their neighbors for many years were the Archbolds, who lived just down the hill. The Archbolds, another Standard-Oil-founding family, are far richer than most Auchinclosses. Yet Archbolds tremble when Auchinclosses frown. At Bar Harbor, the Archbolds kept horses for their children, though the Auchinclosses did not. Horses involve stables, stables involve a manure pile, and a manure pile entails flies and certain odors. Lydia Archbold — now Mrs. Archbold Foote, a horsewoman of some note — recalls that one of the most agonizing duties of her childhood was writing her first social note. It was a note to Mrs. Auchincloss. Since they were Lydia's horses, her mother explained, little Lydia should write to Mrs. Auchincloss apologizing for the way the manure pile smelled, and hoping that the scent did not make its way into the Auchincloss garden.

Auchinclosses have become arbiters of elegance and, in their quiet and unassuming way, standard-setters. Mrs. J. Howland Auchincloss recalls the years before she married into the clan, when she was Priscilla Stanton, and her parents occupied a brownstone opposite the first Hugh D. Auchinclosses in East Forty-ninth Street. The present Hughdie Auchincloss was then a baby of approximately the same age as Miss Stanton's little brother, William, and Priscilla's mother often posted her at the window to keep an eye on the Auchincloss house across the way. "Mrs. Auchincloss," said Mrs. Stanton, "has a *hospital-trained* nurse for little Hughdie. And when you see that nurse take little Hughdie out in his carriage, I want you to tell me exactly what she has him dressed in." Priscilla remembers running to her mother with such news as, "She has little Hughdie in his little fur coat and fur bonnet!" There was nothing to do but hurry out and buy a fur coat and bonnet for baby William.

So powerful is the Auchincloss name in Newport that, when it was decided to combine the coming-out party of Jacqueline Bouvier with a christening party for her half-brother — and invitations read, "Also honouring Mister James Lee Auchincloss" — baby Jamey received invitations to dinners, dances, and cocktail parties all over town.

In the summer of 1966, the most waited for event in Eastern Society was the Auchincloss-Rutherfurd wedding in Newport — he, tall, handsome, splendidly educated (Buckley, St. Paul's, Princeton), and impeccably pedigreed (directly descended from Peter Stuyvesant, New York's last Dutch Governor); she, like her step- and half-sisters, dark-haired and beautiful and, of course, "an Auchincloss," Hughdie's youngest daughter. Socially, it was a long way from another wedding of the same season — that of Luci Johnson to Pat Nugent. In fact, the only notice taken in Newport of the Johnson-Nugent nuptials was when someone commented, "In that heat? Will anyone *go?*"

While Washington sweltered, a crisp breeze blew across Narragansett Bay. The green lawns of Hammersmith Farm, where the reception was being held, swept down to the blue water's edge. The family ponies romped in the fields, and the Black Angus herd posed decoratively against the sky as, indeed, they are supposed to do. (The Black Angus are actually a decorative herd. Both Mr. and Mrs. Auchincloss like to look out their windows onto grazing animals and so, to indulge this fancy, Hughdie Auchincloss buys eighteen or twenty head each spring and sells them again in the fall, before returning to his winter home in Washington.) A white oval tent was set up on the lawn for the reception party. Inside, there was music and laughter and champagne and, outside, little John-John Kennedy, in the costume he had worn as a page (the bride was his mother's half-sister) — blue linen shorts, white silk shirt, blue satin cummerbund, high white socks, black patent leather shoes with silver buckles — chased the Auchincloss ponies while a brace of Secret Service men chased him. (He had been a perfect page throughout the ceremony until the very end; as the wedding party was leaving the church, John-John could not resist throwing a quick punch into the ribs of a young contemporary.) As six hundred guests wandered in and out of the tent, through the spectacular gardens, admiring the dazzling sunshine of the day, the evident happiness of the young pair, and the auspiciousness of the match, everyone was saying that it was the most beautiful wedding anyone had ever seen. Then, suddenly, into the Bay, at the foot of the long cascade of lawn, swept the New York Yacht Club's sailing cruise — hundreds of sails billowing, like a host of huge white butterflies composing a backdrop for the party. "How like the Auchinclosses to get this to happen — and for nothing," someone murmured. And of course Janet Auchincloss, senior, had known that the cruise was scheduled, had hoped it would arrive to help decorate her daughter's wedding. It did, and in the colors she had chosen for the wedding's theme — blue and white.

"Obedience to the unenforceable." It was a phrase that governed the life of Dr. Hugh Auchincloss, who died in 1947, and which governed the lives of many Auchinclosses before and after him. It might be said to be the motto — the moral law — of the family. "We've always been more like a fraternity than a family," Louis Auchincloss once commented and, if so, this phrase is the fraternal password. Each of Dr. Auchincloss's children and grandchildren was required to memorize the phrase as soon as he or she was able to talk, and so were all Dr. Auchincloss's nieces, nephews, grandnieces, and grandnephews. The children were asked to repeat the phrase before sitting down at Dr. Auchincloss's Sunday dinner table.

The phrase, which in Dr. Auchincloss's opinon, encapsulated the code of a lady or a gentleman, is today carved in stone in the chapel of the Groton School, of which Dr. Auchincloss was a trustee. The words have gazed down upon a full generation of Groton boys, including a good many Auchinclosses. "Obedience to the unenforceable" — a principle first uttered in an address significantly titled, "Law and Manners" by Lord Moulton, a British jurist and parliamentarian, Minister of Munitions at the outbreak of the First World War — meant, as adapted by the Auchincloss family, that a man or woman's first duty was to obey that which he cannot be *forced* to obey. Such matters as a person's morals, or his human obligations, in other words, cannot ever be legislated by others. A government cannot regulate decency of thought and purpose; the right action cannot be found by consulting a rule book. Obedience to the unenforceable, Dr. Auchincloss reminded the children, is the great unwritten law of any worthwhile society, or Society, and each individual is the enforcer, and the *only* enforcer, of that unwritten law upon himself. "Obedience to the unenforceable" is, one might argue, a slightly more noble principle than that of *noblesse oblige,* and the Auchinclosses have, as a family, done their best to abide by it.

"Obedience to the unenforceable" has been the theme of life at

Hammersmith Farm, where good behavior is expected to be automatic, and where one's duties are expected to be assumed without question or complaint. Today the amenities of Hammersmith Farm are in the hands of soft-spoken, soft-slippered servants, but it was not always thus. When Janet and Hughdie Auchincloss were married, it was 1942, wartime, and among the other difficulties to be assumed by the new bride — such as helping her two young daughters make the transition to a new home and stepfather who already had three children of his own — was the problem of Hammersmith Farm itself. Janet Auchincloss's mother-in-law had, as part of her staff, employed fourteen full-time gardeners to keep the Hammersmith landscape tidy; she had belonged to an era of Newport Society when gardens were placed a goodly hiking distance from the house, and they were part of a daily ritual: one strolled to the garden after lunch and, when there, sat in the shade of vast pergolas to be served tea brought on a wagon by the "second man." In wartime Newport it was impossible to find a *first* man, much less a second and the fourteen gardeners were a quaint and distant memory.

Young Mrs. Auchincloss put her little girls to work — pruning rosebushes and fruit trees, clipping hedges, and cutting grass. It was very nearly a hopeless task (there were five hothouses of growing things), but the children tackled it with spirit. It would have been easier to give up the big place, but Hughdie Auchincloss was sentimentally attached to it, and still is. He was born there and says, without a trace of gloom, that he intends to die there.

Gradually, under Janet Auchincloss's supervision, the scale of the gardening operation was reduced. The huge old gardens were photographed for posterity, then plowed under. A smaller garden was built next to the house, considerably shortening the old garden trip. But there were other inconveniences. Wartime restrictions meant that the house could have only one telephone. The children took turns doing telephone duty, which meant staying within earshot of the ring. Cooks and maids were hard to find, and the children learned the techniques and disciplines of cooking and housework.

Sometimes guests seemed to forget how much work the old place was. There was one — an old friend — who always insisted on bringing his own linen sheets, pillowcases, and blankets when he visited. The sheets were so deeply hemmed that when folded down across the blanket, they extended fully halfway down the bed and, to satisfy these whims of his, a guest bedroom had to be dismantled and re-made on his arrival. Janet Auchincloss took on the chore herself. She has always been fond of dogs — she presently keeps two poodles and two pugs — but one of her poodles had a curious habit. Whenever he disliked a person, he registered the fact by wetting, rather pointedly, on some article belonging to that person. One evening, the special-sheets friend had come to Hammersmith Farm for the night and, while Janet Auchincloss was making up the bed with his linen, the dog suddenly leaped on the bed. The rest may be imagined. As much to save her dog's reputation as her own as a hostess, Mrs. Auchincloss rose — like an Auchincloss — to the occasion. She seized a bath towel, dried the damaged pillowcase as much as possible, reversed it, and prayed that her guest would not turn it over before retiring. Apparently, he didn't. When he left, he had a special word of praise for "your beautifully behaved dogs."

To teach her children obedience to the unenforceable, Janet Auchincloss had her own methods. When her daughter Lee was about ten, the child was caught telling a fib. Her mother thereupon sat her down and began telling her the classic tale of George Washington and the cherry tree. When she got to the point of the story where George's father asks him who cut down the tree, Mrs. Auchincloss paused and said, "Now, Lee, when his father asked him that, what do you suppose little George Washington answered?" Without a moment's hesitation, Lee replied, "He said, 'I don't have any idea who cut it down, of course!' " "Why, Lee," said her mother, "I'm surprised at you. That wasn't the truth. No, he said, 'Father, I cannot tell a lie. I did it with my little hatchet,'" "Well," said Lee, "I think that was an awfully foolish thing for him to say when his father was so mad at him."

Each of the two Bouvier girls had her own personality and her own style and, though close as sisters, they were not a bit alike. Jacqueline was the quieter of the two, the more reserved and the more determined. She would spend hours over her sketch pad and in scrapbooks at Hammersmith Farm are some of the drawings she made as a child of the others in the family — drawings with such titles as "Mummy," "Uncle Hugh," "Yusha," "Lee," and "Me." As a girl, Jacqueline Bouvier also seemed to be genuinely ashamed of the fact that she was bright. With boys, particularly, she went out of her way to make them think that they were smarter than she, and her mother would overhear her saying — to a young man who had flunked his math exam — "Oh, I'm terrible at math, too!" even though she was excellent at it. It was something her mother — a great advocate of "Be yourself" — never quite understood. "She was so afraid of being thought a bluestocking," her mother says now.

Lee was the more volatile, a creature of sudden whims and enthusiasms. As a girl, she considered herself a champion of social justice, and her mother was always finding her on the telephone to city officials, or writing letters to Mayor LaGuardia to tell him what was wrong with New York and how to correct it. Once her older sister Jackie walked into a room to find Lee telephoning orphanages. She had become interested in orphans that morning, and was trying to find a group she could take with her to the theatre.

Though both girls were voted, by such authorities as Cholly Knickerbocker, "Number One Debutante" of their respective coming-out years, it was Lee Bouvier, not Jackie, who was considered the beauty in the family; Jackie, despite her best efforts to establish a contrary reputation, was known as the brainy, creative one. Then Jacqueline Bouvier married John F. Kennedy, and the Auchincloss family history entered on a new chapter. "This is the most beautiful spot on the Atlantic seaboard," the President used to say as he stood on the terrace of Hammersmith Farm. With a wink at his mother-in-law, he would say, "Mrs. Auchincloss, don't *you* think this is the most beautiful spot on the Atlantic seaboard?" Since she has had to deal with some of the housewifely problems of the place, she insists she has merely "put up" with it. Still, those were exciting days with the President spending holidays there, entertaining such guests as Prime Minister Nehru. The Auchinclosses' guest book of that period reads like an international *Who's Who*. To be sure, there were always crowds of tourists at the foot of the drive, and boats in the bay coming in close for a look, and the retinue of staff and Secret Service men who attended the President to be housed and fed. "Still," says Hughdie Auchincloss, "I think we got the best of the deal. We got wonderful telephone service. All our calls, you see, went through the White House switchboard." Friends, calling the Auchinclosses from down the street, had to call via Washington, but it was fast. Mail delivery was speedier, too.

In the summer of 1963 Janet Auchincloss, Jr., whom many con-

sider the most beautiful of Mrs. Auchincloss's three daughters, made
her debut at Hammersmith Farm. The long drive was lighted by flares
and white Chinese lanterns, and in the big "deck room" — the main
entertaining room of the house — the chandeliers were festooned with
flowers and velvet ribbons. Outside, in the tents set up on the lawn
facing the bay, everything was Venetian red, blue, and gold, with the
center tent poles garlanded with swags of flowers and sparkly lights.
Meyer Davis and his orchestra played from behind a thirty-foot red-
and-black Venetian gondola filled with baskets of flowers, and the
band and its leader were dressed as gondoliers. There were over a
thousand guests, including seven foreign ambassadors, two United
States Senators, a retired Associate Justice of the Supreme Court,
along with the Angier Biddle Dukes, the David E. K. Bruces, the Har-
vey Firestones, the Winthrop Aldriches, the Sheldon Whitehouses,
and virtually everybody who was anybody at all in Eastern Society
including, of course, dozens of Auchinclosses. It was the most festive
and lavish debutante ball of that or any other Newport season anyone
could remember. The President and Mrs. Kennedy did not attend, but
they sent Janet the bouquet of flowers she carried, and announced that
they would entertain for her at the White House during the Christmas
season — a Christmas that did not come for President Kennedy.

Hughdie Auchincloss was lunching at the Metropolitan Club in
Washington when the news of the event in Dallas was brought to him.
He hurried downstairs to have it confirmed on television, then sped
home and gathered his children around him. Later in the day, he and
his wife went to the White House where they met Jacqueline Kennedy when she arrived. Still later, when the President's body was
brought to the White House, there was a short family service. At Mrs.
Kennedy's request, the Auchinclosses spent the night with her.

When John Kennedy was President, with Hughdie Auchincloss's
stepdaughter as his wife, the Auchinclosses were swept into a kind of
international celebrity. All named Auchincloss in America found
themselves in this curious position. They accepted it with good grace,
even enjoyed it. They put aside the traditionally Republican Auchincloss political stance, and spoke out for the President and his party.*

* During the Kennedy campaign, Hugh D. Auchincloss telegraphed numerous
friends who were prominent Republicans, urging them to support Kennedy.

Now, in Mrs. Kennedy's much publicized widowhood, her mother and stepfather have been flung into a share of the spotlight that surrounds *the* most famous woman in the world, and so have all the other Auchinclosses. Mrs. Kennedy's position in the Auchincloss clan is now an odd one. Just as she seems somewhat out of place among the Kennedys, so does she seem out of keeping with the Auchincloss style and manner. She lacks the Kennedys' Irish exuberance and competitiveness; she also blends uneasily with Auchinclosses who have, by tradition, been Scottishly conservative, understated, and aloof. What, for instance, would Aunt Ellie have thought of her in her miniskirt — Aunt Ellie, who disapproved of men and women swimming together in the same pool. It is clear that Jacqueline Bouvier Kennedy is, after all, her father's daughter. Her sensitivity as well as her certain sentimentality, her sense of drama and her sense of fashion, her poise which often conceals her Gallic temper, seem to have come from the opposite side of the English Channel.

Auchinclosses have never been in the business of producing giant public personalities. Like the occasional Vanderbilt, Roosevelt, Rockefeller, Adams, or Saltonstall who has chosen a career in government or politics, the Auchinclosses have produced one such family member — James Coats Auchincloss, Republican Congressman from New Jersey for many years. He seems decidedly a maverick. To prove, however, that Jim's political adventures were not entirely frivolous, Auchinclosses remind themselves that for twenty-five years Jim was a member of the New York Stock Exchange, and a member of its Board of Governors for eighteen. By nature reticent when outside the realm of "people we know," the Auchinclosses now find Mrs. Kennedy's face on the cover of every magazine.

On the ferry-crossing from Jamestown to Newport, Hammersmith Farm, smiling down on the bay, is one of the tourist sights. The little windmill guest house that Mrs. Auchincloss is building at the water's edge is announced as "where Jackie stays," though this is not really the case. Rubberneckers park outside the entrance to Hammersmith Farm with cameras, and some drive boldly up the drive itself, hoping for a glimpse of their beloved. Needless to say, this is a nuisance to Hammersmith Farm's owners, nor are others in the family pleased with these developments. It is not that they are jealous of "the fuss," as one cousin puts it, made over Hughdie and Janet. It is just that they are

afraid the family is becoming famous for the wrong things. Auchinclosses were Auchinclosses, after all, long before Kennedys were Kennedys.

Life at Hammersmith, meanwhile, continues to be decorous and
seemly. In the mornings, which Hughdie Auchincloss spends at his
desk, slippered servants move efficiently through the sunny, airy
rooms, speaking in whispers. Before lunch, Hughdie and his wife
meet for a Daiquiri in the desk room. Then lunch is announced. After
lunch, Hughdie may drive around Hammersmith in his blue Bentley,
stopping to speak with his head gardener or his superintendent. Or he
may sit for an hour or so at the water's edge, fishing for mackerel. If
there is a professional football game scheduled, he will head back for
the deck room and the television set. Upstairs, his wife works at her
desk. Both Auchinclosses nap before dressing for dinner, and at these
times the house grows very still.

The house, too, now wears something of the air of a memorial.
Framed, in the entrance hall, is the Presidential flag which flew from
the lawn when the President visited, and photographs of him are
everywhere — there he is with his wife, there with his children, there
with Yusha Auchincloss's twin sons. Upstairs, in the study off the room
he used, is a desk with a bronze plaque listing the various bills he signed
into law there. Everyone in the family speaks of him respectfully as
"The President," only occasionally slipping and referring to him as
"Jack." On the third floor, the children's floor, the rooms of Yusha,
Nina, Jackie, Lee, Janet, and Jamey are often empty now. The long
hallway is lined with photographs of departed Auchinclosses. One is
struck with a sad sense that the greatest days of the great house may
now be past, or that its history must now enter another new phase.

Janet Auchincloss, Sr. — a handsome, vivid, slender and auburn-
haired woman with a bouyant step and a quick smile who looks far too
youthful to be a grandmother — may sense this too. In 1965, she em-
barked upon a new project. The old windmill, which once lifted water
for the house, was standing idle, and she had an idea: why not move it
down to the edge of the bay and remodel it? She and her daughter
Jackie spent weeks hiking around the acreage at Hammersmith in
search of the perfect spot and, when they thought they had one, the
two women had themselves raised on a work-lift tractor so they could
inspect the view, as it would be, from the top. Working with walkie-

talkies between the main house and a prospective site, she and Jackie tried to place the windmill where it would do the most for the *house's* view. It was a familiar sight, that summer, Mrs. Kennedy and her mother — one woman, leaning from an upper window of the main house, gesturing and shouting directions, and the other, skirts blowing, perched high on the platform of a fork-lift, half a mile away. At last they settled on a site. A workman, helping to prepare to move the building, was using an acetylene torch. A gust of wind blew his flame under a shingle. The windmill caught fire instantly and burned to the ground.

But Mrs. Auchincloss is a woman of determination. Undaunted by the catastrophe, she decided to build a new windmill which became, in the process, quite a bit more than the old one was to be. There are four floors, with an elevator between — a large room for entertaining on the ground floor, a living-dining room on the next, a bedroom on the next and, on the top, a glass-walled studio room that takes in the entire bay and a generous portion of the Atlantic Ocean. Two kitchenettes and a sundeck are staggered between the floors. From now on, according to Mrs. Auchincloss's plan, she and her husband will retreat for the summers into this diminutive, elegant, fairy-tale castle. The children and grandchildren may use the big house as they wish.

There are no outward signs that being the mother of the most publicized woman in the world has been a strain, but certainly it has been. Janet Auchincloss is often recognized and approached by strangers who, as often as not, are well-meaning, and who ask the question, "Pardon me, but aren't you Jackie Kennedy's mother?" Mrs. Auchincloss visibly stiffens before murmuring a polite, and poised, affirmative, and moving on. The publicity and the recognition that went with being connected to the White House, which the Auchinclosses once accepted, is now merely something to be endured.

There is a further matter that privately worries the family. "When," asks one member, "will the Kennedy publicity begin to deteriorate and run downhill?" When, in other words, will it take on a yellow-journalistic cast of the "intimate-secrets-of-John-F.-Kennedy" variety? Alas, it has had a way of happening, following a decent interval, after the deaths of many other famous men, and a number of the family are now grimly steeling themselves for this kind of lurid and leering press.

The Auchinclosses' distinguished brother-in-law, Wilmarth Lewis, feels that in most eventualities, Auchinclosses will emerge triumphant. Having married one, he has particular admiration for the Auchincloss women and their particular sense of balance and rightness. They have acquired this sense, he feels, partly through family tradition and inheritance, and partly through their education. This, of course, has been outwardly superficial — with the mandatory year in Europe — and consistently upper class. Women, by tradition, have gone to Miss Porter's School in Farmington, just as Auchincloss boys have traditionally gone to Groton, and, says Mr. Lewis, "Porter certainly isn't the worst school in the world, but it's hardly the best, either. And yet it has somehow been able to teach these girls to go to the heart of complicated problems — and to rise to occasions." It teaches them, he feels, a sense of *themselves,* a sense of duty, of obligation, of responsibility. It teaches them that there is more to "being a lady" than manners, or Manner. It teaches them to tell what is important from what is not, what needs doing from what doesn't. It supplies them with a certain toughness of fiber. It is this upper-class toughness that is so often mistaken for simple coldness, even arrogance.

Mr. Lewis cites the example of his late wife, Annie Burr Auchincloss, who, when the Second World War was declared, put down her needlepoint and her interest in collecting eighteenth-century prints, and went to work for the Red Cross and other wartime services. No previous education or training — no provisional year with the Junior League doing volunteer work — had prepared her for this. She simply *was* prepared, and did what needed to be done, providing leadership.

"In other words," asked a friend, "there is something to be said for aristocratic values?"

Mr. Lewis looked briefly alarmed. "Oh, yes!" he said quickly, "But of course you must never call them that. An aristocrat would never *call* them that. The minute you use that *word,* the hackles rise."

The crisis the Auchincloss family faces now, in terms of Mrs. Kennedy, comes from without, and from an unimaginable number of possible directions. It is rather like a war. The Auchinclosses would certainly like to go back to lives of sedate, ritualistic predictability, respectably affluent, grandly reticent, to the "second-best" world of Scroll and Key which, as everyone knows, is really better than the best. They would like to become, again, the kind of family who, as a friend puts it, "One would never dream of speaking to without an introduction." But they will certainly, for a while, be prevented from doing so and becoming so by their enemy, the public. Of course, as standard-bearers and standard-setters, conveyors of values that are particular to the American Social Establishment, one expects that they will be able to carry on like . . . well, like Auchinclosses.

Whether or not one is worthy of being considered an aristocrat — that word never to be used — depends, in large part, on how one conducts oneself in the face of adversity. When the chips are down, blood will tell. It is then that one is judged by how automatically, and how well, one obeys the unenforceable.

In *The Late George Apley,* the late John P. Marquand offered his portrait of upper-class life in Boston, and caused his hero's Aunt Amelia to utter the statement: "Whenever I am depressed I remember I am an Apley." To upper-class Boston, however, the remark was puzzling, and tended to cast doubt upon Mr. Marquand's qualifications as a chronicler of the real upper class. Would a *real* upper-class person ever talk that way? As Marietta Tree commented not long ago, "Anyone who has to keep reminding herself what her family stands for can't really be very secure." A good point, to which Mr. Marquand, were he still with us, might have replied, *"Touché."*

Upper-class values are not confined to any family, nor to any city. And yet Mrs. Tree recalls that the "first and only" time her grandmother ever slapped her was when, as a young girl, Marietta referred to an acquaintance as "very middle class." After the slap came these stern, grandmotherly words: "There are no classes in America — upper, lower, or middle. You are never to use that term again."

Mrs. Tree is eminently well-equipped to be called a member of the American upper class. She is a daughter of the venerable Peabody family of Salem; her grandfather was the celebrated Rector of the Groton School, and four other of her antecedents were on the school's first board of trustees. She is related, by blood and marriage, to such great New England families as the Lorings, the Searses, the Lawrences, the Endicotts, and the Bowditches who, in turn, are married or related to such as the Higginsons, the Cobbs, and the Howlands who, in *their* turn, are related to Auchinclosses — a lacy network of interrelationships that floats outward from Boston and New York and Philadelphia over the entire continent. In addition to headmasters of schools,

Mrs. Tree's ancestors include a comfortable complement of Episcopal Bishops and New England Governors.

Mrs. Tree speaks of her family as "The people who built and administered the schools, universities, boys' clubs and hospitals. They were the sinews of society. They gave generously of themselves for the public good and prudently lived on the income of their incomes. They valued educated women as well as educated men; daily exercise; big breakfasts; president Eliot; beautiful views; portraits by Sargent; waltzing (known as the 'Boston' in Boston); Harvard; travel; England; comradeship between the sexes; Patou dresses for 'swell' occasions; long correspondence with family and friends; J. P. Morgan; mahogany and red plush; and, most of all, they believed that if you tried hard enough, you could make the world a better place. And you *must* try." Few better, or more succinct, lists of upper-class values have been compiled.

And yet, at the same time, Mrs. Tree resolutely insists that there is "no such thing" as an upper class in America, and that her family consisted of, most of all, "Good, hard-working ministers, teachers, and community people." When the term *upper class* enters a conversation, she cites her grandmother's slap, and the solemn words that followed it.

Is it possible that the wise and witty Mrs. Tree has missed what surely was her grandmother's point, her grandmother's lesson — which is that to call someone "middle class" is in itself *very* middle class? No upper-class person would do it. No upper-class person would ever admit that such a thing as "class" exists. Those who continue to deny Society, then, continue to confirm it — in generation after generation. On this firm foundation of paradox — not unlike those that have formed the bases of the world's great religions — Society exists.

Index

Astor
Ryan   Gouverneur Gracie   Vanderbilt
Auchincloss Baylies   Appleton Rutherfurd Schermerhorn Post Cushing   Quackenbush
Delano McAllister Van Rensselaer Newbold Burden Hutton Van Zandt Wilmerding Zabriskie
Irving Nichols Bliss Porter Randolph Thayer Phillips Stokes Blauvelt Choate Mills
Flagler Houghtaling De Peyster Blagden Lorillard Bayard Crosby Griswold Lispenard
Morris Dana Hoagland Duer Havemeyer Lanier Kip Jay Francklyn Beekman Read
DeForest Roosevelt Van Cortlandt Van Pelt Sebring Winthrop Lindsay Buchanan
Murray Tooker Whitney Van Alen Twombly Rhinelander Otis Oelrichs Satterthwaite
Pennoyer Webb Rockefeller Tiffany Schuyler Schley Alexander Field Nelson
Lydecker Andrews Gurnee Kernochan Osterhoudt Pratt Schieffelin
Carnegie Suydam Guest Bulkeley Gould Goelet Irvin Allen Bancroft
Brownell Cooper Verplanck Archbold Baker Elliott Belmont
Jennings Livingston Bouvier Depew Hasbrouck Bowdoin   Spreckels
Agnew Brevoort Cutting Talleyrand Wysong Rogers   Wallace Church
Perkins Seton Wickes Coster Gardiner Morgan Cary   Stephenson Baldwin Deering
Berryman Canfield Leiter Payne Clarkson Bostwick   Witter Cartan Roth McAllister
Munn Cravath Brokaw Harriman Delafield Duke Fish   Russell Stanford Norris Verdier
Iselin Frelinghuysen Harkness Talbott Pell   Coleman Howe Mein Lapham
Hamilton Potter Howland   Monteagle Wilson Swinerton
Vanderlip Rutgers   O'Brien Alioto Crocker Ross
Ritchie Sloan Robbins   Baldocchi Kittle Ghirardelli Nickel Fay
Tailer Whitehouse Reid   Pancoast   Livermore Hopkins Metcalf Henderson
Van Tassel Van Winkle Stillman   Stotesbury   Hearst Tobin Huntington Hills
Knowlton Ledyard   Greer   Converse Vaux   Redington Fuller Fair Folger
Howard Hewitt   Ingersoll McLean   Boyd Tucker Benoist Sutro Hall
Cromwell Clews   Drexel Baldwin   Hooper Flood Kent Lyman
Gerry Dodge   Biddle Coxe Wynne   Livingston Sanford Newhall
                Wanamaker Borie   King Morse Van Strum
                du Pont Cadwalader   Mackay Miller DeGuigne
            Bingham Jayne Coates   Theriot Cameron Blyth
            Consanguine Taylor Lippincott   de Young de Bretteville
            Geist Drinker Cope Lennig Wood   Black
            Powel Morris Rush Penrose Scott   Haas
    Shippen   Lewis Dolan Strawbridge Chew Elkins   Noble
Willing Houston Mitchell Merrick Cassatt Widener Dallas Baird
Cooke Meigs Wetherill Disston Kent Hopkins Furness Clark
Meade   Penn Willcox Ridgeway Hopkinson White
    Harrison Roberts Knox Wheeler Pemberton
    Baer Clothier Wister   Wharton Norris
    Lea Pepper   Pennington
    McMichael   Brown Dorrance
    McKean   Weightman

New York   Philadelphia   San Francisco

The RIGHT PEOPLE: a Casua